About the Autho

John T. Reed is a real estate investment book and newsletter author. He was a real estate investor for 23 years.

Mr. Reed's real estate work experience includes brokerage and management of properties ranging from single-family homes and building lots to large apartment complexes, industrial, and office buildings.

He has been interviewed about real estate investment on *60 Minutes,Good Morning America, Larry King Live,* and other tv and radio programs. And his real estate investment analysis has appeared in such publications as the *Wall Street Journal, Newsweek, The New York Times, Forbes, U.S. News & World Report, Changing Times, Money,* and in many real estate trade journals and newsletters.

Mr. Reed is the editor and publisher of the newsletter, *John T. Reed's Real Estate Investor's Monthly* and author of the books:

Aggressive Tax Avoidance for Real Estate Investors (10 editions)
Apartment Investing Checklists
Office Building Acquisition Handbook (2 editions)
How To Increase The Value of Real Estate
How To Manage Residential Property For Maximum Cash Flow And Resale Value (2 eds.)
How To Use Leverage To Maximize Your Real Estate Investment Return (2 editions)

He holds a bachelor of science degree from the United States Military Academy at West Point and a master of business administration degree from Harvard Business School.

Other material by John T. Reed

- Aggressive Tax Avoidance for Real Estate Investors
- Coaching Youth Football Defense
- High-Leverage Real Estate Financing (cassettes)
- How to Buy Real Estate for at Least 20% Below Market Value Volumes I and II (cassettes)
- How to Buy Residential Property (cassettes)
- How to Find Deals That Make Sense in Today's Market (cassettes)
- How to Increase the Value of Real Estate
- How to Manage Residential Property for Maximum Cash Flow and Resale Value
- How to Do a Delayed Exchange
- How to Use Leverage to Maximize your Real Estate Investment Return
- John T. Reed's Real Estate Investor's Monthly
- Offensive and Defensive Tactics for Distressed Real Estate Times
- Office Building Acquisition Handbook
- Real Estate Investment Strategy
- Real Estate Investor's Monthly on Investment Strategy
- Residential Property Acquisition Handbook
- Single-Family Lease Options

For more information, see the order forms in the front and back of this book or contact John T. Reed, P.O. Box 27311, Concord, CA 94527. Telephone toll-free 800-635-5425.

Thanks to...

John Beck, Ron Starr, George Coats, George Rohmeyer, Jr., Lloyd Walters, Gary DiGrazia, Paul Thompson, Jose Leon, Dwain Sachs, Dan Kinter, Richard Gardiner, Lana Balou, Bob Bruss, Leigh Robinson, Jim Stephenson, Ted Thomas, Stephen Kapit, John Schaub, Bill Manley, Larry Kaplan, Jane Garvey, Marc Goodfriend, Mike Scott, Ernie Kessler, Craig Lehmkuhl, Robert Wade Brown, Tom Nitti, Steve Roulac for their help with this book.

How to Buy Real Estate for at Least 20% Below Market Value

by
John T. Reed

John T. Reed
342 Bryan Drive
Danville, California 94526

To my son,
Michael T. Reed

Published by Reed Publishing
342 Bryan Drive
Danville, California 94526

Manufactured in the United States of America by Delta Lithograph, Valencia, CA

Library of Congress Catalog Card number: 93-092745

ISBN: 0-939224-24-0

Table of Contents

1

Overview

I hope you're skeptical about the title of this book, *How to Buy Real Estate for at Least 20% Below Market Value*. **I** would have been several years ago.

I never even saw 5% below market

I worked as a real estate salesman from 1972 to 1975. I never saw a property sell for 20% below market value. Not in my four-office company. Not in the entire Camden County, New Jersey Multiple Listing Service. I never even saw one sell for **5%** below market value. The market was too "efficient," to use a Wall Street term.

If you listed a property **at** its true market value, it sold promptly. If it was 1% or 2% **below** market value, it sold **fast**. In a matter of days or even hours.

So having watched thousands of transactions from the insider's perspective of a real estate office—and never seeing any sell for 5% below market—how can I now write a book which purports to tell you how to buy for at least **20%** below market value?

A whole other world of real estate

I can do it by revealing to you that the multiple listing book is **not** the whole world of real estate. I thought the MLS book—along with assorted for-sale-by-owners and commercial real estate brokers—**were** the whole real estate world when I was a real estate salesman. I continued to think that for many years **after** I was a real estate salesman even though I later had the additional insider's perspective of being a nationally-known real estate investment guru.

It finally penetrated my consciousness that there is a whole other world of real estate out there. A world largely unknown to the public. And even unknown to the vast majority of real estate insiders like agents, attorneys, developers, and landlords.

To be sure, the public and the insiders have **heard of** parts of that world. Like probates, foreclosures, and OREOs. But even the insiders know little about the bargains that are really available in that hidden world—or the details of **how** to go about actually buying those properties. Rather they are only vaguely aware of the bargains available and how to get them.

Most real estate people have tried to buy a probate, foreclosure, or OREO property—with no success. In my early years as an agent, I tried writing to dozens of local banks about buying their OREOs. A book I had read recommended it. I did not get a single response.

St. Louis Realtor® Dwain Sachs knows a woman who decided to specialize in buying probate property. She devoted months to it without success and concluded probate bargains were a myth. Others have put considerable effort into other methods of making bargain real estate purchases and drawn the same conclusion.

They're wrong. As I was when I drew that conclusion.

There are tricks to it

The problem is there are **tricks** to making bargain purchases through these off-the-beaten-track channels. I've learned many of the tricks by interviewing men and women who make their living doing these kinds of deals.

It's a numbers game

Another problem is that laymen and real estate insiders aren't used to the ratios in bargain purchases. That is, the ratios of properties **considered** to properties **bought**.

The typical home buyer looks at three to five houses before buying. The typical investment property looks at a dozen or two dozen properties for every one he buys.

But if you try to apply either of those ratios to the bargain purchase field, you will fail. The investors who consistently make bargain purchases consider far more properties for every one they buy. Their properties-considered-per-purchase ratios range from about 50 to about 1,000.

Mind you, they do not physically inspect that many properties for every one they buy. That would be impossible. Indeed, efficient screening out of inadequate bargains is a crucial part of bargain purchasing because of the high number of properties which must be considered. The bargain purchasers typically physically inspect about the same number of properties per purchase as a regular retail investor. But they communicate with far more sellers by mail and phone prior to the physical inspection than the retail investors do.

Can you use what's in this book to buy your dream house for 20% below market?

Upon seeing the title of this book, some would-be, but heretofore frustrated, home buyers may think, "Hey, maybe this book will tell us how to get a big discount on that house on Meadowbrook Lane. The one we want but can't afford."

Sorry, but I can't tell you how to buy **any** property for at least 20% below market value. I **will** tell you how to buy **many** properties for such discounts. But **not** any property.

You have to deal **only** in certain **situations** to pull off the 20% or greater discount trick. But there **is** a way you can use this book to buy your dream house.

Do it in two steps.

Let's say you are $50,000 short of having enough to buy your dream house, 356 Meadowbrook Lane which is listed for $275,000. But you **do** have $5,000 in cash.

Step one is to do a bargain purchase (or a series of bargain purchases) which produce $50,000 after-tax profit. In step two, you use the $50,000 you made on the bargain purchase(s) to buy 356 Meadowbrook.

What might step one be? Oh, you might buy a house that's due to be **torn down**, move it to a new lot, and resell it. Done selectively, that technique often produces a property which is worth twice what it costs to buy and move it. For example, you find a deal where you can get a house moved to a new lot and ready to sell at a total cost to you of $75,000. When you're done, the finished product will be worth $150,000. You persuade a bank of the above and they make you a $70,000 construction loan. Some lender will make the loan in spite of its high loan-to-**purchase-price** ratio because it has a low ($70,000 ÷ $150,000 = 47%) loan-to-**value** ratio. That together with your $5,000 cash is the $75,000 total you need to do the deal.

When you're done, you sell the property for $150,000, pay off the $70,000 construction loan, pay federal income taxes of $25,000 and walk away with the $55,000 you need to put down on your dream house. (Yes, I know I left out a few things like state income taxes, carrying costs, and resale transaction costs. But you get the idea.)

Screening

Every real-estate buyer screens potential acquisitions. Even home buyers scan the multiple listing book or listen to agents telephonic descriptions before making an appointment to see a property.

Professional bargain purchasers, however, take screening to a much more refined level.

They often subscribe to **on-line, computerized, real-estate data bases**. That lets them tap into real-estate information in computers by telephone. They see the information on their computer screen at home or in their office. They then search and manipulate the information as needed for the particular technique they are employing.

Proper sequencing is an important part of the screening process. In general, you have to do all of the following to buy real estate in any approach—bargain purchase or otherwise:

- physically inspect the property
- negotiate price and terms
- draw up purchase agreement and have reviewed by attorney
- title search
- arrange financing

If any kind of construction or renovation is involved, you also have to get bids from contractors. Preforeclosure buyers often have to perform the added step of helping the seller find a place to live. Foreclosure-auction buyers often have to perform the added step of evicting a holding over foreclosee.

The temptation is to go physically inspect the property. That's the fun part. But it's also one of the most time-consuming parts. As such, the pros know they must have the discipline refrain from inspecting the property until the last minute.

Many professional bargain purchasers draw up their purchase agreement and have it reviewed by their attorney before they even think about a particular property. In that, they are like Realtors® who have their forms drawn up by an attorney and mass produced as part of going into business.

Professional bargain purchasers often arrange their financing in advance, too. That is, they set up lines of credit or working relationships with lenders or equity investors. Then, when they find a property, they produce the financing with about as much effort as a baseball manager motioning to the bullpen for a relief pitcher.

Once those preliminaries are set up, they typically negotiate next. Only after a satisfactory agreement has been tentatively reached do they physically inspect and do a title search. In some cases, like those who buy at foreclosure auctions, they don't inspect until after they become the owner. And sometimes not even then if the previous owner is a hostile holdover.

Foreclosure-auction buyers also postpone their final title search until the absolute last minute before auction in order to pick up eleventh-hour subordination agreements and other extremely important documents. Because postponements are the rule not the exception, foreclosure-auction buyers also have to add to their sequence calling the trustee or whoever is holding the auction, the day before the auction, to see if it's still on.

The proper sequence is somewhat similar between the various bargain-purchase techniques. But it varies for certain techniques in some respects. The objective is to minimize the number of steps taken in unconsummated deals. As I said, all real-estate buyers share that goal. But professional bargain purchasers usually cull through such huge numbers of properties that they absolutely must develop optimally efficient screening sequences and systems and have the discipline to stick with them.

Why 20% below market

You may wonder why I decided to use the number **20%** below market. Most people would be thrilled to save just **10%** on such a large purchase.

Not the pros.

I've encountered a few pros who will accept a 15% discount on **prime** properties. But the vast majority insist on at least 20%. And I think the ones who will accept 15% on "prime" properties are making a mistake.

The reason is that you generally cannot flip a property (immediately resell) it for a profit if your discount is less than 20%. Transaction costs, especially commissions, and carrying costs, totally consume smaller discounts.

Profitable flipping is this book's main criterion. If the technique in question won't get you a big enough discount (20% or more) to allow you to **immediately** resell the property at a profit, it's not good enough to be in this book.

Actual case histories

Whenever possible, I will give you actual case histories of investors who have done the technique in question. The actual discounts achieved are as high as the **99%** (Yes, that means he paid just 1% of market value. He bought a $58,000 duplex for $577.77.) which a client of John Beck got in one executed-judgment-lien deal. Lloyd Walters systematically acquired interests in real estate (not quite equity but almost as good) for an average of 8% of face value.

Using actual case histories is a discipline I have developed as a how-to journalist. By forcing myself to find actual case histories as much as possible, I accomplish two things:

- a more interesting story
- a more believable story.

On a couple of occasions, I have come up with what I **thought** was a good technique for making bargain purchases. But when I tried to find an actual case history, I not only could not, I was told by experts that they had tried to do what I suggested or something close to it, but they could **not** because of this or that problem. So the discipline of finding actual case histories sometimes reveals that my idea was fundamentally flawed and unworkable. None of those ideas are in this book.

Some theoretical ideas

However, that does **not** mean that I insist on actual case histories for **every** article. Sometimes I get what seems like a sound idea—but I cannot find anyone who has done it. However, when I talk to experts in related fields, they agree that the idea would probably work. Those ideas **are** in this book.

To a degree, that is a manifestation of my maturation as a how-to writer. In my early years as a writer, I was afraid to write theoretical articles because I felt my reading audience of real estate investors was too practical and hard nosed to accept a mere theory.

The borrowing builder who never sells

But I did let a couple theories creep in here and there. One was my "borrowing-builder-who-never-sells theory." It wasn't in one of my newsletter articles or a book chapter. I just threw it into an appendix of my tax book, *Aggressive Tax Avoidance for Real Estate Investors.*

I was trying to answer the question, "Is it possible to pay zero tax?" At the time, there was a book out called *Pay Zero Tax.* I said, "Yes, if your 'income' consisted entirely of increasing the value of real estate which you never sold and only refinanced." I didn't mean it as a suggestion to be followed so much as I meant it as an intellectual exercise.

But after I spoke at a real estate conference, a young couple came up to me and thanked me for "changing their lives." "How?" I asked.

Turned out they had decided to become borrowing-builders-who-never-sold. And they were doing quite nicely, thank you. That's when I lost my reticence to share with readers my as-yet-untested real estate theories.

But in each such case, rest assured that I have run the theory through my own mental filter, which is based on twenty-two years of experience in real estate. And in each case of a theoretical technique, I have run the idea by a number of other real-estate experts.

If they had denounced it convincingly, I would have dropped it. As I have with a number of ideas. So the theoretical techniques in this book are only those which have passed both my tests for practicality as well as those of other gurus I respect.

The two categories

There are two categories of properties which can be bought for at least 20% below market value:

- properties which **no one wants** and
- properties which **no one knows are for sale.**

Leper properties

I call properties which no one wants, "**leper**" properties. The obvious question is, "If no one **else** wants them, why would **I** want them? Sure, you can buy them cheap. But then you can't sell them. So what's the point?"

The answer is that you don't just buy properties which no one wants willy-nilly. Most of the properties which no one wants are terrible investments. Rather you are going to buy properties which no one wants very **selectively.** To be specific, you are only going to buy properties which no one wants when the **reason** no one wants them can be **corrected** at a **low enough cost** that you make a profit.

For example, you'll read in this book about John Beck's purchase of a property with a title problem. Virtually all real-estate agents, lawyers, and investors have been told throughout their career that you don't buy properties with **title problems.** It became a property which no one wanted, a leper.

Beck, on the other hand, figured he could **fix** the title problem in question at little or no cost. He was right. And he made a substantial profit as a result.

Overreaction

The key word is "overreaction." You are looking for situations where the market **overreacts** to a problem. The market means both the seller of the property and the people other than you who might buy it.

The word overreacts is key to distinguishing between problem properties which offer profit opportunities and problem properties which don't.

For example, **radon gas** is a problem at many properties. Unfortunately for bargain hunters, the market has **not** overreacted to that particular problem. Most people know that radon gas problems can be corrected for a few thousand dollars so they just get an estimate from a reputable radon-gas-mitigation contractor and knock that amount off the purchase price. You can't buy a radon-affected house for 20% less than market value because of radon.

Market distress, as in the **Oil Patch,** is also a problem. But again, it's **not** the bargain purchase opportunity so many people seem to think it is. The reason is the market has not overreacted. If anything, it has **under**reacted to that particular problem.

Throughout the '80s, Texas real estate suffered high vacancies and much lowered rents. But it has sold for prices which give the buyer break-even cash flow at best—and often negative cash flow—throughout the period of rent distress.

You can get break-even or negative cash flow **outside** the Oil Patch. So what's the bargain in Oil Patch properties? In fact, those properties are **not** bargains as defined by this book. They are **speculations** by people who believe that Texas, Arizona, and so forth will come back economically, thereby causing their properties to go up in value.

Two necessary ingredients of profitable lepers

So in order to buy leper properties for at least 20% below market value, two things must be true:

- The problem is correctable at a cost low enough to permit a profit
- The market erroneously thinks the problem is either uncorrectable or that the cost to correct would be prohibitive.

There are many such problems and properties. And some readers of this book who understand that underlying principle will probably think of some new opportunities I've overlooked.

Properties no one knows are for sale

Some people underestimate the value of their property. The most familiar kind of property owners, owner-occupant home owners, are generally **not** in that category. But there are many more categories of property owners than home owners. Obviously, if someone underestimates the value of his property, you have an opportunity to buy it from him or her for less than its market value—sometimes as much as 20% or more below its market value.

However, most people who underestimate their property's value **suspect** they may be underestimating it. They then check with knowledgeable people and learn that they were, indeed, underestimating. End of bargain opportunity with that person.

But that still leave a few people who underestimate their property's value and either don't fail to get a second opinion or they get their second opinion from an incompetent person.

Bingo!

Desirable properties

In the no-one-knows—category you are buying **desirable** properties. These are generally **not** properties which no one wants. Lots of people would like to buy them—even at market value. They would love to buy them at less than market value. The reason you can and they can't is that you know the property is for sale and they don't.

How does that happen?

Generally, techniques in the no-one-knows—category involve asking hundreds or even thousands of property owners if they are interested in selling. It's the numbers game described above.

You approach the owner **directly** rather than through a real estate agent. You do **not** wait until the owner in question gives some indication he plans to sell. You simply contact all owners of the property location and type you're working on.

You behave very much like a real estate salesman looking for **listings**. That is, you make hundreds of "cold calls." Only one of your selling points to the owner is that you are **not** a real estate agent, so no commission will be due.

Again, you must be selective

You can't cold call just any category of owners. For example, as I said above, owner occupants of homes generally know what their property is worth. So that category would probably prove to be such "low-grade ore" for a bargain seeker that it would not be worth "mining."

Rather you must confine your cold calls to categories of owners who are less likely to know the value of their property—like out-of-area owners of raw land.

Out-of-area owners

One particularly fruitful category is people who own real estate but live far away from it. They are typically pressured by difficult management chores if the property has buildings on it. And they are typically less aware of the fair market values than local owners would be.

Unaccustomed speed

Real estate buyers like to perform what lawyers call "due diligence." That is, they like to check out the property thoroughly before they buy it. Things like the title, the structure, the neighborhood, the tenants, etc. Due diligence is even required by law in some contexts like defending yourself against toxic clean up liability or living up to your fiduciary responsibilities when you are investing the money of others.

But due diligence takes time.

Unfortunately, there is rarely "enough" time in **normal** real estate deals to perform due diligence as thoroughly as you would like. And that's true **in spades** in the bargain purchase realm.

When we talk about buying real estate for at least 20% below market value we're talking about sellers who leave money on the table. Lots of money. For example, let's say a property is worth $150,000 and you can buy it for $120,000. That means the seller is leaving $30,000 on the table.

With that kind of money lying around, each minute that passes before you complete the deal can be hazardous. So bargain purchasers are accustomed to moving with great speed. Unaccustomed speed to most people, especially when you consider the amount of money being spent by the purchaser.

"All appropriate inquiry"

One of the disadvantages of the unaccustomed speed aspect of bargain purchases is your inability to perform environmental due diligence. Ten years ago, you could do a fast deal figuring you were taking a chance on missing a construction defect or some such. Missing something like that could be costly. But rarely ruinous.

Environmental liability can easily be ruinous. As Michigan Bankers Association consultant Jud Moran said, "It's very easy to do millions of dollars worth of [environmental] damage to a $100,000 property." Environmental liability has created many situations where a formerly valuable property not only loses all of its value—it has negative value! That happens when the cost of a required clean up exceeds the value the property will have **after** the clean up.

In some bargain purchase situations, the pertinent laws conflict. For example, trespass laws prevent you from setting foot on a property without the owner's permission. And in the typical foreclosure, the owner is not inclined to let anyone inspect his house.

On the other hand, section 101(35)(b) of the Comprehensive Environmental Response, Compensation, and Liability Act says that in order to invoke the innocent purchaser/landowner defense, you must make

"all appropriate inquiry into the previous ownership and uses of the property consistent with good commercial or customary practice in an effort to minimize liability."

No one knows what "all appropriate inquiry" means. Neither the Congress nor the courts have defined it. But many think it includes not only a physical inspection of the premises in question but also of the surrounding properties!

One might be able to point to the words "customary practice" in the law and note that it is not customary to inspect properties which are being foreclosed or sold through some other legal forced sale. But the court may say that by going ahead with the purchase in spite of the fact that you were not permitted to inspect the property you chose to risk environmental liability, and you lost.

Deedless real estate investing

One of the approaches to real estate which often crops up when I interview professional bargain purchasers is what I call deedless real estate investing. That is, they do profitable real estate deals in which their **names never appear on a deed**. Not that they use a straw man or some such. Rather they simply never take title to the property *per se*—in their own name or any other. Rather they **assign** their right to make the bargain purchase to a third party and make their profit that way.

That's a good way to avoid environmental liability. When contamination is discovered on a property, the current owners will typically try to sue all previous owners since the contamination occurred. By making your money through deedless real estate investing, your name will not show up in the chain of title.

Deedless real estate investing is also a good way to minimize closing costs. Since bargain purchases are often intended to be flipped, the transaction costs of a normal purchase have to be paid twice in a short period. If you can avoid those double transaction costs, you should. By selling (more accurately called "assigning") your right to buy the property instead of buying the property itself then reselling it, you avoid double transaction costs or maybe transfer all or most of what would be your transaction costs to your buyer.

Financing ramifications

Arguably, this book could be called *Nothing Down*. Robert Allen wrote the famous book of that title. And I do not want to be confused with him or his book. I debated him on *Good Morning America*. And I criticized his book at length in newsletter articles and in my book, *How to Use Leverage to Maximize your Real Estate Investment Return*. I do not like his book **at all**.

One problem with the nothing-down approach as it has been taught by cable television gurus and authors is that most of the techniques either require you to **mislead** an institutional lender or bamboozle an unsophisticated person by getting them to trade valuable real-estate equity for a piece of paper which is worth far less than it says it's worth and far less than the equity it was traded for is worth.

The other problem with the nothing-down approach is that the deals are **not profitable**. You would think that was a pretty basic requirement. But no. The nothing-down crowd assumes that all the properties they buy will appreciate at 10% per year or more. So they don't much mind latching onto property with either negative cash flow or negative mortgage amortization because they figure appreciation will more than make up for the negatives and they'll come out ahead in the long run. That has happened in only a minority of five-year periods since World War II.

Nothing down

That brings me to **this** book, which I believe is more of a legitimate "nothing down" book than Allen's *Nothing Down* was.

In general, you cannot borrow more than 80% of the value of a piece of real estate unless there is a **high-credit guarantor** on the loan. Some person or entity whose credit is so strong that they could qualify for an **un**secured loan of the amount above 80% of value. That's what you have with high-loan-to-value-ratio FHA and VA mortgages. Uncle Sam is co-signing. So the loan is secure from the lender's perspective in spite of the high loan-to-value ratio.

Also, in general, you cannot get positive cash flow from a building where the loan-to-value ratio is greater than about 75%. With bigger loans, the interest charges are so great you have negative cash flow or negative amortization.

But suppose you buy the property for at least 20% below market? Let's say you buy a property worth $100,000 for $75,000. You could get a 75% loan-to-**value**-ratio loan from a bank without great difficulty. In fact, it would probably be one of the safer loans they made that month. Most of their loans are 80% of value.

But although a $75,000 mortgage would be just 75% of the value of the property, it would be 100% of your purchase price. In other words, nothing down. Furthermore, you would probably have positive or at least break-even cash flow because of your relatively low, 75% loan-to-value ratio.

No institutional lender has to be misled to get the loan. No unsophisticated seller has to be bamboozled into taking back paper which is worth far less than it says its worth. And the deal is profitable two ways. You could immediately flip (resell) it for a profit. Or you could keep it and rent it out for its positive cash flow.

The lower of value or price

Now I know that many lenders have policy manuals which limit the loan to 80% of value **or** purchase price, whichever is **lower**. Such policies are simply expressions of lack of confidence in appraisers. But I believe that if you ask enough lenders, you will find one who will loan on **value**, not the lower of purchase price or value. Indeed, if you truly know how to buy real estate for at least 20% below market value, you are "movin' on up" financially and therefore a desirable customer for a bank to court.

As your successful track record lengthens, you should use it to persuade skeptical bankers that you are for real.

Tax ramifications

Bargain purchases have no special tax ramifications. In fact, there is one tax ramification which many people **assume** they have which they do **not** have. That is the notion that you cannot do a tax-free exchange into many bargain-purchase situations—like purchases made at foreclosure auctions.

Oh, yes you can. I personally watched that particular transaction done once. And I know a delayed-exchange facilitator who has participated in many deals in which the exchanger was exchanging into property bought at a foreclosure auction.

Auctioneers at government, foreclosure, or other auctions do not care where the money is coming from as long as the source is legal and the form of the payment is cash or cashiers check.

Dealer property

There **is** a tax ramification if you resell the property or assign your agreement to buy it quickly. The property will probably be considered dealer property by the IRS and the courts. That means you can**not exchange** into or out of it. Nor can you claim **depreciation** on it. But those restrictions are not as bad as they once were.

In order to exchange, you have to own property for **long periods**. That is increasingly risky in the current climate of toxic liability, personal injury liability, tax reform, and so forth. Holding for long periods also requires that you engage in such low-paid but time-consuming activities as **renovation** and **property management**. So exchanging looks great when compared to paying tax on the sale of a property. But it looks less great when you see it part of a larger package in which you are forced to engage in management-intensive, risky, long-term holding rather than more profitable, less risky flipping.

Depreciation ain't what it used to be

Depreciation deductions ain't what they used to be. The current depreciation schedules are the **least generous** we've ever had. Furthermore, since the Tax Reform Act of 1986, the **passive loss limitations** and the **alternative minimum tax** tend to prevent many investors from deducting even the meager depreciation allowed under the Modified Accelerated Cost Recovery System.

If you **flip** the property, your holding period is so short that the depreciation deductions wouldn't amount to much any way.

The notion that dealer property is *per se* bad is a residue of the **pre**-Tax Reform Act of 1986 real-estate world. Back when there was also a long-term-capital-gains exclusion that made capital-gains tax rates much lower than ordinary-income tax rates, which are what dealers pay.

There have always been a lot of people who were dealers and very rich in spite of their obligation to pay tax at ordinary rates. People like developers, car dealers, owners of retail stores and restaurants. Real-estate people are the only ones who are in the habit of thinking that paying tax at ordinary-income-tax rates is reason to slit your wrists.

You often must withstand attack

Time after time when I have interviewed bargain purchase practitioners they have told me of this person or that person trying to steal their deal.

Frequently the seller wises up to the bargain and tries to get out of the deal. Or an attorney or agent tries to kill it. Or another would-be buyer tries to overbid. Successful bargain purchasers have to make sure their original contract is tightly drawn and that they strictly comply with it. They often must firmly refuse to let the seller out of a signed deal.

Mostly smaller, lower priced properties

The bargain techniques in this book cover all sizes of property. Some of the actual case histories involve multimillion-dollar office buildings. Others involve large apartment complexes or industrial buildings. Some involve sellers you would think would be too sophisticated, like major corporations or professionals.

But the majority involve single-family homes. And the professionals who make their living pursuing bargain purchases generally find they do best focusing on lower priced homes. For example, pre-foreclosure buyer Ted Thomas says he found most affluent people who get into financial difficulty string him along before ultimately filing bankruptcy to prevent losing equity in foreclosure. The less affluent buyers he has dealt with are generally more honest in their dealings with him and less likely to declare bankruptcy.

In general, the bigger the property, the more money a 20% or greater discount represents. The more money, the more the people involved are likely to consult lawyers and other professionals to make sure they are doing the right thing. That doesn't insure they'll not sell for 20% below market. But it's a numbers game and those categories have less attractive numbers (too many deals considered for every bargain actually purchased).

Sometimes rare birds

Some bargain-purchase techniques work because the type of property or interest is rare. For example, one-bedroom houses, two-on-a-lot houses, life estates and remainder estates, and so forth. There aren't many people who understand such properties or interests because there aren't many such property or interest in **existence**.

In order to find them, you typically have to "farm" a much wider geographical area than other investors.

Bad shape

Everybody and his brother has heard of the **fixer-upper** strategy. You buy a property that needs cosmetic renovation cheap, fix it up, and resell it for a profit.

In general, that does **not** work. Too many people are trying to do it. Many of them are rank beginners who grossly **under**estimate the costs and grossly **over**estimate the after-renovation resale value. You can**not** bid against such incompetents and make an adequate profit.

However, if the property in question **really** needs work, then you've got a chance. I'm talking condemned gut rehabs or severe foundation problems or toxic-substance contamination. Those properties **scare off** the beginners and other incompetents. If it's in such bad shape that virtually every other buyer is scared off, it may offer a bargain opportunity. That's why I call them "leper" properties. Although the bargain techniques in this book cover acquisition of properties in all conditions from mint to condemned, a disproportionate number of bargain purchase techniques involve properties in extraordinarily bad shape.

A career or a deal

Most of the techniques in this book can be used in two ways:

• you can **specialize** in a particular technique
• you can file all the techniques in the back of your mind to be used only when you encounter an appropriate **situation**.

Many people will use the book both ways. For example, they may decide to **specialize** in pursuing over encumbered properties which are about to go to foreclosure or tax sale. But they may run across an opportunity to buy a tenant-in-common interest. Whereupon they think, "Reed wrote that tenant-in-common interests were often super deals in that book, *How to Buy Real Estate for at Least 20% Below Market Value.* Before I say 'no' to this guy who's offering to sell me a tenancy in common, let me go back and see what the book had to say about them."

I have encountered people who made careers out of techniques I advocated. And I suspect that many more did deals which they would have shunned if they had not read in one of my books or articles that there were good deals to be had in such situations.

"Sellers" who don't care

Many of the techniques in this book involve sellers who don't care. For example, real estate is often sold by someone who does not own it and whose pay for selling the property is the same or almost the same no matter what the sale price. That's true of all forced sales like foreclosure auctions, tax sales, IRS seized-property sales, etc. It's also true in some probates where the decision makers are either not heirs or are heirs who would only get a small percentage of the equity in the property. It's also true of real estate owned by large entities like corporations or non-profit institutions.

The easy-come-easy-go syndrome

Sometimes you can get a bargain even though the seller owns the property and will get the equity. That often happens when he got the equity easily.

For example, John Beck once bought a partial interest in a house for just 2.5% of its fair market value. But the guy to whom he **sold** it got a heck of a deal, too.

John sold it to the owner of the **other** part of the house for just **50%** of market value. Surely, John would never sell his own home for 50% of its market value. But since he had only paid 2.5% for his part of this particular property, 50% looked like a heck of a deal to John.

I have come across many similar case histories where one person got a property for 20% or more below market value from another person who had recently bought the property at an **even better** discount.

The easy-come-easy-go syndrome also manifests itself when **heirs** are the property owners. They typically want to convert their inheritance to cash as soon as possible. They are far less interested in getting the last dollar out of the property than they are in getting cash fast.

The "We-wrote-it-off" syndrome

"Wrote it off" is a phrase one often hears. It refers to the accounting practice of reducing an asset's value to zero in the accounting books of a business. Individuals sometimes have assets which they "write off" in their minds if not in a set of books.

Once a person or company has written off a piece of real estate or an interest in real estate as worthless, any equity which appears in that property (typically as a result of your offering to buy it) seems like easy-come equity. So the easy-come-easy-go syndrome arises. You'll find that some of the techniques in this book work because they involve buying real estate or interests in real estate from persons or entities who have written them off.

Specialized expertise

There is no free lunch. You don't get to buy real estate for 20% or more below market without effort.

A 20%-or-greater discount on a purchase as large as real estate produces an extraordinary profit. You don't get such extraordinary **output** without extraordinary **input**. That extraordinary input is mainly **specialized expertise**. You must acquire the specialized expertise for the particular technique you plan to use.

For example, Craig Lehmkuhl does **workouts** where the threat of **bankruptcy** or actual filing bankruptcy is routine. So it should come as no surprise that he has a copy of the bankruptcy code on his desk or that he is well versed in bankruptcy law.

Paul Thompson buys **foreclosures** at public auctions in California (they're called trustee sales there). He is well versed in the California laws pertinent to trustee sales.

Dwain Sachs buys **probates** in the St. Louis area. He not only knows Missouri probate laws, he also knows the attorneys who handle probates in that area.

Expertise can be **technical** as in legal or construction knowledge. Or it can be **personal** as in relationships which produce early knowledge of deals or which make deals go more smoothly.

Secrecy

Another element which is common to bargain purchases but nearly unknown in purchases at retail is secrecy.

Properties are often more valuable to one person than they are to anyone else. For example accumulation of many small parcels for a large project. That's called assembly. It can produce huge profits because the value of the whole large parcel is greater than the sum of the separate values of the parts. One of the most famous assemblies was the one done to create Disney World in Florida. Extremely profitable assemblies are also done in big cities like New York.

The secrecy in these deals is extreme.

As I said above, bargain purchasers often need to withstand attacks from sellers who change their minds or from other would-be buyers who would also like to buy the property and would be happy to pay even a little more than you paid.

Some bargain-purchase techniques involve buying interests in properties, like liens. Investors who practice these techniques often use **straw men** or separate corporations to conceal the connection between their attempt to buy the interest at a discount and their other interest in the property in question.

Buy-very-low-sell-low

An investor who makes bargain purchases systematically typically makes $100,000 to $300,000 a year. Consequently their time is more valuable than most people's. That, in turn, means they cannot afford to spend time on those aspects of real estate which are time consuming but low paid. Property management, renovation, and selling property at market value are prime examples of time-consuming, low-pay real estate activities.

To avoid those activities, many bargain purchasers employ what I call the buy-very-low-sell-low approach. That is, they sell at quick-sale value instead of market value. Quick-sale value is about 90% to 95% of market value.

At quick-sale value, you can generally sell:

- without a real estate agent
- to an all-cash buyer
- within days or weeks.

By selling quickly you minimize carrying costs. By selling without an agent, you save the commission. And by selling to an all-cash buyer, you avoid waits for lender approval and expensive lender requirements.

Buyers waiting in the wings

Another unique aspect of many bargain purchasers' programs is that they have buyers waiting in the wings to buy their bargains from them. For example, preforeclosure buyer Ted Thomas has a waiting list of people who buy property from him. Indeed, he demands a $5,000 earnest money deposit to get **on** the list. One of his buyers, Jesse Carranza, has bought many properties from Ted. And why not? Ted sells at **quick-sale** value. That's not as good as **bargain** (20% discount or greater) value. But it's better than paying **market** value.

Persistence

Another element that crops up more often in bargain-purchase techniques than in normal purchases is persistence.

Preforeclosure buyers like Ted Thomas send letter after letter to the same person during the period when the foreclosure is proceeding. OREO buyer Ernie Kessler calls the bank OREO officer in charge of the property he's after every Monday. Foreclosure-auction buyer Paul Thompson has to keep track of foreclosure auctions which are postponed time and again. Probate buyer Gary DiGrazia constantly rechecks the public probate files on the properties he's pursuing to find helpful information.

"The weird of the world"

Any rational person's first question about buying real estate for at least 20% below market would be, "Why would anyone in their right mind sell so cheap?"

That was **my** first question. John Beck, who was the editor and publisher of the no-longer published *Distress Sales Report* newsletter (510-523-6115) as well as the *Forced Sale Workbook* is often asked the same question. One of his answers is that, "the weird of the world pass through the foreclosure process."

He once told me that many of the seller of bargain purchases were **not** in their right mind in the sense that they were drug addicts or alcoholics. I investigated and found he was right. And that you can legally buy from such people. (Always have the deal handled by an escrow company. They will take special pains to make sure the seller is sober when he or she signs the papers which is the only legal requirement of such deals.)

Some bargain deals arise from the **spite**ful actions of divorcing spouses, business split-ups, or feuding family members.

Other bargains arise from behavior which is not insane but certainly **kooky**—like the otherwise normal couple who let their roof leak for years and let numerous cats live and relieve themselves in the attic. The property was condemned by the city and sold at a bargain price even considering the fix-up cost.

Some professional bargain buyers deal in **useless land**—which they resell at substantial profits. Why would anyone in his right mind buy such a thing? Apparently, some people just can't believe that there is any such thing as worthless real estate.

There is a lot of irrationality in the world and the real estate world has its share. The bargain-purchase part of the real estate world has more than its share of weirdness. Yours is not to reason why. Yours is but to negotiate and buy.

Unique risks

Some bargain purchase techniques present risks which are either unheard of or far more rare elsewhere in real estate. And, in some of those cases, those risks cannot be reduced. You just have to take your chances.

I've already mentioned one: the risk that you'll be liable for toxic contamination on a property you were not permitted to inspect before purchase.

Another, which also crops up in foreclosure auctions, is the fact that you cannot ascertain the balance owed on liens senior to the foreclosing lien. In all other deals, the seller produces a **pay off statement** from the lien holder.

Several bargain-purchase techniques are **not eligible for title insurance**.

Deals involving life estates or remainder estates expose you to risk of **premature death** or Methuselah-length **longevity** of the life tenant.

Sellers who are in financial distress often declare **bankruptcy** after they sell to you. The bankruptcy court may then pull the property back into the bankrupt person's estate.

The big picture

So there you have the big picture.

You were skeptical that this book or any other book could deliver on the promise to tell you how to buy real estate for at least 20% below market value. But now that you've read the broad overview, it probably sounds less far fetched—and probably also less easy than you had hoped.

It's **not** easy. The cable-TV real estate gurus and some book authors are in the get-rich-quick business. I'm not.

Extraordinary output requires extraordinary input. To buy real estate for at least 20% below market value, the extraordinary input takes the form of extraordinary **expertise** and, in some cases, extraordinary **risk**.

By buying this book and reading it, you have taken a major step toward acquiring the extraordinary expertise you need. However, this book alone does not contain all the expertise you need. Entire books can and have been written about some of the individual techniques in this book. And even those books probably do not tell you all you need to know.

But neither is the expertise you need accessible only to the proverbial rocket scientist. Many of the professional bargain buyers I have interviewed are ordinary folks. Most are college graduates. But not all. And a college education is not necessary for any technique I know of. The main thing that distinguishes them from ordinary investors is a large store of **self-taught** knowledge about how to find and close deals in their chosen specialty. Knowledge derived from both study and experience.

The message of this book is **not** that I have found new, easy ways to get rich quick in real estate. Rather it is that there are a great many ways to make extraordinary profits in real estate. They include many approaches which have been widely overlooked or entirely overlooked by the vast majority of real-estate practitioners, not to mention the vast majority of laymen.

Neither this book nor any other can make it **easy** to profit in real estate. But it can and most certainly does make it **easier** than it would have been if you had **not** read this book or other well-researched books which cover the same subjects.

2

Ethics

Buying real estate for at least 20% below market value sounds unethical to some. Some refer to such deals as "stealing" property.

Certainly real estate purchase negotiations are zero-sum games in which neither party can gain except at the expense of the other party. That is, the buyer wants to buy for as **little** as possible and the seller wants to sell for as **much** as possible and neither can make any progress toward their price goal without moving the other party away from his opposite goal.

"Win-win" negotiations

Most people are uncomfortable with zero-sum games. They do not like seeking to better their position at the expense of someone else—at least someone who is known to them. (Although when they other guy is **out of sight**, as in the case of the U.S. taxpayer, most people shamelessly lobby for increased government benefits which better their position at the expense of others.)

Sensing this discomfort, many real-estate people and negotiation teachers have claimed that they only favor "win-win" negotiations. The notion that both parties can win a negotiation is nonsensical.

All negotiations contain two elements:

- a zero sum game
- mutual interest.

My *Webster's New Universal Unabridged Dictionary* says a zero sum is a...situation...in which gain for one must result in a loss for another. So, by definition, a zero-sum game cannot be "win-win."

On the other hand, there are elements of mutual interest in **all** negotiations. That mutual interest is the **basis** for the negotiation. On the other hand, if there were **no** mutual interest, there would be no **reason** to negotiate.

In the simplest house sale for cash, you can see both elements:

• The price is the zero sum game.
• The mutual interest is that both parties would like see the house have a new owner.

"Win-win" advocates point to the ever-present element of mutual interest and say, "See, both sides benefit."

Big deal. That's true of **every** negotiation which is successful at arriving at an agreement. If it wasn't, the parties would not have signed the deal. If **any** mutual satisfaction is evidence of "win-win," then **all** negotiations are "win-win." If all negotiations are "win-win," the "win-win" concept is meaningless.

If there were no zero-sum aspects to the negotiation, there would be no **need** to negotiate. The parties would simply agree on everything and sign on the dotted line. The very fact that the parties are negotiating proves the existence of the zero-sum game.

So forget the notion that there is such a thing as a "win-win" negotiation. A "win-win" negotiation is an oxymoron, a contradiction in terms, a self-canceling phrase.

The best deal you can get

Your goal in a negotiation, including the purchase of real estate, is to get the best deal you can. The seller's goal is to get the best deal he or she can get. Neither of you owes the other an apology for pursuing that goal. Indeed, where fiduciary responsibilities are involved, **failure** to pursue the best deal you can get is illegal, unethical, and immoral. Even absent fiduciary responsibilities, failure to pursue the best deal you can get has negative implications. For example, a person who carelessly paid much more for real estate than was necessary to make the purchase could arguably be committed to a mental institution for such irrational behavior.

The mundane admonition to "Shop around" is universally accepted as good advice. This book simply shows you how to shop around with extraordinary efficiency and in markets where bargains mean extraordinarily large savings.

My ethical code

The ethical code I try to live up to has three tenets:

• Tell the truth.
• Keep your promises.
• Treat others as you want to be treated.

I urge you to adhere to the same standard. This book will adhere to that standard.

Don't misrepresent value

In the course of negotiating a bargain purchase, you may be tempted to make a false statement—especially to say that the price you want to pay is fair market value.

Do **not** do that. It will cost you some deals. But so be it. Claiming you are paying market value when you believe you are paying 20% or more less than market value is plain dishonest. That's **unethical** and **immoral**. It's also **illegal** in most cases. And not just illegal in a **civil** sense. It's also illegal in a **criminal** sense. It's fraud.

There are even some specific statutes aimed at would-be bargain real estate purchasers. One is California's Home Equity Sales Contract Statute (California Civil Code § 1695) which is aimed at investors who buy from property owners against whose real estate a notice of default has been filed. The portion of that law where they state its purpose contains the following:

"During the time period between the commencement of foreclosure proceedings and the scheduled foreclosure sale date, homeowners in financial distress, especially the poor, elderly, and financially unsophisticated, are vulnerable to the importunities of equity

purchasers, who induce homeowners to sell their homes for a small fraction of their fair market values through the use of schemes which often involve oral and written misrepresentations, deceit, intimidation, and other unreasonable commercial practices."

Now that sentence contains some political rhetoric which is completely or mostly baloney. Like the notion that the "poor and elderly" are special targets of preforeclosure buyers. That's nonsense based more on Dickensian novels than reality. The poor don't own homes and the elderly don't default for the most part. Also, the word "induce" is always a tip-off. It means the same as "persuade." But it **sounds** sleazier. So it's frequently used by politicians and lawyers to cast aspersions on behavior which they don't like but which is moral and legal.

But the California legislature's purpose sentence also contains **legitimate** complaints, i.e., those about misrepresentation, deceit, and intimidation. You should not misrepresent, deceive, or intimidate in your eagerness to make a bargain purchase.

The Golden Rule

The third tenet of my personal code of ethics is commonly known as the Golden Rule. Some might say buying real estate for at least 20% below market value violates that rule. Not so.

Negotiations for real estate or anything else are **adversarial** activities. Athletic contests are also adversarial activities. No one would accuse an athletic opponent who tried his best to beat you of violating The Golden Rule. Adherence to The Golden Rule does not require adversaries to take a fall.

Any mentally competent adult knows that someone who is bidding on his real estate wants to get it for the lowest possible price. No sensible adult expects a buyer to offer more than he thinks he has to for a property. As long as you do not try to convince the seller that you are doing something **other** than trying to buy for the lowest possible price, your behavior in seeking that lowest possible price is ethical.

The problem comes if you make statements like, "I will pay you fair market value for your property." or "You won't do any better than my offer." or "I'll help you save your equity." or even, "I'm offering a fair price."

Rather you must simply say, "I am willing to pay X dollars." or you can ask the other party to name his price then either counteroffer or accept it.

Never, never say or imply that the price you are offering is market value or fair or anything similar.

Just make your offer. You are entitled to point out such undeniable advantages as the fact that your offer is all **cash** (if it is) or that you are willing and able to close **fast** (if you can). Those are accurate statements and cash and/or speed are genuinely valuable to many sellers. If you can help the other person save their credit rating, that, too, is a legitimate advantage you could point out.

Buying at bargain prices is ethical. **Lying** about bargain prices is not.

Suitability

Suitability is a Wall Street word. It ought to be a real estate word, too. But the only time it crops up in real estate is in limited-partnership prospectuses.

The idea is that some investments are not suitable for some people. That generally happens when the prospective investor is unsophisticated. Options are the type of investment which is most commonly the subject of unsuitability disputes between stock brokers and their clients.

Options are simple. They give you the right to buy (call) something or sell (put) something at a specified price for a specified time period. If the market price is higher than your call option or lower than your put option during the option period, you make a profit. If it's not, you lose all your money.

The problem is that **un**sophisticated people will listen to that explanation, nod their head, swear they understand, they sue your butt off when they lose their money.

It's not that they don't understand the definition of an option or how they work. They do understand that. Rather they **don't** understand on a gut level the **probability** of loss and how **bad** they'll feel if they lose. They understand—but they don't understand.

Suitability in bargain purchases

In my real-estate finance book, *How to Use Leverage to Maximize your Real Estate Investment Return*, I said I had no problem with high-leverage acquisitions involving unsophisticated sellers as long as the unsophisticated seller got **all cash** for his or her equity. But I most certainly do have a problem when the technique in question pays the unsophisticated seller, in whole or in part, with "**paper.**" That is, a mortgage taken back or some more exotic document. In brief, the problem is that the immediate cash resale value of the paper is invariably much less than the value of the equity which was traded for it.

So one of my special ethical rules for bargain purchases is that you must pay all cash. That's not to say you shouldn't borrow money to do the deal. Just don't borrow it from an unsophisticated seller. I urge you to finance as much of the purchase as you can. 100% or even more if you can find a lender to go along. Just make sure that you do no deal in which an unsophisticated seller ends up with something other than cash in return for their property. The rule I put in my finance book was,

"Thou shalt not do a high-leverage, seller financed deal unless the seller is at least as sophisticated in financial matters as you."

For bargain purchases, the rule is,

"Thou shalt not make a bargain purchase in which an unsophisticated seller receives anything other than cash."

The definition of sophisticated

The seller is sophisticated in financial matters if:

• He or she has a net worth of at least $75,000 and
• He or she has a net worth as least as high as yours and
• he or she earned that net worth themselves as opposed to obtaining it by inheritance or winning the lottery or some such.

OR

the seller is sophisticated in financial matters if:

• He or she is a **professional** who works in finance or a related field—regardless of their net worth

Examples of finance professionals include:

• attorneys
• real estate agents
• title insurance company officers
• loan officers
• syndicators

- accountants
- appraisers
- officers of businesses (vice president or higher)
- owners of businesses with employees
- stock brokers

Clerical staff in those same occupations are not sophisticated, as a group, in my opinion. Basically, my list is a list of people who would generally not be willing to file a lawsuit which was based on the theory that they were taken advantage of by a more sophisticated person. Lawsuits are public documents. These people generally hold themselves out to the public as knowing what they are doing in the business world. If they are willing to sell you a property at 20% or more below market value and take back some cockamamie paper in the process, that's fine with me.

In fact, some of the techniques in this book specifically involve profiting from the lack of real estate sophistication of people who regard themselves as financially sophisticated in general. For example, the discount-lien-release technique frequently involves persuading a big corporation to release a lien on a property for a large discount—a larger discount than they would give if they knew what you know.

Taking advantage

Successful business people are often accused of evil. Critics use phrases like "taking advantage of the ignorance of others" or "taking advantage of shortages." But **all** economic activity can be accused of that.

In a sense, what this book is about is **out appraising** the other guy. He thinks the foundation problem is hopelessly expensive. You know it will cost $23,000 to fix—which is much less than the $58,000 discount you're getting because of the problem. Are you taking advantage of the seller's ignorance when you do that deal?

You bet you are. You're also taking advantage of the ignorance of the others who might have bid on the property if there were no foundation problem or if they knew what you know about the cost to repair it. You're also taking advantage of the ignorance of the guy who buys the property from you on resale. After all, if he had known what you know, he could have bought it at the bargain price which you paid.

But there's no dishonor in such a "taking advantage." Doctors make money by taking advantage of their patients' ignorance of medicine. Plumbers make money by taking advantage of their customers' ignorance of plumbing. Everyone whose job requires knowledge not possessed by laymen makes his living by taking advantage of the ignorance of others.

Every additional bidder helps the "victims"

The fact that I and other gurus are teaching the techniques in this book **helps** the sellers who are foolish enough to sell at 20% or more below market value. Because we are **increasing the number of bidders**. In some of the techniques I teach, like life estates and remainder estates, there are literally **no** bidders at all for what the seller has to sell. To the extent that my book causes **some** people to become willing to buy such interests, the people who own them are better off.

To the extent that we send more people after properties that already have **some** buyers like probates, foreclosures, and such, those properties will sell for **higher** prices than before our teaching because of the increased number of bidders. So we who teach bargain purchases—and you who make bargain purchases—**help** the people whose properties you buy cheap. Because if you didn't buy them as cheap as you did, someone else (the people you outbid) would have bought them even **cheaper**.

Unconscionability

Another political word which occurs in anti-rich-people rhetoric and legislation is "unconscionable." Some would say, "Hey, we don't begrudge a guy who buys foreclosures making a profit for his time and effort. We just think it's unfair, obscene even, that he make $256 an hour (to use the figure I calculated on Paul Thompson, an actual foreclosure-auction buyer). A 'reasonable' profit would be OK."

In fact, there is no definition of unconscionability or reasonable or obscene or unfair. Like the word "induce," they are mere dysphemisms (opposite of euphemisms) which say **much** about the **speaker's feelings** toward the person of whom he speaks—but say **nothing** about the **behavior** of which he speaks.

In general, the free market takes care of excess profits. There is a saying in economics that profits beget competition and excess profits beget ruinous competition. Indeed, this book is a manifestation of the truth of that saying.

I am writing this book because I think the profits available to bargain real estate purchasers are extraordinarily attractive. Many of those who pursue the sort of bargains described in this book are unhappy that I am spilling the beans. Apoplectic might be a more accurate description of their feelings. They've got a good thing going and they don't want competition.

The laws of economics

The people who criticize those who buy real estate for 20% or more below market value generally do so out of ignorance of economics. They understand dollars per hour. They understand the concept that profit is an entrepreneur's "wages." But they do **not** understand **risk**.

In general, the techniques in this book are extraordinarily profitable because they are extraordinarily risky. Take the bad-foundation example above. The seller agrees to sell you his house with severe foundation damage for $92,000. It there were no foundation problem, it would be worth $150,000. No one but you will touch it. You get an estimate from a foundation repair contractor who says he'll fix it for $23,000.

Ostensibly, that's a good deal. After repair cost, your cost would be $92,000 + $23,000 = $115,000 which is only 77% of its post-repair $150,000 value.

But the best-laid plans often go awry. What if the contractor fails to fix it for that price? That could happen if he's incompetent or dishonest. Or it could happen even if he is competent and honest if his health failed and you couldn't find a substitute willing to do the work for as low a price.

If you pull it off, and make the $150,000 - $115,000 = $35,000 quick profit, it may look like you took unconscionable advantage of a widow or orphan. But that's hindsight. Hindsight is blind to risks.

The deal that looks like a risk-free slam dunk in hindsight invariably looked much riskier at its inception.

In foreclosure buying, you get no payoff statements or title insurance—a fact which has cost many foreclosure buyers to lose all the money they put into the deal.

Many of the factors which are characteristic of bargain purchases—speed, all cash deals, other people trying to kill your deal, special expertise—increase the risks dramatically. The incremental compensation bargain purchasers get above, say, $50 per hour, is compensation for the risk they take. Anyone who thinks that compensation is excessive, is welcome to enter the business. That's free enterprise. That's also calling their bluff.

Crybabies

Consumers are also crybabies. When oil prices go down, they couldn't care less about the plight of people in the oil business. But when oil prices go up, they howl about "obscene, excess, windfall profits."

If people truly think the oil business is so excessively profitable, why aren't they rushing to buy stock in oil companies? Same thing applies to bargain purchases of real estate. If they're such super deals why aren't more people doing them?

The answer is they take a considerable amount of extra effort, expertise, and risk. It is the extraordinary effort you make, the extraordinary expertise you acquire, and the extraordinary risk you take that entitles you to the extraordinary profits you will make if you execute one or more of the techniques in this book competently.

And that proves another of the Laws of Economics: There is no free lunch. Not in this book or anywhere else.

3

Title problems

Most real estate people are taught to **run** from title problems.

Not so fast. There's money to be made from **some** title problems—precisely **because** everyone **else** runs from them.

Actual case history

John Beck (510-523-6115) didn't run from the title problem I'm about to tell you about. And he made about $24,000 as a result.

The house was sold and the papers signed. Then the preliminary title report came back. It said the **sellers did not own the property!** They never did.

The sellers protested that they **did** own it and produced papers to prove it—a **land contract**—an unrecordable (not notarized) land contract. That means the **previous** owner still had legal title. A land contract typically provides that the buyer will get **legal** title (the deed) when they pay off the seller financing.

The real estate agent tried to locate the previous owner to straighten out the problem—but could not find him. So the buyers and the agent walked away from the deal.

Enter John Beck

That's when John Beck came in. He is an attorney turned real estate investor. As an **investor**, he smelled a profit in the situation. A seller who needed cash fast—and whose property was essentially **unsaleable** because of a title problem.

As an **attorney**, he saw the title problem as finite and solvable. Not the invulnerable monster it seemed to be to the others.

Half price

He agreed to buy the property for $19,000—less than **half** the price agreed to in the sale that fell through. To protect himself, John got the seller to agree to take part of the purchase price in the form of an **unsecured note**. The note provided in part that John could deduct from his payments to the seller any arrearages he had to pay on the property. Arrearages like back taxes, unpaid interest, water bills, and so forth.

It turned out that the arrearages amounted to about $200 **more** than the $4,000 note—mainly interest payments that the sellers had not made to the previous owner. So as careful as John was about protecting himself—he was **not careful enough**.

Solving the title problem

John located the previous owner by making a more diligent search for him than the real estate agent had. But finding him was not all it took. The land contract buyers had not made all their payments. And the previous owner was mad about that.

On the other hand, he welcomed the opportunity to recover a debt he had written off. So John was able to get the previous owner—who was still listed in the county records as the **current** owner—to deed the property to John by paying the loan and the interest arrearages off.

When that occurred, the county records showed that the property was deeded **directly** from the pre-land contract owner to John. So except for the fact that John recorded his purchase of the land contract buyer's interest, a new title search would not show any trace of the land contract buyers.

Sold with a clear title

After John had acquired clear title to the property, he sold it for its full market value of about $43,000. His profit was about $24,000 less the $200 excess arrearage. So he got the property for $23,800 ÷ $43,000 = 55% below market value.

"Marketable" title

The standard wording of most purchase agreements says that the seller must deliver "marketable" or "merchantable" title to the buyer. If he can't, he has a title problem. What does marketable title mean? In *The Current Law of California Real Estate 2d*, Miller and Starr say at §2.52,

"If there is any reasonable doubt that there may be litigation regarding the title, then the title to the property is not 'marketable' because the buyer is not required to take the risk of matters that are not part of the public record or to assume the risk that litigation may be won or lost." Hardy v. Admiral Oil, *366 P 2d 310*

In another case, the court said a seller's title was not marketable because there was a recorded lease option against the property. The court said this in spite of the fact that the lease was in default and the option to purchase was thereby void and probably not could not be exercised. *Dennis v. Overholtzer*, 178 CA 2d 766

The point I'm trying to make is that buyers are **ultra sensitive** to the slightest hint of a question about the title to a property. And the courts have generally upheld the right of the buyer to get out of the deal when there was some slight question about the title.

In chapter one, I said one way to find bargains is to find problems which cause the others in the market to **overreact**. Lack of "marketable" title is clearly such a problem in many cases.

Unclear title = profit opportunity

To buy title-problem property at 20% or more below market, you buy or get control of a property which does **not** have marketable title. Since you are generally the only one willing to bid on it, you get it **cheap**. Then you **correct** whatever title problem there is—and sell the property for its normal, "clear title" market value.

Since clearing title problems is a somewhat uncertain proposition, you should try to **control** the property with an option to purchase or a purchase agreement contingent on your solving the title problem. Do not actually buy or even control the property unless you're pretty sure you can correct the title problem cheaply enough to make an adequate profit.

You can also reduce your risk with the following if the seller will agree:

• secured or unsecured **indemnification agreement** from the seller

• escrow company **impounds** money at closing to cover the problem

In some cases, you can pay the title company extra for a **special policy** covering the title defect which is scaring everyone else away.

50% discount

A November 27, 1985 *Wall Street Journal* column by Robert Guenther on "vulture funds" told of a case in Boston in which a building was "impossible to sell" because of a cloud on the title. The investors bought it for $50 a square foot and expected it to be worth **twice** that after the expenditure of a sizable amount for legal fees to clear up the title.

In his book, *How To Make A Fortune In Real Estate: The Land Game*, Albert Winnikoff tells of James Lick, who specialized in buying properties with clouded titles "dirt cheap" in the San Francisco area around the time of the 1849 Gold Rush. He must have done well. There's a freeway named after him.

Flooded property

A Southern California title company attorney I interviewed told me of a large area which had its titles screwed up by a flood. Many of the owners subsequently abandoned the properties and there were many tax deeds in the chains of title. Tax deeds arise out of the government auctioning off the property for nonpayment of property taxes.

Over time, the area became much more desirable. But no developer would touch the once-flooded portion because the title companies refused to issue clear title policies on the affected lots. The title companies figured the problems were fixable, but didn't want to front the massive number of man-hours which would be required.

Ultimately, one title company and one developer **teamed up** to tackle the property. The developer was willing to put up some front money to defray the title company's extra front-end costs—and to guarantee the title company that they would get the regular title insurance and escrow business when the lots were built upon and sold to their ultimate owners.

Lender unavailable case history

In 1988, investor Dan Kinter (916-965-6716) was contacted by a friend who had a friend who had a title problem. The individual had bought a house and the seller had taken back a $3,000 mortgage. Now the seller/lender could not be found therefore he could not be paid off therefore the house could not be sold to normal buyers who want such things taken care of.

The mortgage had been created in 1982 and was supposed to have been paid off in 1985. So it was in default.

Kinter agreed to buy the house for $55,500. It was worth $70,000. Kinter was subsequently able to find the brother of the seller/lender. Through the brother, Kinter negotiated with the seller/lender, who apparently did not want anyone but a relative to know where he was. The seller/lender insisted on being paid $4,500 to release the lien. The brother brought the notarized, signed document to Kinter who turned over the $4,500 in return. So Kinter's total purchase price including paying off the note was $60,000.

How to find these deals

Title companies and **real estate agents** become aware of these problems. So you could make your willingness to buy such properties known to the title and real estate brokerage companies in your area. That could be done with a quarterly post card or letter to the office manager of each office. You could try to make an occasional **speech** to the local Realtors® board and/or to the sales meetings of the larger brokerage companies.

Your speech in such situations would focus on how keeping your name and phone number might enable the agents to salvage a commission and help a seller in need. Do **not** tell the agents how much money you are making. All they need know about your bottom line is that you are a profit-seeking investor.

Try an "I buy problem properties" ad in the newspaper classified section, *Yellow Pages*, or trade media.

Try hiring **clipping services** to clip newspaper articles about title problems and send them to you. Clipping services are listed in the *AT&T Toll-free 800 Directory* under clipping bureaus

There are now **electronic clipping services** which periodically search computer data bases for articles containing words specified by you. Dialsearch is one (800-843-6476). For example, you could try running a weekly search for the phrase "title problem." Every time you got a likely clipping, you could contact affected parties and tell them of your interest in buying their property.

Ask title and real estate brokerage people if they know of any properties in the area which have **long been unsaleable** because of title problems. Sometimes, as in the case of the flooded property mentioned above, such properties are well known to long-time real estate people in the area.

Your local **Multiple Listing Book** may list an occasional property with a title problem mentioned in the comments section of the listing.

As I said above, recorded **lease options**—even when they have expired or been breached—are considered a cloud which renders title unmarketable. As you may know, lease options have become quite popular among single-family rental house owners in recent years. Nationally syndicated real estate columnist Robert Bruss frequently advocates them in his weekly column. He also advocates recording a memorandum of option when you are the lessee/optionee. So you might be able to find clouded titles by looking for recorded options.

Secrecy

You may find it wise to not mention that you buy property with title problems when you are talking to someone whom you **already** know has a title problem. Rather, just express interest in their property. And when they tell you of the title problem, tell them that you are still interested. Then investigate before you buy to get an idea as to how much time and money it will take to correct the problem.

If you tell people you buy properties with title problems, they may reconsider the very panic which creates the bargain opportunity. Of course, when you are making your interest in such properties known to real estate agents and title companies, you cannot be secretive.

Title claim litigation

A suit by a property owner against a title insurer who refused to pay a claim would red flag a property with a title problem. For example, in California there is a two year statute of limitations on such claims [CCP §339(1)].Whenever there are statutes of limitations, there are suits over when the statute of limitations began to run. It may make sense to buy out a person who lost such a suit where the discount obtainable seems big enough to more than cover the cost of clearing the title.

Systematically seek *lis pendens*

Lis pendens is Latin for lawsuit pending. It means there is a legal question as to whether the property seller has the right to sell the property. You could systematically seek out *lis pendens* situations by periodically looking for them in the public records.

Legal training helpful

Legal training would be helpful for a person pursuing title problem property. But legal training is not necessary. Just understand that by the time you learn what you need to learn to play this game, you'll become a quasi attorney if you are not a real one. Not to mention a quasi title search expert.

An oversight in searching the title of a property you buy can be disastrous. And in the techniques described in this chapter, you'll have to do most of your own title work, because title companies either won't work on the situations in question—or you won't have time to hire a title company—or there will be so many properties involved at the screening (pre-purchase) stage that it would cost too much to pay a title company to search all their titles.

Sellers without title insurance

If the guy you're buying from bought title insurance when he bought the property, there may be no opportunity for you to profit by clearing the title. Because the seller can just call the title insurance company and tell **them** to solve the problem. That's what title insurance is about.

Who does **not** have title insurance?

There is no title insurance in Iowa. And it's rare, by custom, in Massachusetts. Also, there are always a few penny-wise folks who refuse to get title insurance in other parts of the country. But mostly the sellers who do not have title insurance are people who were **unable** to get it when they bought the property.

How come? Typically because they acquired title by buying the property at a tax or lien foreclosure auction. Title insurance companies will not insure such titles until the redemption period is over—if ever.

In some states where the government's seizure procedure is questionable from a Constitutional-due-process standpoint, title insurance for a property which has been sold out of a government seizure is extremely difficult, if not impossible, to get. So you may have to sue for quiet title.

One investor bought a property from another investor who was also a friend. He did not get title insurance. Then when he went to sell, he discovered many judgments recorded against the same name as the previous owner. The person with all the judgments against him was **not** the previous owner. But it took mucho effort to get the statement of identification from the previous owner to prove it to the new title company.

Title insurance companies often fix slowly

Title companies are supposed to cure title defects which they failed to list as exceptions when you bought the property—or compensate you for them. And they generally will do what they're supposed to do. But it often takes time.

One large condo development I know of discovered after it had sold out that the survey and legal descriptions were all screwed up. Hundreds of condo owners had deeds and title policies showing the wrong property description for their parking space or their living unit. As a result, the whole development became untouchable for a year or two. During that time, a title company worked to correct the problem. Presumably, you could have picked up some of those condos for far less than market value if any of the owners had been forced to sell during that time.

In that case, the original title company bugged out. But if the original title company agrees to fix the problem, they will typically agree to insure the title of the new owner— thereby eliminating the opportunity to profit from an uninsurable title. Even though no other title company will insure the same title until the problem is cleared up.

Condo litigation

I know of another condo development which is on a hill. Some of the units slid down the hill in heavy rains. The owners of those units sued both the builder and the condo association. The suit dragged on for years. As a result, the entire condo development was untouchable for a while. Even though most of the units appeared to have no soil problems.

Clearly, you could have bought cheap there then.

The point here is that condos are excellent candidates for profit opportunities from title problems because the condo associations with their insurance policies and involvement in overall management tend to act as **title cloud collectors**.

It's safe to say that most of these clouds will eventually be dispelled. In the interim, you could buy a unit cheap. So cheap that you might be able to rent it out for positive cash flow (because your mortgage payment is so low). Then when the cloud is removed, you sell for normal market value.

An all cash business

To a large extent, buying untouchable properties is an **all cash** business. You're getting a bargain because buyers, lenders, and real estate agents won't touch the property. Note the word, "lenders."

If lenders are among those who will not touch the property, you won't be able to finance the purchase the way you normally do. You'll need all cash. Or at least all cash for the seller's equity if there is an assumable mortgage.

It's possible you could arrange **unsecured** financing if you had a strong relationship with a lender or other property which you could pledge as security for a line of credit. You might have such a relationship because of either your track record in turning title problems into profits—or your financial statement.

Forgeries and other frauds

You'd be amazed how common forgery and other fraud is in real estate sales. It's not a matter of master forgers running around copying signatures to create phony deeds. Rather the forger is usually a **relative** of the owner of the property.

Maybe a divorcing husband does not want to ask his estranged wife for her signature—so he forges it on the deed. Or an 80-year old owner is too sick with Alzheimer's disease to sign his name—so his wife or son sign it for him. In many, maybe most, of these cases, the person whose signature is being forged would **not object**. It doesn't matter. Only the owner in question or his or her legal guardian can sign.

According to Chicago Title Insurance Company, forgery is on the upswing. Less than 4% of their claims involved forgery or fraud prior to 1979. More than 25% did in 1984.

Title changes from legal proceedings

A great many title problems arise from title having changed by way of involuntary **legal proceedings**. That's because relatives of the owners who lost their property—and the owners themselves—can claim the property was taken **without due process**. In reality, there probably **was** due process. But that doesn't mean someone can't allege that there was not due process.

The greater the owner's equity at the time he lost the property, the greater the probability that he will sue to get it back. These suits create the kinds of problems that make people shy away from the property. California may have more such situations because an anti-foreclosure-abuse law aimed at people who buy property scheduled for foreclosures has made title companies and others even more gun shy than in other states.

Examples of involuntary title changes include

- divorces
- deaths
- appointment of guardians
- partition suits
- bankruptcies
- tax sales
- foreclosures

• judgment sales and so forth.

Lawsuits and patience

The correction of title problems like these is often a **quiet title** suit. That's where you file a suit to get the court to say unequivocally that **you** own the property and that these other people who claim ownership are full of baloney. Once you win that, you're generally squared away and anyone to whom you sell can get title insurance.

Depending upon the calendar, it may make more sense to wait until the **statute of limitations** runs out. Virtually all laws have statutes of limitations—time periods during which suits must be filed. Once the time period has expired, title insurance companies can generally be persuaded to resume insuring a title they refused to insure previously. And, if not, the quiet title suit would then be much simpler and cheaper.

Or if you buy an interest in a property in someone else's possession, you can simply record your interest then wait until the occupant tries to sell or refinance. At which time you will be contacted and asked what you'll take to execute a quitclaim deed.

Then there are **statutory expiration dates**. In California, for example, there are three kinds of involuntary liens and each expires unless renewed as follows:

- Attachment lien   three years
- Judgment lien   ten years
- Execution lien   two years

Also, your state may have statutes which wipe out "ancient" voluntary liens if they are not renewed. California's (CC §880.020-886.050) works like this:

- **trust deeds** and **mortgages** expire **ten years** after maturity or 60 years after recording if the maturity date is unknown
- **options** expire **six months** after the expiration date in the option or after recording if the option expiration date is unknown
- **land contracts** expire **five years** after the date provided for conveyance of title or five years after the last date specified in the contract.

Often patience is more cost effective than suing.

Sus Niimi's title problem

One of my newsletter subscribers, Sus Niimi, had an unusual title problem. And he solved it in an equally unusual way.

On July 1, 1988, a man called Niimi to ask him if he was aware that an $18,000 second trust deed had been recorded against his home. Niimi said he was not. The man then said his mother had been the victim of some fraud in which a phony second trust deed had been recorded against her home and that when the son investigated, he found a total of ten such trust deeds to the same "lender" all recorded on September 4, 1987. He had been calling the owners of each of the ten properties and each said the trust deed was a fraud.

The perpetrator had forged the signatures of the home owners on second trust deeds on ten Manhattan Beach, CA homes which had low loan-to-value ratios. The notary stamps were also forged. No one could find any record of the individual named as beneficiary (lender) in the trust deeds. And the "lender's" address was a private post office box which evicted him in February of 1989 for nonpayment of box rent.

In order to sell or refinance any of the ten properties, their owners would have to post a deposit or bond typically of 150% of the amount of the lien with the title company. Only then would the company remove the title exception for the $18,000 second trust deed.

Niimi's solution

Niimi tried to get the title company which had recorded the fraudulent trust deeds to solve the problem. They showed little interest in doing so.

He called me to see if I had any ideas. I said **publicity** probably wouldn't hurt. The story sounded newsworthy to me so I called the *Los Angeles Times* and told them about it. They did a story. As did other local newspapers.

Niimi says the publicity got the title company to get off their duffs and start working on the problem.

The story also brought four or five "ambulance chaser" type attorneys out of the woodwork. Each bragged about his experience in such matters and offered to pursue a quiet title suit for the victim. The average fee quoted was $7,500.

Niimi and six other victims declined to pay that sum. Instead, they agreed to let Niimi jawbone the title company and the supervisor at the county hall of records. However, three victims **did** hire attorneys.

The records supervisor finally gave in to Niimi's common-sense appeal and just pulled the fraudulent trust deeds from the records—no charge. One of the attorneys sheepishly called Niimi to see if his client could get the same treatment. Niimi got all ten trust deeds removed.

The police never found the perpetrator or discovered his motive.

Can you do this part time?

Investors often ask me if a particular technique can be pursued by part-time real estate investors. In general, the answer is "yes" with any leper property technique. Leper properties are properties which no one wants. Since no one is competing with you for the property, you can generally make the seller wait until evenings and weekends to do business with you. Title problem properties are leper properties.

Incidence of title problems

I do not know of any statistics on the incidence of title problems too difficult to be handled routinely in escrow by title companies. But my impression from 21 years in real estate is that they are quite rare. You might be able to systematically seek them out especially if you were a full-time real estate investor. That would probably require that you search over a wide geographic area.

Most people will probably find that this technique is best filed in the back of their mind to be recalled when a target of opportunity presents itself.

The key combination

Because title problems are generally solved eventually, you're looking for a combination of two things:

- problem which renders the property **unsaleable**
- seller who must sell **now**.

Get title insurance

You ought to get title insurance whenever you buy real estate. That includes when you buy a property with a title problem whenever possible. The title company may be willing to write a policy which excepts the one problem which is making it unsaleable but covers all other potential problems. You should buy that less than full coverage for the same reason you buy title insurance in a normal deal: there are lots of ways your title could be screwed up. And you need protection from them.

In the *California Title Insurance Practice* book published by the Continuing Education of the Bar, they list 50 different title defects which do not appear in public records but which are covered by title insurance. Here are some examples from that list:

3. Documents signed under a fabricated or expired power of attorney.

12. Notary signed before his commission began or after it expired.

18. Misinterpretation of wills.

29. Mistakes made by recording clerks, like incorrect indexing or loss of documents.

33. Failure to include necessary parties in judicial proceedings.

42. Person who signed deed was a convicted felon.

49. Unrecorded land contract sale (What John Beck made a profit on).

The fact that the property has one big, **un**insurable title problem doesn't mean it has no other insurable ones.

Toxics

By the same token, the fact that a property has a title problem does **not** mean it cannot also have a toxic problem. Matter of fact, I suspect a distraction like a title problem would be a good way to divert someone's attention **away** from a toxic contamination problem. If you've got a property on which you do not want the buyer to do due diligence—including an environmental audit—offering it at some bargain price for a plausible reason like a title problem or impending foreclosure would probably cause most prospective buyers to **not** do their normal due diligence.

Do not fall prey to that sort of sloppiness. Check the property out thoroughly as you would any other acquisition. My books, *Residential Property Acquisition Handbook* and *Office Building Acquisition Handbook* are good guides to the prepurchase investigation you ought to do.

Ethics

In the ethics chapter, I said you may not mislead the seller as to the value of their property. When you buy property with title problems, there probably is little question as to the value of the building with**out** the title problem. Rather the question is how much the title problem would cost to fix. So in title problem purchases, do not make any statements about how much it will cost to fix the title problem.

You should only do the deal when you believe it can be fixed for far less than the discount you are getting. Obviously, you can't say that. And if you can't say that, you'd better not say anything at all on that subject.

Furthermore, you may not even nod or otherwise agree with the sellers or their agent if **they** make a comment on the subject of how much it will take to fix the title problem. Rather you must respond to any such comment with a totally blank stare. If you are asked point blank how much you think it will cost to fix the title problem, you must decline to answer.

I recommend the following books if you are interested in this area:
John Beck's Forced Sale Workbook $49 and
Foreclosure Super-Bargains in California by John Beck and Ronald Starr $64
Researching the Title of Real Estate by Barry Adams
John Beck Seminars
1024 Regent Street

Alameda, CA 94501
510-523-6115

All About Escrow by Sandy Gadow $10.95 plus tax in CA and $2 for shipping
Express
P.O. Box 1639
El Cerrito, CA 94530
510-236-5496

4

Probate

Most real estate people have heard that you can make money buying probate properties. But there seem to be far more who have tried it and failed than success stories.

Apparently, it can be done. In fact I'm told you can regularly buy real estate out of probate for as much as 30% to 40% below market value. I found four success stories and I'm sure there are more.

How it works

When someone dies, their estate goes through probate. True, some people avoid probate by setting up living trusts. The best-selling book, *How to Avoid Probate* by Norman Dacey tells how to do that. But there are still lots of estates which go through probate.

A dead person's estate often includes real property. When it does, the heirs usually want it sold so they can get the cash. The laws of each state govern how the heirs must sell the property. The typical state law contains provisions which try to make sure that the property isn't sold too cheap. Appraisals and public auctions are commonly required.

Three stages

State laws vary but you can typically buy at any of three stages:

• private auction with probate attorney
• at court hearing to confirm bid obtained at private auction
• from successful bidder at above or heir who receives property instead of cash.

In general, the biggest bargains come from the **private** auctions. But adequate bargains can be obtained at the confirmation hearing (as in Beck's deal below) or by buying from other investors who got a super probate deal and are willing to sell cheap to make a quick profit.

Heirs sometimes receive the property itself instead of cash (called "distribution in kind"). In that case, you may be able to negotiate a bargain purchase from the heir.

Anyone can bid at confirmation hearings. The purpose of the hearing is to make one last check in the form of a public auction to make sure the estate can't get a better price than the one obtained at the probate attorney's private auction. In California, bidders at the hearing must bid at least a certain percentage over the high bid from the **private** auction. So you're better off being the winning bidder in the private auction where the profit margin on the deal is close to your minimum target.

You can bid through a real estate agent. But the estate must compare bids **net** of commission so those who bid through an agent are handicapped by the amount of the agent's commission.

Why you can get bargains

Property is least likely to sell at a bargain if the seller is a local owner who bought it recently for fair market value and occupied the property. With probate property, most of those ingredients are often absent.

The sellers are the heirs. They did not buy the property at all. So they may be subject to the **easy-come-easy-go** syndrome.

Often they are **not local**. They may live anywhere in the world. If they are not local, they probably do not know local property values.

Heirs are accidental owners. They didn't buy or manage the property in question. Their egos are not tied to the property value.

Most probate properties belonged to older people. Older people tend not to move much so they have generally owned the property for **many years** by the time they die. As a result, even a sale price well below market value can represent a large profit.

If the deceased has **multiple heirs**, each heir's share of the net sale proceeds of the real property sales is relatively small. In *The Land Game*, Albert Winnikoff tells of a probate deal he bought where an estate owned half the property and six other people owned interests ranging from 65.4/454ths to 96.2/454ths. Each such heir has only a fractional **motivation** to maximize the price.

So it's hard for any heir to get too excited about the price. Furthermore, each may be reluctant to expend the effort required to sell for fair market value because the other heirs would get part or most of the benefit of that effort.

Heirs are often **cash-oriented**. They are more interested in the speed at which they receive the cash than in whether the amount is X dollars or 80% of X dollars.

Sibling rivalry and long-standing feuds often prevent **communication** between heirs or leadership by any one of them. Heirs behave funny. You don't really know someone until you split an inheritance with them according to one old saying. In his book, *Estate Planning*, attorney Peter Lippett mentions,

"...the often family-wrecking disputes that can come up in an inheritance situation."

The decision maker in the sale of probate property is often a **non-heir** like an attorney or judge or independent appraiser. Human nature being what it is, these folks often accept the most expedient deal rather than the best deal.

Isn't the probate attorney supposed to make sure the estate realizes market value for its property? As a practical matter, probates are usually handled by **paralegals**. The attorney's fee is usually fixed by statute or local custom which, in turn, gives the attorney incentive to standardize and minimize the amount of time spent on each case.

In *How To Avoid Probate*, Norman Dacey quotes the *New York Times* as saying, "there *is evidence...and general agreement among many top legal experts...that the probate procedures in many areas are woefully inefficient, inadequate, and...sometimes bordering on the scandalous."*

Dacey tells of one probate property sold for 42% of its appraised value. And another sold for $80,000 with a person who bid $125,000 being bribed $25,000 to withdraw his bid. The actual market value of that property was not stated but we can assume it was significantly greater than $80,000 + $25,000 = $105,000.

Lawmakers and probate attorneys ought to clean up the probate act. But we real estate investors have neither the power nor the responsibility to clean it up. And until **they** do, probate's inefficiencies, inadequacies, and scandals represent an opportunity for real estate investors. Publicizing those opportunities—as I'm doing in this book—can only **help** estates by increasing the number of bidders for their properties.

How many are there?

Probate buyer Gary DiGrazia (510-276-5331) pursues probate property in four San Francisco Bay Area towns. Those four cities have a combined population of about 400,000. A combined total of about 25 new probates are filed in those three cities each week. That suggests the probate-to-population ratio is about 25 ÷ 400,000 = 6 per hundred thousand per week.

The national death rate is about 9 people per thousand per year so DiGrazia's four cities should have about 400 x 9 = 3,600 deaths per year or 69 per week.

DiGrazia says about 70% of the deceased in his area own real estate.

Success ratio

DiGrazia buys three or four houses per year so his ratio of estates contacted to houses purchased is 52 weeks per year x 25 probates per week = 1,300 probates per year ÷ 3.5 buys per year = 371 to one. That is, if you contact 371 probate estates and pursue them competently, you will probably buy one house for at least 20% below market value.

The typical real estate person who "tried probates and they don't work" probably gave up before he hit 371.

The response to DiGrazia's mailing piece may come in a week—or a year. He still sends **no follow-up letters**. The typical response is noncommittal, resulting, at best, in his inspecting the property.

Dwain Sachs (314-647-0001) contacts about 250 new estates per month in his St. Louis area or 250 x 12 = 3,000 per year. In 1990, for example, he bought four properties for an estates-to-buys ratio of 3,000 ÷ 4 = 750 to one. The difference probably stems from DiGrazia's more intense involvement. He does nothing but probates; Sachs has many other irons in the fire. Also, DiGrazia spends more time per probate since he contacts fewer than half as many as Sachs.

Neither approach is necessarily best. The best measure of efficiency is probably how much each makes per hour of time spent.

How to find them

Both DiGrazia and Sachs are real estate brokers. As such, their approach may be a little different than what a **pure** real estate investor would do. That's because each has a fallback position of accepting a listing on the property. Listings typically produce a commission which is less than the profit on a bargain purchase but still substantial.

The establishment of probates is announced in "newspapers of general circulation." The executor, personal representative, or administrator is listed in the paper. As is the estate's attorney. Here's an example I copied out of my local newspaper for today (10/29/91). I've changed the names to protect their privacy.

NOTICE OF PETITION TO ADMINISTER ESTATE OF:
George W. Armakant, aka G.W. Armakant, aka George Wilkerson Armakant

CASE NO. CV000676-4

To all heirs, beneficiaries, creditors, contingent creditors, and persons who may otherwise be interested in the will or estate, or both of: George W. Armakant, aka G.W. Armakant, aka George Wilkerson Armakant.

A PETITION has been filed by Anita M. Armakant in the Superior Court of California, County of Alameda.

THE PETITION requests that Anita M. Armakant be appointed as personal representative to administer the estate of the decedent.

THE PETITION requests the decedent's WILL and codicils, if any, be admitted to probate. The will and any codicils are available for examination in the file kept by the court.

THE PETITION requests authority to administer the estate under the Independent Administration of Estates Act (This authority will allow the personal representative to take many actions without obtaining court approval. Before taking certain very important actions, however, the personal representative will be required to give notice to interested persons unless they have waived notice or consented to the proposed action.) The independent administration authority will be granted unless an interested person files an objection to the petition and shows good cause why the court should not grant the authority.

A HEARING on the petition will be held on November 18, 1991 at 10:00 A.M. in Dept. 50 located at 5672 Stoneridge Dr., Pleasanton, CA 94566.

IF YOU OBJECT TO the granting of the petition, you should appear at the hearing and state your objections or file written objections with the court before the hearing. Your appearance my be in person or by your attorney.

IF YOU ARE A CREDITOR or a contingent creditor of the deceased; you must file your claim with the court and mail a copy to the personal representative appointed by the court within four months from the date of first issuance of letters as provided in section 9100 of the California Probate Code. The time for filing claims will not expire before four months from the hearing date noticed above.

YOU MAY EXAMINE the file kept by the court. If you are a person interested in the estate, you may file with the court a formal Request for Special Notice of the filing of an inventory and appraisal of estate assets or of any petition or account as provided in section 1250 of the California Probate Code. A Request for Special Notice form is available from the court clerk.

Attorney for Petitioner:
MERLE S. TOMEY
O'MALLEY, WEINSTEIN, & WONG
129 Main Street
Danville, CA 94526
Legal PT/VT/SRVT 0039
Publish October 25, 28, Nov. 11, 1991.

Note that the name of the would-be special representative appears at lines 11 and 12 of the ad. (There are no line numbers in the real ad. I added them to help explain how to read the ad.) Her address does not appear. But note that lines 60 and 61 say you can examine the file at the court. That file will have the personal representative's address.

The name and law firm name and address of the would-be personal representative's attorney appears at lines 70 through 73. You can get the attorney's phone number from the *Yellow Pages*.

You need the case number (line 6) to request the file from the court clerk. Most courts have a numbering system which tells you something about the case. For example, in DiGrazia's area, a case number beginning with H is located in Hayward; one beginning with a 2, in Oakland.

The petition to be appointed personal representative is generally approved at the court hearing. So the hearing has little real significance. The **date** of the hearing, however, **is** significant in that the would-be personal representative usually will refuse to deal with you or anyone else on estate matters until the appointment is made official by the court.

In some areas, you can subscribe to services which will list all the new probates that are filed, court confirmation hearings, and completed sales out of probate. For example, San Francisco has *The Blue Sheet* (415-731-7941).

Screening

As I said in the first (Overview) chapter, efficient screening is important when you are only doing one deal for every several hundred possible sellers considered. DiGrazia is only interested in residential real estate. So he needs to quickly eliminate those probates which have no real estate or which only have nonresidential property.

He cuts out probate ads all week then goes to a title company on Fridays. There he checks to see if the deceased owned any real estate. The tax assessor's list of property owners generally shows what properties, if any the deceased owned, and describes the nature of those properties in words or a code.

Those records are typically on microfiche at title companies or in your local library. If you do a big enough volume, you may want to lease the microfiche yourself. Suppliers of that data include TRW Real Estate Information Services/Real Estate Data, Inc. (REDI). If you lease the fiche, you'll need a microfiche reader. Many professional bargain purchasers buy used microfiche readers for their home office.

Generally, **homes** occupied by **surviving spouses** are a waste of time for bargain seekers. They rarely suffer from any of the heir failings described above, i.e. unfamiliarity with market, fractional interest, easy-come-easy-go.

There is also self screening by the recipients of the mailing pieces. In DiGrazia's case, only about three or four people respond out of each batch of 25 pieces sent. And of course he does **not** buy property from **most** of of those who respond.

Your state law

As with many bargain-purchase techniques, you need to learn the details of your state law and local procedure. For example, DiGrazia has found in California that only estates administered under that state's Independent Administration of Estates Act yield bargain purchases. As you can see in the example ad above, the fact that the estate will be administered under the Independent Administration of Estates Act is readily available right in the ad (lines 24-27).

In California, the Independent Administration Act is a key screening step. Your state may have similar laws and procedures. You can buy DiGrazia's book for the details on how his approach works in California. For other states, you'll have to figure it out on your own perhaps with the help of probate attorneys and/or trips to your local law library.

You can generally buy a paperback copy of your state's probate code from a law book store or by mail. And you should. You may also want to subscribe to a legal service which will keep you up to date on changes in your state's probate law. Local colleges and universities may have extension courses on probate law. If so, you may find it useful to take them. You do **not** need to graduate from law school to buys probates for a living. Neither DiGrazia nor Sachs are lawyers.

How to approach the decision makers

Both Dwain Sachs and Gary DiGrazia communicate by mail to the personal representative. Sachs also sends a copy to the attorney. DiGrazia avoids the attorney but he also sends his letter to each heir who has been willed an interest in the property in question. (He reads the will in the probate file.). DiGrazia says he averages about three letters per estate. Each letter has a "cc" showing who else received the letter.

That's **one** piece of mail to each recipient. Neither Sachs nor DiGrazia sends any further mailing pieces after the first one. Sachs calls **out-of-county** personal representatives. He also calls attorneys. He says the probates tend to be concentrated among a small "hard core" group of attorneys.

DiGrazia uses a reverse directory to find out the phone number of the personal representative. He calls several days after he figures his letter has been received and asks if they plan to sell the property.

Sachs' mailing piece is a double post card. The recipient can tear off half and send it back to Sachs postage paid.

Gary DiGrazia's letter is one he created after much trial and error. He found the wording of the letter is extremely important because many heirs are beset by profit-seeking people. In most cases, the deceased was a loved one and the heirs find mercenary hearse chasers to be an annoying intrusion.

I called a new widow once

When I was a real estate salesman, I specialized in cold calling for listings by phone. I would go right down each street calling each house using a reverse directory.

According to the Law of Averages, if you do that, you will eventually call someone whose spouse just died. That happened to me. The woman burst into tears and slammed the phone down immediately upon my saying I was calling to see if she was planning on selling her home.

The next day, when I called someone else on that same street, a person who had not been home the previous day, she said I must have been the one who called Mrs. So-and-So and that was a horrid thing to do and everyone in the neighborhood now hated my company and would never do business with us. I explained that I had no idea her husband had just died. I was simply calling **everyone** on the street to ask the same question. The second woman refused to believe me in spite of the fact that I had called her the next day and no one had died in her family. People enjoy their hatreds and they aren't about to let a little thing like the facts dissuade them. In any event, I learned, inadvertently, that you'd better tread very lightly when trying to do death-related business with close relatives of the recently deceased.

DiGrazia's letter

DiGrazia's letter is not reproduced here because it appears in his copyrighted book, *Diamond Farming, Probate Real Estate.*

In general, it:

• expresses condolences
• expresses interest in the estate's property
• offers to purchase in "as is" condition
• offers to pay all cash
• offers to close within 30 days

• explains that the personal representative does not have to wait until the probate is finished to sell
• points out that the court confirmation process runs up attorney fees.

When to approach the decision makers

With real estate deals in general, and bargain purchase deals in particular, speed is crucial. DiGrazia says your letter should go out with a few days of the probate ad appearing in the paper. "You want to be the first to show interest in the property..." he says.

Within 48 hours of inspecting the property, Gary submits an offer from one of the three investor partners he works with. He won't let the investor offer more than 75% of market value. He puts 30% down in order to get a fast, "easy-qualifier" mortgage.

The offer calls for closing in 30 days, a number of inspections, and gives Gary ten days to remove those inspection contingencies.

He uses the ten-day contingency period for both inspections and another purpose: to find a **buyer** for the property.

Nature of the properties

Different bargain techniques tend to produce different kinds of properties. For example, foreclosed properties are often trashed out. Probate properties tend to be single-family houses which were recently occupied by an old person. A significant percentage are **fixers**. Probate guru Jim Banks says 15% to 18% fall into that category.

They generally are not trashed out or vandalized. About the only problem you would expect would be excess possessions and deferred maintenance. Many senior citizens accumulate tons of stuff—newspapers, tax records, children's possessions, old clothes, trunks, and various family treasures. I listed a probate house once when I was a real estate salesman. It was literally piled to the ceiling with junk.

Volunteers from the deceased's church said they would clean it out for my buyers. But they apparently got tired before the job was done. So on closing day, there were still tons of stuff to be removed and days of cleaning to be done.

Financing

You can finance a probate purchase like any other purchase: conventional, FHA, VA, or seller financing (taken back by the estate). Seller financing is even more feasible than in non-probate deals because most probate property is **free and clear**. In any event, you need not pay all cash. Although Jose Leon says probate sellers give **bigger discounts** for cash than regular sellers. Unlike delinquent tax sales, you can get the **title insurance** lenders require.

One of the reasons you got bargains in probate purchases is that many heirs are eager for fast cash. Accordingly, you may need to come up with fast cash to get bargains. DiGrazia has partners who have **equity lines of credit on their homes**. More established investors could probably get business lines of credit not related to their homes.

When they find a deal, DiGrazia's investors use the equity line to come up with enough for an all cash purchase. Then they sell the house or apply for a regular mortgage after they tie up the purchase.

Tax ramifications

Buying real estate is not a taxable event. If you immediately resell, you are almost certainly a dealer as to that property. That means you may not take advantage of long-term capital gains rates, depreciation deductions, or tax-free exchanging on that property.

Profit per deal

DiGrazia says he insists on a minimum of $15,000 per deal. His average deal produces $20,000 in profit split between him and his investor partner. Plus DiGrazia gets the buyer's broker commission which is typically around $5,000.

I'll give you some actual case histories later in the chapter to further show what profits you can expect.

Part-time?

You **can** pursue probates part time. Sachs does.

Can you do this everywhere?

People die everywhere at approximately the same rate. But I do not know the probate law of every state. It's possible that you cannot buy real estate for at least 20% below market value in some states because of probate laws or customs in those states. In many areas, bargains are scarce because a high percentage of probate properties are listed in the multiple listing service.

In California, it's much harder to buy for 20% below market value if the estate is not administered under the Independent Administration of Estates Act.

The buyer is required to pay at least 90% of appraised value in California in the **non**-Independent Administration of Estates Act probates. On its face, that would seem to prohibit 20% discounts altogether. But DiGrazia says you can still sometimes get a 20% discount if the following are present:

- low appraisal
- you get a commission from the estate (in such cases, state law requires you to say if you plan to resell at a profit)
- estate pays closing costs
- estate credit you at closing for repairs to the property.

Estate appraisers are typically paid very little, for example, less than $100 to appraise a house. And the estate wants the value to be set as **low** as possible for estate and inheritance tax purposes. If the appraiser comes in **high**, the heirs often challenge and force him to reveal such embarrassing details as the fact that he never inspected the property. So the appraiser has incentive to come in low. And even if he's trying to hit market value, he can't afford to spend adequate time digging up the pertinent facts.

You'll have to check your state laws and customs to see if 20% or greater discounts are possible there.

Dwain Sachs deal

In 1990, Sachs bought a property on Dale Avenue which was typical of the deals he gets this way. The estate's attorney called Sachs in response to his letter. Sachs inspected the property then agreed to buy for all cash.

The property was a four-family house with apartments worth $325 a month per unit. That's $325 x 4 = $1,300 per month x 12 = $15,600 per year gross. Assuming a 50% operating expense ratio (half of gross goes to pay operating expenses but not debt service), the net operating income is $7,800.

Sachs figured the property was worth $85,000 to $100,000 when he bought it. He paid $65,000. At that price, his cap rate is $7,800 ÷ $65,000 = 12%, which was extraordinary in the 1990 market.

With a 75%-of-purchase price mortgage (75% x $65,000 = $48,750) at 10%, the monthly payments on a 30-year mortgage would be $427.82 or $5,133.79 per year. That would leave $7,800 - $5,133.79 = $2,666.21 positive cash flow per year. The down payment would be $65,000 - $48,750 = $16,250. So the cash-on-cash return is $2,666.21 ÷ $16,250 = 16%.

John Beck's deal

John Beck (510-523-6115), author of a forthcoming book on buying through probate and previously editor of *Distress Sales Report*, a newsletter for Californians who invest in foreclosures, bought an Alameda, CA home in 1981 by outbidding the private winning bidder at a probate confirmation hearing. Beck paid $80,000. He figured it was worth about $110,000 to $120,000 at the time.

Winnikoff's deal

In the 65.4/454ths deal described above, Winnikoff got 160 acres worth between $2,150 and $5,641 per acre for $1,100 an acre.

Jose Leon's deal

On December 30, 1988, Jose Leon and some partners bought 2106 48th Street in San Francisco for $175,000 all cash in a private probate sale. He spent about $1,500 on the two-bedroom house and sold it for $256,000 within two months. A real estate agent heard about the house from a neighbor. When the heir refused to list it, the agent told Leon in return for a finders fee.

Resale of the properties

DiGrazia employs a technique which many professional investors use: a **stable of buyers and agents** who will either buy or find a buyer for your property quickly.

Quick resale is essential to DiGrazia. He's a deedless real estate investor, a flipper who regards 90 days as long term. He wants no part of either **management** or **renovation**. Local appreciation rates are all but irrelevant to his program.

DiGrazia has a stable of regular buyers and agents he calls when he has a property to sell. He wants to sell the property at **quick-sale value** (about 90% to 95% of market value) for **all cash** as fast as possible because the property is **vacant** and generating no income. Meanwhile, the money borrowed to buy it accrues interest. DiGrazia has keys to the property at this point and shows the property to his own buyers or gives the key to selected, cooperating agents.

He generally gets a buyer fast enough that he **could** double escrow the deal if he wanted. But double escrows *per se* antagonize the probate attorneys too much so he closes the resale **separately**. However, the closings are still close enough that he can pass most of his closing costs on to the ultimate buyer. Among other things, he uses the standard flipper technique of paying 110% of a normal title insurance premium to get a "110% binder." That enables him to get back all but 10% of his title insurance premium when the ultimate buyer gets title insurance from the same company (which DiGrazia requires).

DiGrazia pursues the **buy-very-low-sell-low** strategy rather than the far more well known buy-low-sell-high approach. Selling for quick-sale value makes sense whenever the property in question is **vacant**. Buy-very-low-sell-low also makes sense when the investor's time is valuable. At quick-sale value, you can generally sell in a matter of **weeks**, for **cash**, without an agent.

Time commitment

DiGrazia spends about five to ten hours a week keeping his probate tracking sheets (See his book for details) up to date.

Preparation for inspection

Before he inspects the property, Gary reads the entire **probate file** which is a public record. He also takes every opportunity to build **rapport** with the personal representative including face-to-face meeting whenever possible. That rapport often becomes crucial when other actors like attorneys and other would-be buyers later come into the picture with deal-killing on their mind.

Intimate knowledge of the personal representative's wants and needs also enables Gary to out-negotiate his Johnny-come-lately critics and competitors. As does his general knowledge of what personal representatives want most: things like **speed**, **cash**, and **minimum effort** on their part.

5835 Hooker

One of the responses DiGrazia got in the spring of '89 was from Fred Cucci (not his real name). Fred was the personal representative of his mother's estate which included her home, a two-bedroom, one-bath house at 5835 Hooker Street in Hayward (not the real address). Fred, however, was handling the estate from out of state. DiGrazia would have to establish rapport without a face-to-face meeting.

He did—through numerous phone calls. DiGrazia arranged immediately to inspect the property. Then he quickly made his offer: $150,000 with 30% down and a new, easy-qualifier mortgage.

The house came with a lot big enough to build on. The personal representative knew that but didn't want to be bothered getting approvals. DiGrazia figured the property was worth $200,000.

Court appraisal

The Cucci estate was being handled according to the rules of California's **Independent Administration of Estates Act**. That is the less formal of the two California procedures. It does **not require** a court appraisal. However, most estate attorneys order such an appraisal as a CYA measure. The attorney in this estate ordered such a court appraisal.

The court appraisal is done by the court-appointed estate referee. Estate referees get paid minimal fees. You get what you pay for. Probate experts figure the typical referee does a windshield appraisal. While referee's appraisals are often inaccurate, they can be inaccurate in **either** direction. By law, if the referee's appraisal comes in more than 10% above DiGrazia's agreed-upon purchase price, the deal is off.

DiGrazia held his breath waiting for the appraisal. It came in at $158,000—**within** the 10% allowable range.

Interlopers

Theoretically, that should have sealed it. But as with other bargain purchase techniques, others quickly recognized the bargain and tried to overbid it.

The attorney recommended that the property be listed with a real estate agent so a **new, better** buyer might be found. Plus, a builder who wanted the property for its extra lot tried to get the personal representative to sell to him instead.

That builder was building on other lots around 5835 Hooker. One of those lots had been sold to the builder by the deceased who had taken back a mortgage on it. That mortgage was now one of the estate assets the personal representative wanted to liquidate. DiGrazia and his partner offered to buy that note from the estate for face value. That clinched the deal. As it turned out, the builder got some construction financing and paid off the note so DiGrazia and his partner never had to complete the note purchase.

No court confirmation

Because this estate was handled under the Independent Administration of Estates Act, court confirmation was not necessary. Under the **other** procedure, the public would have to be given an opportunity to bid more than the amount agreed to privately by DiGrazia and the personal representative. Such public auctions often wipe out the private bidder's bargain.

Resale

Gary resold the property through one of his "broker outlets" in May of '89, three weeks after he and his partner closed the purchase from the estate. The sale price was $230,000. The investor paid a 4% commission.

Here's a summary of the deal:

Resale price	$230,000
Selling commission	$9,200
Net sale price	**$220,800**

Purchase price	$150,000
Buyer's commission	$8,000
Closing costs	$1,000
Total cost	**$159,000**

Net investor profit $61,800

Gary got half that profit or $30,900.

Attorneys

Probate attorneys are cultivated by real estate brokers. As a result, many probate attorneys have favorite real estate agents. They generally recommend to the personal representative that he or she **list** the property with that favorite broker.

Listing with a real estate agent usually eliminates any bargain opportunity. Broadly speaking, the two ways to buy property for at least 20% below market are 1. buy property **nobody wants** or 2. buy property **nobody knows is for sale**. Probate properties are generally not in the first category. So locking them up **before** others find out about them is key.

DiGrazia obtains agreement on the sale price and terms **before** the probate attorney persuades the personal representative to list it. On a number of occasions, the probate attorney has tried to kill Gary's deal. So far, none has succeeded—primarily because of the rapport he has established with the personal representative.

DiGrazia asks each person from whom he buys for a letter of recommendation. He asks the personal representative to write a letter in his or her own words generally answering the question, "Did Gary DiGrazia do everything he promised?" DiGrazia puts the letters into a brag book which he shows to future personal representatives and attorneys as part of his sales pitch.

5

Pre-foreclosures

The opportunity to buy bargains as a result of foreclosures occurs at three stages:

• Pre-foreclosure
• Foreclosure auction
• Post auction (OREOs).

This chapter is about the **pre-foreclosure** stage, that is, buying from persons whose mortgages are in default but whose properties have not yet been auctioned off.

How it works

Impending foreclosures must be advertised in to the public. Those ads give the names and addresses of the people who are in default. You then contact them and offer to buy their house. A small percentage will sell to you for 20% below market or more. As soon as you buy the property, you reinstate the delinquent mortgage. That means you pay the back interest and penalties and any other costs due. If you don't reinstate, the foreclosure will proceed and your equity in the property will probably be wiped out. In some states, you have no right to reinstate. You have to negotiate with the lender or refinance the entire mortgage and pay off the one which became delinquent.

Why it works

People who are being foreclosed and who have equity in their homes ought to either sell the home before foreclosure or reinstate the mortgage which is in default. They reinstate the mortgage by paying the back payments, penalties, and other charges they owe.

But people are often **not** rational about financial difficulties. A high percentage go through a **denial** phase about the time the foreclosure process begins. Consequently, they are not taking the steps they need to take to either sell the property in an orderly manner or reinstate the mortgage.

In many cases, they **cannot** reinstate the loan because they have bad credit or inadequate collateral or income to qualify for the needed new loan.

That leaves selling the property. But in order to sell the property fast enough to beat the foreclosure, they must list it promptly with a real estate agent and price it at the bottom of the fair market value range.

Unfortunately, they react to the legal notices of the impending foreclosure as if they weren't real or as if some unknown savior was expected to appear and prevent the foreclosure. Plus they don't **want** to sell their house. They want to **keep** it. So they tend to rule out the orderly-sale alternative.

My late uncle Jack would respond to that by saying, "People in Hell want ice water, too. But that doesn't mean they're gonna get it."

So properties with equity which could have been saved through an orderly sale of the property often go to foreclosure because the defaulting owner simply refuses to believe foreclosure is actually going to happen or because he waits too long to take appropriate action.

Once the owner realizes he really is going to lose his house, he goal shifts to avoiding **homelessness**. When he tries to rent an apartment, he often has enormous difficulty because his credit is bad and he often cannot even come up with a security deposit and first month's rent. Helping the owner find and pay for a place to live is generally part of what the pre-foreclosure investor must do to make his bargain purchase.

Basic principles

As with most other bargain purchase techniques, the vast majority of defaulted homeowners will not sell you their house for 20% or more below market value. So you must contact perhaps a thousand defaulted property owners in order to do one deal.

When you deal with properties-to-deals ratios that high, **direct mail** is generally the only way to go. And, indeed, that's what the professional pre-foreclosure buyers like Danville, California's Ted Thomas do.

You also need efficient **screening**. Thomas uses a carefully designed questionnaire to eliminate the non-bargains as quickly as possible.

Speed is very important. You must complete your due diligence like title search, inspection, and so forth very fast.

And this is an **all-cash** business. People who are being foreclosed need cash fast. Thomas generally only pays cash for their equity. He "assumes" mortgages which are not assumable by just reinstating them. If the lender exercises the due-on-sale clause which is in virtually all mortgages, Thomas refinances the property.

As a pre-foreclosure buyer, you must be sensitive to the peculiar needs of people who are being foreclosed. You contact many, hear back from a few, question them, commiserate a little, negotiate a little, offer to help with their moving needs (typically by cosigning on their new lease and paying their first month's rent and security deposit), and so forth.

Do **not** give them **all** the money you promised until they are completely moved out of the house.

Incidence of this opportunity

There are always foreclosures—even in boom markets. The **number** of foreclosures, however, is cyclical. During hard times, it goes up dramatically. And during those same times, the number of competing buyers drops dramatically. So the pre-foreclosure buyer can get 20% discounts in good times and 40% and 50% discounts in hard times—like when I'm writing this—November, 1991.

How to find them

Lenders must give public notice of foreclosures in every state. That stems from the due-process clause in the Fourteenth Amendment to the U.S. Constitution. Those notices generally must be recorded in the county recorder's office and published in a "newspaper of general circulation" in the county. In some counties, so-called legal newspapers are used. In others, regular newspapers contain the notices. The notices are recorded and published 90 to 120 days before foreclosure in every state I'm aware of.

In many areas with highly organized real estate industries, there are private services which monitor the official notices recorded in the courthouse or published in legal newspapers and publish them in abstracted form for pre-foreclosure investors and others.

Direct mail

Thomas subscribes to a service which reports the filing of notices of default. He operates in Contra Costa, San Joaquin, and Alameda Counties (all east of San Francisco), Santa Clara County (south of San Francisco), and in Solano County (northeast of San Francicso). In 1988, about 100 notices of default a week were filed in Contra Costa County; about 125 in Alameda (which includes Oakland and Berkeley).

Little old ladies

Thomas advertised for and trained little old ladies to hand address and mail letters to the defaulting borrowers. The little old ladies write the name and address of each defaulting borrower on seven different envelopes by hand. Then they insert seven different numbered letters, seal the envelopes, and stick on a bulk rate stamp (19.8¢). They put one envelope in the mail and the other six in dated boxes.

There are boxes with the dates of the Mondays through Thursdays for the next 90 days (the time to cure default under California law). Each defaultee receives one of Thomas's letters about every 12 days (he doesn't mail on Fridays because he doesn't want the letter to arrive on a Saturday).

Ten letters

For example, if Joe Deadbeat appears in the notices of default which Thomas receives on January 2nd, a letter will go out to Joe that day and the other six letters will be placed in boxes labeled January 14th, January 26th, February 7th, February 19th, March 3rd, March 15th—unless any of those are Fridays or weekends in which case it will go in the box for the following Monday.

At the end of the 90-day period—if the default has not been cured—the property is posted for the foreclosure auction and appears in **another** part of the service Thomas subscribes to. The little old ladies write the names and addresses of those folks on **three** items. The first is a 6" x 9", 20-page, self-mailer booklet Thomas wrote called

"Eye-Opening Facts About Foreclosure—18 Ways To Avoid Foreclosure."

In addition to the information promised on the cover, the booklet contains Thomas's name, address, and phone number as well as an ad offering to buy their property. Plus the foreclosee gets two more letters from Thomas during the 21-day notice period.

The envelopes are placed in zip-code order in the boxes as required by the post office to qualify for bulk rates. Whenever a box's mail date arrives—and the box has at least 200 envelopes (the minimum for bulk rate)—Thomas's little old ladies mail it. If there are fewer than 200 envelopes in a box, that box gets combined with the following day's box. They drop a batch in the mail about three or four times a week—about 600 to 1,000 letters a week.

The response

About two to five people a week (1% to 2%) respond to Thomas's letters—usually at the third to fifth letter. Of those, he buys about one property every week.

Thomas tried customized computer-printed letters. It didn't work. The printer ran constantly. It was too expensive.

The cost-effective approach is the **handwritten** envelope and licked stamp (to get the envelope opened)—but printed form letters inside. Each piece in the series is different—to avoid the sort of repetition that gets thrown away without being read. But each contains letters which emphasize **quick cash** for the defaultee's equity, no commission, and each contains a different **testimonial** from a previous defaultee who took Thomas up on his offer. Recipients are invited to respond by calling Thomas or writing to him.

The cost

Thomas has two part-time women (different from the ladies who address and mail the letters) on staff. They answer the phone, type documents related to the purchases and sales, and coordinate the occasional renovation. Thomas hates to hold a property long enough to have to rent it or renovate it. But the best-laid plans...

The cost per letter is

postage	19.8¢
letter	1.0¢
envelope	2.0¢
labor	5.0¢
Total	27.8¢

If you figure it takes 1,000 letters for each deal done, that's 1,000 x 27.8¢ = $278 per deal. If the average deal is $150,000—and the average profit per deal is 20% of that or $30,000—that's $278 well spent. (Office overhead, of course, consumes some of that profit, too.)

Financing ramifications

Cash is the name of the pre-foreclosure financing game. You generally need to offer fast cash in your letters to the property owners who are being foreclosed. You may want to pay only for their equity and buy subject to the existing mortgage(s). Technically, the mortgage lender can demand pay off of the mortgage when the property is sold to a pre-foreclosure investor or anyone else. That's because virtually all mortgages these days contain a due-on-sale clause which gives them that right in the event of a sale.

But as a practical matter, the lender does not always pay enough attention to notice that the property has been sold. Also, if the mortgage interest rate is at or above current market rates, and you have rescued it from foreclosure, the lender may choose not to exercise their right to demand immediate pay off of the mortgage.

Even if the lender **does** choose to foreclose under the due-on-sale clause, the pre-foreclosure investor can often resell the property at a profit **before** the lender's foreclosure is completed.

Ethics and laws regarding the due-on-sale clause

There is an **ethical** consideration here. Heck, it's a **legal** one, too. You had better not take any action whatsoever to **mislead** the lender as to the fact that the property has been sold. Matter of fact, you'd better not even take any action which is aimed at merely **concealing** the change in ownership from the lender.

In his book on the subject of pre-foreclosure investing (*Your Complete Guide to Foreclosure Profits* 510-837-2106), Ted Thomas gives an example in which he has the owner who sells to him request a new mortgage payment book from the lender. The letter says the reason is "...we have misplaced ours."

In fact, Thomas's book says the **real** reason for requesting the new payment book is that the old owner threw the original one away. Furthermore, the letter saying the old book was misplaced and requesting the new book is signed by the previous owner and leaves the false impression that the post office box to which the payment book is requested to be sent is the previous owner's box.

I would not send such a letter. A court might find that sending such a letter violated federal laws against:

- mail fraud (18 USC 1341)
- conspiracy (18 USC 371)
- false statement in connection with a federally-related lender (18 USC 1014)
- concealing a material fact in a federally-related matter (18 USC 1001)
- racketeering (18 USC 1961).

These are **felonies** punishable by fines, prison sentences, or both.

I have had several mortgage in which the lender forgot to send me a payment book one year. I simply sent the checks in without any payment coupon. Writing the loan number on the check was enough for the lender.

Where to get fast cash

Pre-foreclosure investors typically finance their purchases with cash on hand or **lines of credit**. Then they pay off the loan when they refinance the line of credit with a regular long-term mortgage. Or when they resell the property quickly to a new owner who gets a traditional mortgage or arranges to assume the existing mortgage.

Some pre-foreclosure investors have partners waiting in the wings. Whenever you bring other equity investors into a deal, you'd better check whether what you are doing is governed by **real estate license** or **securities** laws. Failure to have a proper license or registration can be legally devastating.

Tax Ramifications

There are no special tax ramifications to buying pre-foreclosures. It's just a purchase like any other. If you **resell immediately**, you are almost certainly a **dealer**. That means you cannot take advantage of tax-free exchanging, depreciation deductions, long-term capital gains tax rates, or installment sale treatment.

Some see that list of disadvantages and think, "Well, I guess I'd better not resell immediately." Not at all.

I recommend that you **do** resell immediately in spite of the four income tax disadvantages. The reason is in order to qualify for exchanging, depreciation, long-term capital gains, and installment sales, you must be a long-term holder and manager of properties. Long-term holding is extremely risky because you cannot predict the future. Property management is time-consuming and extremely poorly compensated. Having to manage properties will waste time more profitably spent buying pre-foreclosures or other bargain purchases.

Kill ratio

Ted Thomas says he buys about one property for every thousand letters he sends. Since he sends about seven letters to each owner during the pre-foreclosure period, that's about one bargain purchase for every $100 \div 7 = 143$ properties pursued.

Special expertise required

To do pre-foreclosures, you need to study the foreclosure law in your state. That includes buying a copy of the pertinent statute and subscribing to some sort of loose-leaf service that will keep you up to date. You also need to master efficient direct mail technique. You need to have a salesman's ability to close the deal—typically over the property owner's kitchen table.

Full-time or part-time possible

I don't know of any part-time pre-foreclosure investors. But I know of no reason why it could **not** be done part-time. Ted Thomas chases pre-foreclosures in five counties full-time. It seems like you could chase them in one county part-time.

One problem for a part-timer might be the need for **speed**. Thomas once got a call Thanksgiving morning from a pre-foreclosure seller who had decided to respond to Thomas's letter. He asked Thomas, "Can you close by 4:00 PM today?" Thomas could and did. A part-time investor could probably do likewise on Thanksgiving. But he'd have trouble doing that on a weekday when he was at work.

Regional variations

There are regional variations because of different state laws and foreclosure procedures. There are also temporary regional variations because of differences in regional economies. For example, there have been a lot of foreclosures in the Oil Patch in the eighties and in New England in the late eighties and early nineties. But in general, the opportunity to buy pre-foreclosures is nationwide.

Actual case histories

Thomas did the following deal in Solano county in 1989. His price: $101,000. Market value: $145,000. Thomas resold for $116,000 in less than 14 days.

In San Joaquin County, he bought a house for $117,000 and sold it for $132,000 three weeks later. Local brokers say that property is worth $155,000.

At the other end of the price spectrum, he bought a house for $22,000 in Stockton and resold it for $31,000 three weeks later. Market value was about $45,000. On that deal, Thomas got his cash down back and took back a six-month mortgage for his profit.

In May 1989, Thomas did four deals with profits in the $5K to $10K range.

In his book, *Your Complete Guide to Foreclosure Profits*, Thomas tells of a house he bought in Martinez, CA in May 1988. He agreed to pay $14,550 for the seller's equity. But Thomas's standard agreement deducts amounts he has to pay for roof and termite repairs, reinstating the mortgage, clean-up, and liens not disclosed by the seller when the agreement was signed. As a result, Thomas ended up owing the seller **minus** $696.05 for the house. Thomas's total cost of buying the house was still $8,887.93 which went to reinstate the $54,000 mortgage, pay construction, termite, and roof inspectors and an appraiser, clean up the property, and to carry it for one month. When he sold it for $78,000 six weeks after he bought it, his net proceeds were $19,542.31 giving him profit of $19,542.31 - $8,887.93 = $10,654.38.

In another actual case history in that book, Thomas tells how he bought another pre-foreclosure house earlier that year for a total cost of about $96,500 and resold it within six weeks for $136,900, a $40,000 profit.

In 1974, George Davidson, a Louisville, Kentucky investor, bought a run-down house which had an FHA mortgage. The mortgage was delinquent and going into foreclosure. Davidson paid $15,000 putting $1,000 down and buying subject to the delinquent FHA mortgage. He reinstated the loan, spent about $4,000 fixing up the house then sold it for $24,000 six months later.

Ethical considerations

Do not tell the owners of a pre-foreclosure that you are trying to buy that you will pay them market value. The title of this book is how to buy for at least 20% below market value. Pre-foreclosure owners like other owners want top dollar for their property. So there will be a powerful temptation to assure them that you are paying market value or that they won't be able to do any better.

Up above, I discussed the temptation to mislead the institutional lender so you can preserve a non-assumable mortgage. You must resist that temptation.

Misleading either the seller regarding fair market value or the lender regarding the ownership of the property is unethical. It also arguably violates various criminal and civil laws.

Screening procedures

When you are contacting 600 to 1,000 people a week as Thomas does, you obviously have to have some way to efficiently screen out the vast majority. Thomas uses a questionnaire.

When a recipient of one of his mailing pieces responds by calling, Thomas asks them the following questions:

1. Where is the property located?
2. What kind of property is it?
3. Age of property?___ # bedrooms? ____ # of baths? ____ Sq. Ft? ____
4. How much do you owe on it?
5. Are the loans assumable?
6. How much is the property worth?
7. Is that what homes in the neighborhood are selling for?
8. Do you have a recent appraisal?
9. Are you behind in any payments?
    If yes, are you in default of foreclosure?
    If yes, when is the property going up for auction?
10. How old is the roof?
11. Have you had a recent termite inspection?
12. What condition are the carpets and draperies in?
13. How long has the property been for sale?
14. How much will you take for the property?

If bargain purchase appears possible then he asks:

15. Directions to the property.
16. Name, address, day phone number, evening phone number.
17. Appointment date, time (Try to make the appointment for daylight hours. It's easier to inspect the house in daylight.).

Takes seller's word

At this point, Thomas takes the caller's word for everything. If the amount they want for their equity is small enough that Thomas can resell for a quick profit, he makes an appointment to inspect the property and meet the seller. But if, for example, their answers indicate they have $30,000 equity and they say they'll take $30,000 for it, Thomas forgets about the property.

I questioned the phrase "in default of foreclosure" in question number nine as being garbled. But Thomas said he found that particular phraseology worked best.

Non-Californians should note that it is normal for Californians to know the square footage of their homes. (In New Jersey, where I'm from originally, a home owner would be no more likely to know the square footage of his home than he would the BTU rating of his furnace.)

Non-Californians should also note that **termite inspections** are a big deal and a racket in California. Virtually all California home sellers are required by termite inspectors to replace the floors of all bathrooms when they sell.

They also typically require a thousand or two thousand dollars worth of repairs to such nit-picky problems as fungus spots on the underside of a deck. California termite inspections are required to be registered with the state and lenders generally require the work be done before they will make a mortgage on the property.

Hidden liens

Thomas does not worry about hidden liens until **after** he signs the purchase agreement. That's because his purchase agreement contains clauses which state that the price will be reduced by the amount of any additional liens above and beyond the ones identified by the seller.

He says the price gets adjusted downward about 40% of the time because people forget about some liens. But he says he has never lost a deal because of liens requiring downward price adjustments.

After he and the seller have signed the purchase agreement—and during the five-day rescission period required by California law in pre-foreclosure situations—Thomas has a title company do a normal title search.

He says Chicago Title gets him a preliminary title report on the property and the seller within 48 hours. Thomas gets a title insurance policy as if he were buying a house in a normal (non-pre-foreclosure) deal. Consequently, any hidden liens become the title company's problem. (He always buys a **binder** title insurance policy. A binder policy costs 110% of normal. But it has the advantage that if you resell within two years—and require the buyer to use the same title company—you get a refund of all but the 10% extra premium you paid. Thomas usually resells within a month.)

Appraisal

The other side of accurately estimating the equity he's buying is the value of the property. If the property is in an area Thomas is familiar with, he knows the values from experience. In **new** areas, he can call upon three on-line, appraisal data bases:

- Damar (415-692-1261)
- Dataquick (213-306-4295)
- Six different multiple listing services

On-line means that Thomas can call up the data base in question on his computer screen. Like an appraiser, he can then get comparables: similar properties which have sold, are still for sale, or expired listings. The computer gives the price, terms, and a detailed description of the property.

Thomas is a licensed real estate broker and a member of the multiple listing services of each of the areas he "farms" for bargain purchases.

Post cards

Thomas's system worked on hand-addressed envelopes containing form letters. As with all good direct mail practitioners, Thomas constantly experiments with new approaches.

He has preliminary indications that **post cards** work as well as the hand-addressed envelope and form letter. That saves postage, paper, labor, and printing on each piece.

Ted Thomas seminars

Last I heard, Thomas was doing seminars ($5,000—no kidding). I have not attended the seminar so I do not know if it is worth the money and time.

Thomas's background

On August 13, 1989, *The Contra Costa Times* (Walnut Creek, CA) did an expose´ article on Ted Thomas. Since I have written about Thomas's system for buying pre-foreclosures in this book, even though few of you saw the *Times* article, I feel I should respond to the *Times* article.

The article's main points were that Thomas used to be a syndicator of conspicuous prosperity, that many of his limited partnerships are in bankruptcy or foreclosure, that he filed bankruptcy in October of '86,—that many of his limited partners are mad at him, and that he was, at the time of the *Times* article, being touted by Howard Ruff as a "street smart" foreclosure expert.

I knew Thomas was a syndicator who had gone bust. He switched to pre-foreclosures because he concluded the traditional approach of buying income property and holding it hadn't worked. I did not and do not think his syndications were relevant to whether his technique for buying pre-foreclosures works.

In the *Times* article, a disgruntled limited partner points to Thomas's failed syndications as evidence that his approach to foreclosures is "B.S." That's not logical. The syndication properties were in over built markets (e.g., Phoenix apartments, California office buildings) and had fallen in value until they were worth less than their mortgages. Neither Thomas nor anyone else can fix an over built market. The expertise needed to make bargain-purchases of pre-foreclosures is useless when it comes to properties with negative equity.

Ruff, who declared bankruptcy himself once, said in his seminar brochure promoting Thomas that his brochure statement that Thomas is "very rich" was inaccurate. Both Thomas and Ruff had a responsibility to make sure the brochure advertising their joint seminar venture was accurate.

One deal did not check out

I asked Thomas for the address of one of the properties I wrote about in a November 1988 article in my newsletter, *Real Estate Investor's Monthly*, so I could verify it. Thomas had told me in November that he bought a condo in September for $200,000 and resold it for $259,000 three weeks later to an investor who regularly buys his resales.

On August 16, 1989, I went to the county recorder's office to check that deal. In fact, Thomas took title on November 1, 1988; purchase price, $200,400. The $259,000 resale fell through because the buyer could not qualify for a mortgage according to Thomas. The deed says the transfer tax paid on the "full value" was $235.40 which, at a rate of 55¢ per $500, indicates a resale price of $235.40 ÷ $.55/$500 = $214,000.

Before I print an article, I read it to the source or sources to make sure it is accurate. The **actual** profit made on that Thomas deal was impressive even after taking into account the carrying costs for 3 1/2 months. But it was **not** as impressive as the $59,000 Thomas claimed and reconfirmed before I went to press on November 21st.

Thomas's deposit from buyers

Thomas requires a $5,000 **deposit** from investors who would like to be in line to buy his resales. He says that's to weed out the time wasters. Weeding out time wasters is necessary and a $5,000 deposit is probably a good way to do it. But as I have often said in articles and in my other books, you should not give a deposit to anyone but a top-tier, third-party escrow or title company.

It would also be wise for an investor buying from Thomas or any other seller who claims to be selling **below market** to make his own appraisal. Before I wrote my Thomas

It would also be wise for an investor buying from Thomas or any other seller who claims to be selling **below market** to make his own appraisal. Before I wrote my Thomas articles, I checked him out with distress property guru John Beck and I talked to a man who had bought one of Thomas's resales. Beck still recommends the Thomas System. The resale purchaser was very happy with the purchase. Jesse Carranza of San Francisco bought eight properties from Thomas in 1989 and told me he was very pleased with the deals.

Still a sound system

Overall, it still appears to me that the Thomas System is an excellent way to make money in real estate. I do not **know** whether Thomas treated his former limited partners properly. I did **not** appreciate his telling me that he made $59,000 on a deal when the actual profit was only $14,000. However, I **do** appreciate the real estate expertise, ingenuity, and persistence which Thomas used to make his pre-foreclosure system work. And I appreciate his willingness to share it with me and my readers.

Low end best

Thomas says his system works best at the low end of the price range. (In metropolitan California, $100,000 **is** at the low end.) He finds the owners of higher-priced homes generally take a lot more of his time, offer unacceptably small discounts, and frequently file bankruptcy at the last minute—thereby delaying foreclosure. That's why he expanded **east** into rural San Joaquin County instead of **west** into high-priced San Francisco County— which is closer.

Main problem

Thomas's main problem during good times is incompetent competitors. These are people who have heard foreclosures are a good deal—but who haven't done their homework on the particular property—or who have profit margin targets which are too small—and bid too high as a result.

During hard times, his main problem is finding buyers for his resales.

Sequence

Thomas investigates the **liens** on a property **after** he agrees to buy it. But he **appraises** the property **before** he signs the purchase agreement which means before he arrives at the property. He inspects the property to see if it is in such bad shape that the appraisal needs to be revised downward. Then, if possible, he strikes his deal with the seller on the spot.

Thomas visits the property just **one time** before closing (not counting the pre-closing inspection). Because he does so many deals a month (four to ten), he must do one-stop-shopping. So the sequence is:

1. Fill out property evaluation questionnaire over phone.
2. Appraise the property.
3. Inspect the property and sign purchase agreement at that time.
4. Get title report.
5. Do pre-closing inspection and close.

Toxic liability considerations

The possibility that you will become liable for the astronomical cost of a toxic clean up is always a danger when you buy real estate these days. Unlike some other bargain purchase techniques, the danger is less in pre-foreclosures because you get to inspect the property inside and out.

The need for speed can cause you to overlook a contamination problem.

Thomas buys only homes. The toxic liability laws regarding homes are much more favorable than those which apply to commercial property. So if, like Thomas, you restrict your purchases to single-family homes, you will avoid most of the dangers of toxic liability in real estate.

Need for secrecy

Thomas's competitors sometimes find his sellers during the five-day rescission period (required by California Civil Code § 1695 for post-notice-of-default purchases), ask to see the contract with Thomas, and outbid him by a small margin—or perhaps offer to close in **less** than five days (in violation of that California law), or both. So to the extent possible, you should keep your offers secret until they are binding on the seller.

Unique risks of pre-foreclosures

People in financial difficulty often declare bankruptcy or are forced into bankruptcy by their creditors. That could happen to someone who sells you a pre-foreclosure. If it does, laws regarding fraudulent transfers could be triggered.

A fraudulent transfer is one in which:

1. property is transferred for less than fair market value (that's our aim)
2. the old owner owed or could have anticipated that he would owe money to a third party(ies)
3. the old owner did not have enough money to pay the debt after he transferred the property.

The idea here is that a pre-foreclosure seller can be stupid enough to sell you his property so cheap that it hurts him. But he may not be so stupid that he hurts his creditors by selling the property to you cheap. In other words, the creditors claim that all or part of your profit is being made off equity which belonged to them, not the seller. And they want it back.

The law says, roughly speaking, that the creditors are entitled to have the property in question brought back into the bankruptcy, sold, and the proceeds divvied up among the creditors.

Another way to put it is that once the liability arises, a sort of invisible lien arises and attaches itself to everything the seller owns. When you buy from such a person, it's possible that the invisible lien may be foreclosed upon, thereby forcing you to return your profit to the bankrupt's estate. If you acted in bad faith, you could lose not only your profit but also your investment.

On the other hand, I was unable to find anyone who had become involved in a fraudulent transfer situation. John Beck, who is an attorney and publisher of *Distress Sales Report* newsletter, says he never has had a problem with fraudulent transfer law. And none of his subscribers has ever told him that they had a problem with it. Ted Thomas says he's has never encountered fraudulent transfer problems.

Arnold Goldstein, author of *The Complete Asset Protection Guide*, says that as a practical matter, you can pay as little as 70% of the value of a home and you will probably not have it taken back as a fraudulent transfer.

For more information on fraudulent transfers, see my *Special Report, Offensive and Defensive Strategy and Tactics for Distressed Real Estate Times.*

Another unique risk of buying pre-foreclosures in some states like California is special laws which pertain to purchases of properties against which foreclosure proceedings are pending. California Civil Code Section 1695. Last I heard, Missouri was considering passing a similar law. You can buy special forms which purportedly comply with California's law from the monthly California real estate law magazine, *first tuesday* (800-235-5522). Also, Professional Publishing (122 Paul Drive, San Rafael, CA 94903 415-

472-1964) plans to offer a form which complies with the California laws pertaining to real estate agents listing homes which have had a notice of default filed against them.

Resale

Frequently, Thomas **double-escrows** properties. That is, he has a buyer for the property before he closes on it to buy. As a result, Thomas buys and sells the property at the same closing.

Limited by time

Thomas says the limit to expanding his system is his time. He feels he must do all the negotiating and property inspections **himself**. Only administrative work and initial screening can be handled by outsiders or his part-time staff. If he added a fourth county, he says he wouldn't have enough time to talk to all the responding defaultees or to inspect all the offered properties.

Lucier's book

Thomas Lucier sells a book called *How to Make Money Buying Pre-Foreclosure Properties Before They Hit the County Courthouse Steps*. I do like or recommend Lucier's writings. I think they generally are of poor quality. I feel like I've seen virtually every idea previously in the books and newsletters of others. Some of the ideas I see in his writings are things I've previously written in my own books and newsletters.

56

6

Foreclosure auctions

How it works

When a mortgage or trust deed borrower defaults on their loan, the lender usually forecloses. (Sometimes, when they suspect or know of toxic contamination, they refuse to foreclose.) To comply with the due-process clause of the Constitution, notice of the foreclosure auction must be advertised to the public. That's typically done in legal newspapers. In many areas, there are private companies which publish abstracts of the official notices.

You investigate the property and its title as best you can. You can only set foot on the premises and go inside if the owner permits you. That is in the owner's interest, but the professional foreclosure buyers I've talked to have never asked the foreclosee to permit such an inspection. And even if they allow you to inspect, there is no agreement requiring them to keep the property in the same condition until you become the owner the way there is in a normal purchase.

You can only find out the current balances owed to non-foreclosing lien holders if the foreclosee gives them written permission to release such information to you.

If you decide you want to bid on the property, you take enough money in the form of cashiers checks to the auction and bid. Make sure your checks are drawn up as required by the trustee or other auction holder. If you win, you fill out some paperwork, turn over your check and wait for a deed and refund of any overpayment by mail or Federal Express or some such.

Why it works

Some properties sell for 20% or more below current market value at foreclosure auctions because:

• sales are poorly advertised by private standards
• real estate agents refuse to help because there are no commissions
• buyers must pay all cash
• buyers may not set foot on the property before purchase unless they have permission from the owner who is usually in a uncooperative mood
• sales are usually postponed or canceled at the last minute
• about half the properties are still occupied by the defaulted home owner after you buy and must then be evicted
• foreclosees with equity should sell in a more orderly fashion before the auction but they often fail to take timely action.

Basic principles

Many are defaulted by few are actually auctioned off—especially among properties with substantial equity—the only kind you're interested in. So you need to monitor thousands of properties which are announced for foreclosure even though you know the vast majority will be reinstated or stayed by bankruptcy before the auction. That requires efficient screening and sequencing your property investigations and evaluations.

You must evaluate the property and its title at **high speed** at the **eleventh hour** before the auction. You cannot do it sooner at a more leisurely pace because most of the properties are pulled off the action track at the last minute. And if you ignore checking the title or doing a windshield appraisal, you could easily pay tens of thousands of dollars for nonexistent equity.

In theory, foreclosure wipes out liens junior to the foreclosing lien. As a practical matter, it's not that simple. Wiped-out lien holders tend to be very unhappy about that and sometimes try to overturn the foreclosure auction as improper. IRS and other governmental liens often either survive foreclosure of senior liens or have reinstatement rights after foreclosure. In the case of IRS liens, they survive on the property even if they were recorded after the foreclosing mortgage unless the foreclosing lender gave IRS at least 25 days notice of the foreclosure sale.

In general, buying at foreclosure auctions is a high-speed, low-kill-ratio, all-cash business. It is somewhat risky because of your inability to physically inspect the property or obtain current payoff statements from non-foreclosing lien holders.

Incidence of this opportunity

The incidence of foreclosures is **cyclical**. The December 25, 1991 *San Francisco Chronicle* says California foreclosures were up 74% for the year ended September 30, 1991 compared to a year earlier. The nationwide increase for the same period was 20%.

San Mateo County, California had 336 foreclosures during the first eleven months of 1991 compared to just 126 for all of 1990. The number of notices of default filed in that county in the first eleven months of 1991 was 2,133 compared to 1,451 in all of 1990. Those numbers suggest the ratio of notices of default to actual foreclosure auctions ranges from 2,133/366 = 5.83 to one and 1,451/126 = 11.52 to one. No doubt both ends of those ranges have been exceeded in other counties and at other times.

According to the *Statistical Abstract of the U.S.*, the percentage of savings institutions' mortgage portfolios which were **delinquent** ranged from 1.48% in 1970 to 5.56% in 1987. That apparently includes a considerable amount of **commercial** mortgage loans on apartment and office buildings because 1987 was not that bad a year for home mortgages but it was terrible for commercial mortgages.

The savings institutions' **foreclosure** rate, as opposed to the delinquency rate, ranged from .13% of all savings institutions' mortgages held in 1970 to .74% in 1987 and 1988. Those figures indicate a default to foreclosure ratio of 1.48%/.74% = 11.38 to one to 5.56%/.74% = 7.51. Actually, there's some apples-and-oranges mixing there because the delinquency rate is a percentage of the dollar value of the savings institutions' portfolios and the foreclosure rate is the percentage of the number of mortgages foreclosed regardless of the amount of each mortgage.

The number of savings institutions' mortgages foreclosed in the late eighties was about 100,000 nationwide. Given the national population of 250,000,000, that's about one savings institution foreclosure per year for every 2,500 people. So you can get a rough estimate of the number of foreclosures in your target area by dividing its population by 2,500. Of course, there are other kinds of lenders in addition to savings institutions so the actual number is somewhat higher.

Affluent San Mateo County's population is about 700,000 so the foreclosure rate there of 126 in 1990 and over 336 in 1991 represents a population-to-foreclosure ratio of about 700,000/336 = 2,083 to one to 700,000/126 = 5,555 to one.

In their book, *Foreclosure Superbargains in California*, John Beck and Ron Starr say that if you pursue foreclosures full time, you can expect to find about two superbargains a year. They define a superbargain as a property you get for at least 33% below market value. I will add that you can make a nice living of deals where the discount is less than 33% as long as it's at least 20% or more. And I will also add that the incidence of superbargains seems to be cyclical. In 1991, with real estate in the investment dog house, a full-time foreclosure investor could probably buy more than two superbargains a year.

Regional variations

I don't have figures for depressed areas like Texas, Denver, or New England in the eighties. But it is noteworthy that newspapers in those areas had so many foreclosures that they added foreclosure-only sections to their real estate classified ad sections. California got bad in 1991 relative to its own high-flying real estate history. But it never got as bad as Texas, Denver, and New England.

Ethical considerations

Bid chilling is an agreement between prospective bidders to stop bidding at a prearranged, artificially low level.

> *It is unlawful to offer or accept consideration not to bid at a foreclosure sale or to fix or restrain bidding in any manner at a sale of real property conducted under a power of sale and a deed of trust.* California Civil Code § 2924h(g) [California Real Estate Law 2d §4:14]

Bid chilling is a misdemeanor punishable by a fine of up to $10,000 or up to one year in the county jail or both. There is a one-year statute of limitations. (PC §802)

In the typical scenario, the conspirators agree in advance on which one of them is to bid. After the designated wins the bidding at an artificially low price as a result of no one else bidding, they repair to a nearby coffee shop immediately after the **public** auction and hold a second, **private** auction among themselves. The high bidder at that private auction gets the **property;** the other bidders split the difference between the two auction prices equally among themselves in **cash.**

Other than bid chilling, I know of no other ethical consideration for those who buy at foreclosure auctions. Indeed, that's one of the beauties of foreclosure auctions for some investors. You do not need to sit face to face with a distressed person or family and try to negotiate a great deal for yourself at their expense.

Win-win

Real estate gurus are fond of claiming they only believe in win-win negotiations. That's a bunch of poppycock. When you negotiate with a seller to buy a preforeclosure, you are trying to buy it as cheaply as possible. The cash involved is a **zero-sum game** in which each party can win only at the other party's expense. The people who do such negotiations are fond of pointing out that they **helped** the distressed person. They cite their help as evidence that it was a good deal for the seller.

Baloney. This book is about good deals for the **buyer**. And so are the seminars and other books done by the "win-win" gurus. The fallacy behind the win-win concept is that the win-win advocates fail to acknowledge the cost of their "help." It's true that a preforeclosure buyer can save a foreclosee's credit—or at least prevent further damage to it. But preforeclosure buyers, in effect, charge tens of thousands of dollars to do what the seller could have done for himself for far less if only he were not paralyzed with denial.

There is nothing ethically wrong with making a bargain purchase from someone in distress as long as you do it as I've outlined elsewhere in this book. But spare me the win-win line.

At foreclosure auctions, at least, the win-win pretension is refreshingly absent. You simply bid. You don't make any representations or implications. Indeed, the foreclosure auction is a good model for you to follow when making bargain purchases in other situations. Simply offer a bid. If the seller takes it, fine. If not, wait for the next "auction." It's when you start telling the seller you're her friend or that you're offering fair market value, that you cross the ethical line.

Toxic liability considerations

I cannot give you much comfort in the toxic liability area when it comes to foreclosure auctions. At foreclosure auctions, you are required to bid on a **pig in a poke**. This is a carry over from the colonial days when the real estate which was auctioned was generally farm land. A prospective bidder need only inspect it from a distance to know all he needed to know. If there were any unknowns like whether there was a well, he could discount his bid to assume the worst.

But nowadays, unexpected toxic contamination can bankrupt the buyer. And you cannot discount your bid to take into account the worst because that would result in a huge **negative** bid. And the guys who do the foreclosures don't sell properties for minus bids as far as I know. In the toxic contamination era in which we live, they probably will have to start.

Price: $380, Clean-up cost: $600,000 or $25,000/day

Kenneth Groves bought an old street car barn in Kansas City, KS for $380 at a delinquent-property-tax-sale auction, not a foreclosure. But the same thing could happen at a foreclosure.

The 500' x 100' building, which was built like the proverbial brick outhouse, previously housed a chromium plating company.

After Groves bought it, he was informed by the EPA that it was contaminated with chromium and needed to be cleaned up. EPA estimated the clean-up cost at $600,000 to $1,000,000. Furthermore, EPA said they would fine Groves $25,000 per day starting in six months if he failed to clean it up.

Groves complained to the county that it was unfair to sell him such a thing. The county commission voted to seek a court order deeding the property back to the chromium plating company. As is typical of delinquent-property-tax sales, Groves had no opportunity to inspect the property before he bought it. Also typical is the county's claim that he bought it "as is."

Groves says he thinks the EPA estimate of clean-up costs is grossly exaggerated. That EPA is, after all, part of the same federal government that pays $400 for hammers and $1,200 for toilet seats. Although **any** estimate of the clean-up costs is likely to dwarf his $380 purchase price.

Groves was the lieutenant governor candidate on the Democratic party's losing ticket in last November's Kansas election. I asked if he thought that had anything to do with his EPA troubles. He said, "I don't like to think so."

The environmental movement has created laws and hysteria which cause many properties to have huge **negative** values. This is unprecedented. The laws pertaining to seizure and sale of properties on which mortgage payments are delinquent are obsolete as a result of the environmental movement's successes. If the problem is not fixed somehow, lenders will—at worst—be holding auctions which no one attends and at which no one bids. At best, they will be selling only at extremely low prices to judgment-proof speculators. When contamination is found, the judgment-proof speculators will abandon the property. One way or another, the taxpayers are going to pay for the environmental movement's monstrously expensive agenda.

As an individual investor, you'd better take what precautions you can to avoid buying contamination in a poke at a no-inspections-permitted foreclosure auction. If a drive-by inspection leaves any doubt as to whether the property is contaminated, you have to pass. You could spend money on an investigation of the property's history. But your budget would be limited by the long-known need to bid low on no-inspection property to cover the possibility of unexpectedly bad physical condition. And it would be further limited by the need to take into account the possibility that you will only buy **some** of all the properties you investigate.

There was one court case in which the successful bidder at a trustee sale (trust deed "foreclosure" auction) sued to give the property back after they discovered it would cost $350,000 to repair the soil movement problems in the house for which they paid $173,000 at a trustee sale. They sued the lender for not disclosing the problem to prospective bidders at the trustee sale. The first Circuit Court of Appeals in California ruled the suit should not be thrown out. (*Karoutas v. Home Federal Bank*, CA 1st, No. A050085, 7/23/91)

Need for secrecy

Unlike most other bargain purchase techniques, there is little need for secrecy in foreclosure auction buying. In theory, secrecy is **impossible**. These are public auctions pursuant to public notice and all that.

However, in reality, there is one little twist that comes up at times. Auctions are sometimes **postponed**. And the new auction is less publicized in many cases. Often this is done by private lenders who hope to get the property cheap and resell it for a profit. California has laws regarding postponements to limit these kinds of shenanigans. But you may still encounter them in California and elsewhere.

When you are dealing with postponed auctions, the new location and date and time are valuable information. It is in your best interest to keep track of postponed auctions. They are more likely than normal auctions to produce small crowds. Furthermore, it is also in your interest to keep the location and time of the postponed auction to yourself.

Criteria

Paul Thompson (510-443-1927) is a 50-year old, former computer specialist for the Lawrence Livermore National Laboratory, a top-secret, federal facility believed to be engaged in the design of thermonuclear weapons. He's also a real estate investor who specializes in acquiring foreclosures by buying them at the public auction.

That's one of the three stages at which you can profitably buy a foreclosure. I've written about the other two: **pre-foreclosure** and **post-foreclosure** (OREOs) elsewhere in this book.

Thompson lives in Livermore, California and does his foreclosure buying in California's Central Valley (roughly Sacramento to Fresno). He has **tried** buying foreclosures in the San Francisco Bay Area, of which Livermore is a part, but he found the greater competition there made the profit margins too narrow.

How to find them

Notice of a foreclosure auction is required to be published in a "newspaper of general circulation." In California, that notice must be published at least **21 days** before the auction. Thompson subscribes to all such newspapers in the counties where he pursues foreclosures. He sits down a couple times a month and clips out the notices pertaining to single-family residential properties. Says it takes him a couple hours.

He pastes the clippings onto a sheet of paper and keyboards four pieces of information from them into a computer data-base management program (Lotus 123):

- date the auction is to be held
- address of the property
- estimated minimum bid (amount owed to foreclosing lender)
- date the trust deed being foreclosed was originated.

Thompson says he can guess how much equity the property has just from the address, minimum bid, and origination date. He then sorts the properties by auction date thereby creating a computerized tickler file.

Sequence

About a week before the auction is scheduled to take place, Thompson calls the trustee (listed in the newspaper notice) to ask if the auction has been canceled or postponed and, if not, whether the estimated minimum bid has been revised. He says the trustee's staff are specifically trained to give out **no** other information.

Calling to see if the auction is still on is important because only one or two out of every thirty properties upon which a notice of auction is filed actually are sold at auction. There are also many **postponements**, especially when the borrower declares bankruptcy. An investor who began to investigate properties as soon as the notice of auction was published would find he was wasting the vast majority of his time on properties that never get foreclosed. Thompson spends about **one hour per day** calling trustees to see if auctions have been canceled or postponed.

Title search

You could have a title company do the search—and even issue title insurance. Thompson says foreclosure buyers who also own real-estate-brokerage companies can do that because they give the title company so much business that the title company will only charge them for the title reports on the properties they actually **buy**. But an **individual** does not have the clout to get so many free title reports.

So Thompson does his **own** title search—usually one or two days before the auction— sometimes even the morning of the auction. He does **not** buy title insurance (which is mainly a search fee) until he refinances, at which time the lender requires it.

Thompson says the title searches are the toughest part of his program.

No payoff statement

The tough part is the lack of a document which is taken for granted in normal real estate transactions: a payoff statement from the lien holders. Sure, you can find out the **names** of the various lien holders, the **origination date** of the lien, and the **original amount** of the lien. But what about the **current** amount?

The current amount can be so much greater than what you expect that it can wipe out your profit or even cause you a loss. One of John Beck's (*Distress Sales Report* 510-527-6115) subscribers bought where a second mortgage was being foreclosed. The FHA had not filed a notice of default on the underlying first. Normally, an investor can assume the borrower had defaulted on the first no sooner than they defaulted on the second. In this case, the borrower defaulted on the second three months earlier. The investor **assumed** the first had been in default no more than nine months.

Beck thought that was ultraconservative. But it turned out the borrower had been receiving credit counseling from the FHA and the mortgage had been in default for **5 years!**

Other surprises can come from local assessments, delinquent taxes and insurance, repairs made by the lender. One way to cut down on the chances of this occurring is to only buy when a **first** mortgage is being foreclosed. And if you bid when junior liens are being foreclosed, demand a bigger profit margin.

Overlooked senior liens

Another special danger of buying at foreclosure auctions is that you may overlook a lien **senior** to the foreclosing lien. Sometimes this happens when the buyer assumes the foreclosing lien is a first mortgage but does not make sure. Or there could be a mechanics lien or some such senior to a seller mortgage. Or a senior citizen owner may have taken advantage of a state law allowing them to defer paying property taxes in return for a lien on the property. Whatever the nature of any senior liens, you must identify them and accurately estimate their current balance. Foreclosure wipes out most **junior** liens. But it does **not** wipe out, or affect in any way, liens **senior** to the foreclosing lien.

Inspection of the property

One of the disadvantages of buying at auction is that you generally do **not** get to set foot on the property before you buy it. You could try to make an appointment with the occupants to inspect it. But they are generally **hostile** to such requests. In fact, it's in their interest to behave like any other owner of a house that's for sale. The more bidders, the higher the sale price. And the higher the sale price, the more likely there will be excess proceeds from the auction.

Excess proceeds are amounts which exceed the amount necessary to pay off the lien holders. Excess proceeds are paid to the junior lien holders then the former owner of the property after the auction. But people who are dumb enough to allow a property with equity to be foreclosed are also dumb enough to discourage bidders and thereby minimize the excess proceeds they will receive.

Windshield appraisals

So Thompson is restricted to windshield appraisals in his preparation for the auction. Fortunately, he says the condition of the **exterior** of the property is normally indicative of the condition of the **in**side. He has only been surprised once—by a bad foundation. Most of the time, he says the houses are messy and dirty but **not** in disrepair. He does not buy properties that need more than cosmetic work—at least not on purpose.

He also said he expected that most foreclosures would be in **bad** areas. But that he has been surprised to find that they are mostly in average or better-than-average areas and that most of the houses are less than 20 years old.

To keep up with values, he subscribes to DAMAR ($50/month minimum, 213-380-7105) which provides comparable sales data on-line to his computer.

Actual case histories

Thompson acquired 17 or 18 properties from 1988 through 1990.

He bids on about **half** the houses that go to auction, which is about 15 to 20 houses a year. And he is the **winning** bidder on five to ten.

In the first half of 1990, he purchased four houses. His total cost was $370,000 plus $40,000 for rehab. He figures the houses are worth about $560,000 after the rehab. So his average profit per deal this year was $560,000 - $370,000 - $40,000 = $150,000 ÷ 4 properties = $37,500 per property.

He says he usually pays 75% to 80% of the market value of a property, as much as 85% for "good" properties. I disagree with the different-criteria-for-"good"-properties approach. Seems to me that 20% below market is the **minimum** acceptable discount. The increased desirability of a property ought to be entirely reflected in its price. So there is no need to think about the desirability when you are setting percentage-of-value criteria. To put it another way, you're better off buying two $100,000 properties for $75,000 than you are buying one more desirable $200,000 property for $170,000. Ratios of what you pay to what you get matter in investing. Not prices.

Thompson's **greatest hit** was a $65,000 house he got for $31,000. It was in a low-income, run-down area.

Here are the actual figures on one of Thompson's recent acquisitions:

Fair market value:	$130,000 after rehab
Auction price:	$82,000
Rehab cost:	$12,000
Profit:	$36,000

Financing ramifications

Thompson pays on the terms the trustees demand: **all cash**. He gets the cash from $500,000 worth of lines of credit which are secured by other properties he owns.

At auction, the money is in the form of a cashiers check. You have to **show** your money to the trustee before you are allowed to bid. Thompson shows the check.

After he rehabs a property, he **refinances** it. He pays off the line-of-credit loan with the proceeds of the refinancing—typically within three months of the day he bought the property.

In at least one state—New Jersey—you put down 10% after you become the winning bidder at the auction. Then you have a certain period of time—ten days in New Jersey—to come up with the rest of the money. But this is not like buying a house in the normal fashion where the purchase agreement contains a mortgage contingency clause. If you don't get the rest of the money, you forfeit the 10% and the property is auctioned off again.

Ten days is pretty short notice for a mortgage. But these days you can yourself pre-approved personally for a mortgage. The rest of the approval is then subject to approval of the property (type, value, and title). You may be able to get the property itself appraised and approved within the ten days. The best thing would probably be to have a cash source, like a line of credit, available in case of failure to get the regular mortgage approved within your state's come-up-with-the-rest-of-the-money deadline.

Four-mortgages-per-person limit

There is a four-mortgages-per-person limit. It is in section 202.05 of the Federal National Mortgage Association conventional mortgage eligibility standards. Specifically, it says FNMA doesn't care how many mortgages you have if they are buying the mortgage on your **principal residence**. However, if they are buying a mortgage on your **second home** or **rental property**, you may **not** have more than four one- to four-family properties—including your home—with mortgages on them.

Properties which you own **free and clear** don't count. Nor do properties with **five or more units** or **nonresidential** properties. It doesn't matter whether FNMA owns any of the other mortgages. Partial ownership of a property is considered the same as full ownership.

By financing your home **last**, you could have as many as **five** small properties with FNMA mortgages.

To go beyond five, you'd have to find a **portfolio** lender. Portfolio lenders are those which keep the loans after they make them rather than sell them to FNMA or another secondary market buyer.

Foreclosure auction buyer Paul Thompson owns about 45 one- to four-family residential properties—almost all with **ARMs**. Virtually all his mortgages are with portfolio lenders, apparently. Even then, lenders typically cut him off when he does **his fifth** loan with **them**. So every six months or so, he has to find a new lender. So far, he has always been able to do so.

He is not, however, optimistic about recent trends.

You can use a home-equity line or other line of credit to buy a sixth or seventh property. Thompson buys properties initially with lines of credit, then refinances with regular mortgages. You can also simply restrict your empire to five properties and flip others you buy.

In short, it ain't easy, but it's still possible, to finance lots of rental houses.

After winning

After he wins a bid at the auction, which is held on the courthouse steps literally, Thompson and the trustee retire to a nearby bench. Thompson gives the trustee the check; the trustee gives Thompson a receipt. If he does not know the trustee (he knows most of them), he gets their drivers license number and such.

In a couple days, he gets the trustee deed by Federal Express.

Eviction

About **half** the properties he buys are **vacant** after the auction. The others are occupied by their former owners.

After Thompson records the deed, he goes to the property to meet them and tells them, in so many words, to hit the road. Thompson also asks to inspect the property, which they usually agree to.

If they don't move, he has an attorney evict them. Because they were never tenants, eviction is faster and easier than in the normal landlord/tenant relationship. The attorneys charge about $400 for such evictions which take three weeks to two months depending upon the competence of the attorney.

When the house is empty, he goes there with a locksmith, picks the locks if necessary to get in, and changes the locks. Acquisition complete.

More actual case histories

Fourteen Syracuse, New York area buyers beat the pants off the other buyers in their region according to a study by a Syracuse law professor. Those fourteen each bought one of the many varieties of "leper" properties: **foreclosures**. Leper properties are properties which virtually all of those in the market shun. As a result of that shunning, some good deals get overlooked. The investors who are the heroes of this article selectively bought the best of the overlooked pile.

The Spring 1988 issue of *Real Estate Educators Journal* (312-372-9800) mentions a study of foreclosures which was written up in the *Cornell Law Review* (volume 70, page 850). I got the Cornell article and reanalyzed its figures from an **investment** standpoint. (The author wrote the article from a protect-the-consumer standpoint.)

Amateurs

The study of all the foreclosures in Onondaga County, New York (Syracuse area) which commenced in 1979 followed each property until August 1, 1984. According to the article's author, Steve Wechsler, only one of the twenty-seven non-lenders who were successful bidders bought more than one of the foreclosures. Thus I conclude that they were amateurs, rather than professional foreclosure buyers. Although when you see how much money they apparently made you'll agree they lost their "amateur status."

All but one of the **non-lender** buyers (77% were bought by the foreclosing lenders) made a surprisingly high gain on resale. The study does not say how much, if any money, was spent on **fix-up** by the buyers before resale. But the **most** spectacular gain was made in a property that was resold so fast—42 days after foreclosure—that fix-up seems unlikely.

1,115% "appreciation"

The indicated **annual** "appreciation" rates on the fifteen resold, non-lender deals in the *Law Review* article ranged from 18.74% to 1,115.81%—with a median of 71.39%—at a time when the Northeast region existing house appreciation rates were:

Year	Appreciation Rate
'79-'80	13%
'80-'81	5%
'81-'82	-.3%
'82-'83	14%

Obviously, the difference between the regional appreciation rates and the "appreciation" rates enjoyed by the foreclosure buyers stemmed from the discount at which they bought the properties originally.

Most lenders lost

The **lenders** in the sample did less well. They **lost** an average $14,000 per foreclosure. Keep that and lenders' traditional conservatism in mind next time you are tempted to rationalize taking back a mortgage with the line,

"The worst that can happen is that I get the property back."

Twenty-two percent of the lenders in this study were **individuals** who had sold the properties and taken back mortgages. The lenders were made whole by foreclosure and subsequent resale in only 44% of the cases. And the study includes no amount for carrying costs. So one can assume that net of carrying costs, the made-whole percentage was even **lower** than 44%.

Some lenders won big

Some of the lenders did almost as well as the non-lenders though. On the deals in which the foreclosing lender resold at a profit, the annualized appreciation rates ranged from 56% to 1,067%.

Any surplus over the foreclosed lien and costs goes to the **borrower** at foreclosure. But when a lender profits by reselling the property **after** foreclosure, the lender can not only **keep** all the profit—they can still go after the borrower for a **deficiency judgment** if the foreclosure proceeds were less than the loan plus costs—where deficiency judgments are allowed under the terms of the loan and state law. A deficiency judgment is a decision by a court forcing the borrower to pay the lender, in cash, the shortfall between the amount realized at the foreclosure auction and the balance of the loan and costs at the time of the auction.

Other observations

Other interesting facts in the study:

• When lenders bought the property, the foreclosure price was **less** than the mortgage more than ninety percent of the time. But when **non-lenders** (investors or home buyers) bought the property, fewer than 39% of the sale prices were below the amount owed.

- Only one lender sought a **deficiency judgment** even though there were apparent deficiencies in 80% of the foreclosures and both the mortgages and state law allowed deficiency judgments. The lender in question won the judgment but could not collect it.
- Author Wechsler, who is a lawyer and MBA, expressed the suspicion that the non-lender buyers *"were snapping up the most attractive properties at foreclosure and leaving the depreciated and neglected parcels for the [lenders]."* What the heck did he expect?
- The median amount owed (for costs, fees, real estate taxes, etc.) above the loan balance was **7%** of the loan balance.
- About a third of the **non-lender** buyers **still owned** the properties at the end of the study period.
- Lenders in Onondaga County who were interviewed as part of the study insisted that lenders **never** made money on resale of foreclosures. When confronted with examples to the contrary, they dismissed them as flukes.

Doable but not easy

I pounced on this study because it purports to show the **entire** foreclosure market in a county for one year. The success of the 14 non-lender buyers who resold proves that the high discounts I urge you to insist on are actually **available**. The fact that there were **only** 14 shows how rare such deals are.

It's a 14-in-118 shot. That was the actual incidence of this particular variety of bargain deals during the 1979 study period. (The non-lender buyers who **held** their properties may also have bought at bargain prices.)

Not in *today's* market

Whenever I use an example from the **past**, some readers grouse that

"Those days are gone. It's much harder today."

Not according to Ernie Kessler. He's been buying foreclosures in the Maryland-DC area since 1981. And he publishes a listing service (*Foreclosure Hotlist* 301-294-2274) for other foreclosure buyers. He won't consider buying a foreclosure property unless it has at least 25% equity. The percentage of foreclosures in his area that **meet** that criterion has been as low as 10% of the 250 to 300 that come up there each month. But in 1988, it was **40%**—the **highest** he's ever seen.

Paul Thompson tells me that in 1991, the number of foreclosures going to auction increased dramatically over 1990 and that the number of competing bidders dropped dramatically. As a result, he was able to buy properties for 40% to 50% discounts below market value compared to the 15% to 25% discounts he got in the 1988 through 1990 period.

"Not in *my* county"

Citing an Onondaga County, New York study will also undoubtedly inspire some to utter those words which are the bane of all nationally-oriented real estate gurus:

*"Well, **sure**, you can do that in Onondaga County. But this is _____!"* [insert your county]

According to the *Almanac Of American Politics*, Syracuse is ,

"sufficiently middle American that for many years it was a favorite test market site."

To hear the typical "It-won't-work-here" heckler tell it, you'd think his local real estate market was Mars compared to where the technique you talk about was used.

John Beck, foreclosure buyer, author of several books on foreclosures, and publisher of the *Distress Sales Report* newsletter is thoroughly familiar with the California and Texas foreclosure markets. Plus he has lectured on the subject all over the country and spoken to foreclosure buyers nationwide. He says the Onondaga County figures are representative of what he sees **nationwide**—in **today's** market.

Another actual case history

When I first interviewed Paul Thompson I mentioned that I had never been to a foreclosure auction. On August 17, 1990 he took me to one.

Stockton, CA

I met Thompson at his Livermore house at 8 a.m. and we drove to Stockton so as to arrive about a half hour early. When we walked up the courthouse steps, I started for the building entrance out of habit. But Thompson just walked over and leaned on the masonry wall. Then I realized these things are **really** held **on the steps**. There we waited under a "No loitering" sign.

Most such auctions are scheduled for 9 a.m. to discourage bankruptcy filings on the day of sale.

Off-duty Rotarians

If you saw the gathering from across the street, you probably would not recognize it as a foreclosure auction unless you had experience in that area. There were 20 men and women in casual clothes, some carrying clipboards with fold-over covers. Several greeted each other by name. Thompson said five were regulars. If a layman had to guess, he'd probably figure they were Rotarians meeting informally on their day off.

The auctioneer fit right in. He wore sneakers, an open collar shirt, and a beeper. His clipboard was fatter than the others. And he greeted several of the would-be buyers by name.

The auctioneer volunteered the information he knew everyone was most interested in: which auctions were postponed or canceled. He announced that only two of the scheduled auctions were going to be held and gave their street addresses. The crowd was very disappointed. Thompson explained that the only properties with enough equity to warrant bidding were all postponed or canceled.

Five checks

Thompson brought five separate cashiers checks totaling $260,809.

Three of the four properties he was interested in were among the canceled or postponed sales. This in spite of the fact that he had called as recently as the day before to confirm that the sale was still on.

Just prior to bidding on each property, the prospective bidders were required to show their money. Thompson showed $140,000 worth of checks to prove he was qualified on the property he bought. The checks are shown **only** to the auctioneer so the other bidders won't know Thompson's maximum bid. No one else showed money thereby indicating Thompson was the only bidder.

Bring **more than you expect to bid** because sometimes a senior lien which you expect to pay **after** you buy the property is paid off **before** foreclosure and the amount which was required to pay it off is added to the minimum bid. To put it another way, the amount of equity in the property may be increased significantly just before the foreclosure auction by the pay off of a lien on the property. That, in turn, increases the amount you should be willing to pay. But if you don't have the new higher amount **with** you—in the proper form—you could lose out to a bidder who bids **less** than you would have been willing to pay.

The actual auction

After checking his watch several times to make sure it was 9 a.m., the auctioneer began reading disclaimers and such from papers in his clip board. Before long, he came to the first property to be auctioned.

Thompson tried to bid but was somewhat confused as to the exact amount of the minimum bid. The auctioneer recognized that Thompson wanted to bid the next dollar amount and said, "You mean $137,639? That's the next even dollar above the minimum." Thompson said, "Yes."

Auctioneers sometimes make mistakes. For example, they may read the address of the foreclosing lender as the address of the property being auctioned off. If you are not paying close attention, you could completely miss out on bidding on the property you came for as a result.

When no one else bid, the auctioneer spoke the familiar, "Going once, going twice, going for the third and final time at $137,639. [Pause] **Sold** for $137,639."

A second property was then auctioned off in similar fashion. Only one person bid. (Thompson did not bid because it was in a bad neighborhood.)

The entire two-property auction was over by 9:04 a.m. Many an investor has lost a bargain foreclosure purchase because he did not allow enough time for traffic or finding parking and arrived too late.

Elm Street

Thompson bought 123 Elm Street (not the real address) in a small central valley town. The minimum bid on the property was $137,638.23. That's the amount owed including principal, interest, penalties, and costs. Thompson bid $137,639 or 77¢ more than the amount owed. The previous owners are entitled to that 77¢ unless there is some statutory minimum amount of excess proceeds or extra fee that has to be paid above the minimum bid.

Market value

Thompson had **driven by** 123 Elm the day before. He could see it was about two years old, in a decent neighborhood, and apparently vacant (dead lawn, newspaper on driveway). He had not gone to the door.

Based on his knowledge of the market and the windshield appraisal, Thompson figured the property was worth about $160,000 to $170,000. The margin over the minimum bid was only $160,000 - $137,638 = $22,362 ÷ $160,000 = 14%.

Tax ramifications

Acquiring a property generally has no tax effect *per se*. Although it has tax ramifications if it is an exchange, for example. See below for more on that.

If you immediately resell the properties you buy at foreclosure auctions, you will probably be a dealer with regard to those properties. That makes you ineligible for exchanging, depreciation deductions, and long-term capital gains treatment. But you are still probably better off getting rid of the properties quickly from the standpoint of avoiding property management and exposing yourself to the many risks inherent in long-term holding.

Delayed exchange

If none of the properties available that day had enough equity, why did Thompson bid at all? He needed a property to complete a delayed exchange. Because of the tax savings, his **overall** margin was larger than was apparent to a person who knew only the value of the property and the liens on it.

He was exchanging out of a foreclosure condo he bought for $63,000. He had received an all-cash offer of $90,000—which he felt he couldn't refuse.

his **overall** margin was larger than was apparent to a person who knew only the value of the property and the liens on it.

He was exchanging out of a foreclosure condo he bought for $63,000. He had received an all-cash offer of $90,000—which he felt he couldn't refuse.

Can you exchange into a foreclosure bought at auction? Sure. Why not? In the event, it was a non-issue.

After the auction was completed, the two successful bidders repaired to the courthouse hallway to complete business. Thompson asked the auctioneer if he would mind coming to the office of Thompson's delayed-exchange facilitator a couple blocks away. The auctioneer readily agreed.

It would not have been a problem if he had refused. All that matters is that the auctioneer receive a check from the delayed-exchange escrow and that the exchangor never have unfettered right to the money. That could have been done in the courthouse. San Francisco Bay Counties Exchange Services' Brandt Nicholson (415-882-4667) says he has handled many similar exchanges. All the auctioneer cares about is that it's a cashiers check.

Thompson had $20,000 in the delayed-exchange escrow. He needed more to buy the property. No problem. Just use **two** checks: one for $20,000 and one for the rest.

On to the property

Having completed the transaction, we set out to see what Thompson had bought. On the way, I asked how many bedrooms the property had.

"I don't know."

How many square feet?

"Don't know that either."

Is it occupied?

"I don't think so."

I began to wonder if the neighborhood would offer good avenues of escape should the former home owner come after us with a gun. On the way to the house, Thompson had to pull over to consult a map. "I don't remember where this house is," he explained. This was definitely not the kind of acquisition I was used to.

3br, 2 1/2 ba, fr, fp

But when we pulled up in front, it looked like your basic house. Almost brand new. Dead lawn, but otherwise in great shape from what could be seen. The house is a two story with an attached two-car garage and a deck in the back. The lot wasn't much bigger than the house. But the house was one of the newest in the neighborhood.

The neighborhood was modest working class with the occasional pickup truck or boat in the driveway.

No answer at the door. Drapes all drawn shut. All doors locked. We went to a phone booth to call a locksmith. He showed up in twenty minutes and picked the front-door lock, a dead bolt, in about 10 seconds. He worked on changing the locks, putting all on one key, while we inspected the property.

Immaculate

Immaculate is not a strong enough word to describe the condition of the house. Mint condition would be too strong—but not by much. The property was perfect on the inside except for a pencil line on the wall where a picture had been hung, two torn vinyl spots where the refrigerator had been, and a slight stain in the tub drain caulk. The oven and microwave ovens were spotless. Same for the toilets and other bathroom fixtures. Not so much as a paper clip was left behind. And someone had obviously spent two or three man days cleaning the place.

I was flabbergasted at the condition of the place. My **tenants** don't leave apartments that clean. And I have a security deposit they want back. I had heard and believed that

In addition to the two-car garage and deck, the house has three bedrooms, two and a half baths, a family room with fireplace, living room, wet bar, dining room, kitchen with dishwasher, disposal, and microwave, central air-conditioning, wall-to-wall carpet, parquet foyer, and drapes or blinds on all windows and glass doors. It had over 1,800 square feet.

Revised value

Thompson said the house was one of the better ones he had bought as far as condition was concerned. But he did not seem as surprised by it as I was. However, upon seeing the condition of the interior, Thompson revised his market-value estimate **up** to $180,000. At $180,000, that would give him profit of $180,000 - $137,639 = $42,361 above his purchase price. That's a $42,361 ÷ $180,000 = 24% discount.

Full-time or part-time possible

I asked Thompson how many hours he had spent **total** to buy this property. Three. Of course, he had also spent additional hours rejecting properties he did not bid on. Thompson figures he spends about 20 to 30 hours a week pursuing foreclosures. In 1989, he bought 7 properties; 6 in the first eight months of 1990. That's 20 months x 4.3 weeks per month x 25 hours per week = 2,150 hours to buy 13 properties or 165 hours per acquisition. This was an average deal so the pay per hour is about $42,361 ÷ 165 = $256 per hour. Nice work if you can get it. And you can get it if you try.

Thompson bought me the usual tycoon's lunch at Arby's. Then, having made $42,361 between 8 and 10 a.m., he took the rest of the day off.

One of the worst times and places

You should note that all of the above took place at one of the **worst** times and places imaginable. California's central valley had high appreciation rates in the late eighties and 1990. Sacramento was one of the very top cities in appreciation in 1990. Those conditions produce the **minimum** number of foreclosures and the **maximum** number of bidders at the auction. In the few years Thompson has been doing this, he has seen the average margin on properties he buys drop from about 35% to 40% to about 20% to 25%. When conditions worsened in 1991, the margins and compensation per hour of foreclosure buyers increased dramatically.

Beginner's luck

In their book, *Foreclosure Superbargains in California*, John Beck and Ron Starr tell of a beginner foreclosure investor who, in 1983, paid $19,101 for his first property—a two story house which was worth about $50,000 to $55,000.

SBA stays home

Beck and Starr tell of another foreclosure in which the property was worth about $75,000 but there was a $20,000 first, which was being foreclosed, and a $58,000 second held by the Small Business Administration. It turned out the SBA did not go to the foreclosure auction to protect their position. The winning bid was $26,000. The property was sold through normal for-sale-by-owner channels three and a half months later for $77,000 by the winning bidder.

Six-unit success story

On page 195 of *Superbargains*, Beck and Starr tell of an investor who bought a six unit property in Fremont, California for $123,100. After spending about $30,000 for fix up, he sold it for $318,000 within a year ($85,000 down, $67,000 seller second, subject to first mortgage put on the property by the investor after he bought it at the foreclosure auction)

Special expertise required

To buy foreclosures at auction, you need to know the **foreclosure law** of your state. You also need to know the laws pertaining to IRS and other governmental liens and the pertinent parts of the bankruptcy code and your state's bankruptcy exemptions. Be aware that your state may have a multi-tiered foreclosure law. In the typical state, there are different laws for owner-occupied homes, commercial properties, and agricultural properties. The laws pertaining to owner-occupied homes and agricultural properties are very favorable to the borrower; those pertaining to commercial properties, more evenhanded.

Since about half the homes are still occupied when you become the owner, you need to know the **eviction law which pertains to holding over foreclosees**. This is different from the eviction law which pertains to defaulted tenants. In general, I am told that it is much easier to evict a home owner who lost his home in foreclosure than it is to evict a tenant to whom you rented a house or apartment.

You do not have time to use professional title search companies because you don't know which properties are actually going to foreclosure until just before the foreclosure. Actually, you don't **really** know until the auction itself since so many mortgages are reinstated at the 59th minute of the eleventh hour. The need to wait until it's too late to use professional title search firm means you have to do your own searches. To do that, you need to know **how to search titles**.

Competent title searches can only tell you part of what you need to know about the liens on the property. You need to learn how to **estimate the current balance of liens** for which the public records only give the **original** lien amount.

You must be able to **estimate** the current **market value** of the property from only a windshield appraisal. And you must be able to estimate the **clean-up and repair cost** from only a windshield appraisal for properties which are in bad shape.

Foreclosures are tricky

Switching from buying regular properties to buying foreclosures is not the same as switching Realtors®. Even **experienced** real estate investors need retooling to enter the foreclosure market. It's a very complicated game—where the rules vary from county to county and state to state. Success requires meticulous record-keeping, efficient investigation of values and liens, willingness to buy buildings you are not allowed to inspect inside, etc.

So you should use this chapter as a springboard to **study** foreclosure investing—not as complete instruction on how to **do** it. Both Beck and Kessler do local seminars which interested investors in the MD-DC or California areas should attend. Also Beck's books on the subject are excellent. (Kessler has not written a book.)

Rights of redemption

In some states, the foreclosee has a **right of redemption** after the foreclosure auction. That means he can redeem or buy back the property from you. In the typical law, he must pay you what you paid plus some statutory interest rate. These rights, where they exist, expire in a matter of months or days. But until they do expire, you will have trouble reselling the property.

If there is an **IRS** lien on the property which is wiped out by the foreclosure of a mortgage recorded before the IRS lien, the IRS has 120 days in which to redeem the property themselves. This applies nationwide.

Sometimes IRS exercises that right of redemption. When they do, you get your purchase price back—and an anemic 6% annual rate of interest. But you may **not** get back money you spent on improvements or acquisition costs like title insurance. So be careful what you spend on any IRS-liened property you buy until after the IRS's redemption period expires.

Other federal government agencies can also have liens on a property and their right of redemption runs for a whole year. Releases from those liens can sometimes be obtained by contacting the agency in question. In California, county recorders are required to tell you in certificate form, if any federal liens are recorded against a property.

Fraudulent transfer in anticipation of bankruptcy

As with pre-foreclosures, the law against fraudulent transfers in anticipation of bankruptcy (Bankruptcy Code § 548) can undo a purchase you make at a foreclosure auction. However, it is far less likely to have a foreclosure auction sale undone because the sale is widely publicized (by government standards anyway) and conducted under a strict procedure designed to protect the interests of creditors and owners. So it's harder for creditors to argue that the property was sold too cheap which is an essential element of fraudulent transfer. Plus there was usually no meeting between the buyer and bankrupt person and the bankrupt person played no role in the sale.

In one case, the bankruptcy court was **not** allowed to void a foreclosure auction where a property sold well below market. The foreclosure auction was allowed to stand because the proper procedure was followed. (*BFP v. Imperial Savings*, 91 CDOS 9056 11/5/91)

In his book, *Forced Sale Workbook*, John Beck says bankruptcy courts generally don't pull the property back after a foreclosure auction unless the sale price was less than 70% of market value.

If your bargain foreclosure-auction purchase **is** pulled back into a bankruptcy, you will get your money back as a secured creditor in the bankruptcy as long as you acted in good faith. If, however, you made your purchase in bad faith (knowing it was an attempt by the bankrupt person to screw his creditors), you will become an **un**secured creditor of the bankrupt estate.

Hazard and liability insurance

The moment you become the winning bidder, you are the owner. As the owner of a property, you need **hazard and liability insurance.** You may think it can wait a couple days. No, it can't. Foreclosees sometimes deliberately burn their houses down out of spite. *Distress Sales Report* editor John Beck has had three properties burn (2 houses he bought through normal channels and one he bought at a distress sale other than a foreclosure). One of John's fire losses was uninsured.

One of his book readers bought a house at an IRS-seized property sale. The former owner deliberately set fire to his own house just before the end of the redemption period applicable to IRS-seized property sales. The former owner was convicted of arson for the fire. But that did the investor no good. The investor was uninsured.

My insurance agent says have your agent try to make a windshield, replacement-cost appraisal and insurability evaluation before the auction. Some insurers simply won't insure certain property types or property locations at all. Because of the high incidence of postponements and reinstatements in foreclosure-auction buying, there is little or no time to get the insurance agent out there. Some agents who want your continuing business may be willing to inspect multiple properties **before** auction even though you don't buy most of them. Most insurance agents will **not** insure properties they have not seen.

Assigned-risk pool

Because the properties are vacant or hostilely occupied, you may have to get your insurance through an **assigned-risk** plan. In California, there is a program called the California FAIR Plan which is many times more expensive than normal insurance.

Unfortunately, the coverage available through assigned-risk plans is generally far more limited than what is available in the free market. So you may not be able to buy all the coverage you want. For example, you may have trouble getting any **liability** insurance at all on an assigned-risk basis. Assigned risk also tends to be bureaucratic and the government agency in charge is slow to issue the policy.

If you have a loss between the time you buy the property and the time you get insurance, you must pay the entire loss out of your own pocket. In the case of a burn-to-the-ground fire, you would have to pay to clean up the debris on your own. And you would only have the lot and foundation left to sell.

Furthermore, the property may have been a **nonconforming use**. That means it was allowed to be built under the zoning law, if any, in effect when the property was built. But now, current zoning says it may not be rebuilt if a certain percentage of it is destroyed— typically 50%. If the lot is too small to build on or unbuildable for other reasons, it is probably worthless or nearly so. And the money you paid for it at the foreclosure auction is lost.

The moral: you'd better find an insurance agent **in advance** of your first foreclosure-auction purchase.

Due-on-sale clauses in mortgages senior to the foreclosing lender

In some cases, the second mortgage is in default but the first is current. The second mortgage lender is the only one foreclosing. If you buy such a property, you may then find that the first mortgage lender can foreclose on you by virtue of a due-on-sale clause in the first mortgage.

Some investors are attracted to second-mortgage foreclosures because much smaller amounts of cash are needed to play in that market. But if, shortly after buying the property, you are required to pay off the entire first mortgage, you may find you have painted yourself into a financial corner.

If you are considering bidding on such a property, you'd better read the due-on-sale clause, if any, in the first mortgage. If it allows acceleration of the mortgage as a result of a forced sale like a foreclosure, try to get the first mortgage lender to agree, in writing, in advance, to let you buy subject to the first at the foreclosure auction.

Transfer tax

In some jurisdictions, you have to pay transfer tax when you record the deed you get at a foreclosure auction. The transfer tax is generally in the .1% to 3.5% range. So in the high-tax jurisdictions, it can throw an otherwise 20%-discount deal into the less-than-20%-discount category. You should pay 3.5% or whatever less for any property you buy in a jurisdiction where there is a 3.5% or whatever transfer tax.

Taking control of the property

In the Paul Thompson case history above, I told how he secured a vacant property which was in good condition in a good neighborhood. When the property or the neighborhood are not in such good condition, it becomes more difficult. In bad neighborhoods, local folks will steal the windows, carpet, plumbing, appliances, etc.

You must secure the property as best you can immediately in such situations. You can do that by occupying the property or having someone else you trust occupy it. Or you can board it up. Do that the way HUD does with thick plywood cut to fit inside the window frames and attached to the house with carriage bolts whose nuts are on the inside of the house.

In climates with freezing temperatures, vacant houses must be winterized immediately.

If the property is **rented**, you must get the tenants to immediately fill out a new credit application, put up a security deposit, sign your lease, and pay the rent for the rest of the month starting with the day you bought the property. They will typically say they already have done all four. (See my book, *How to Manage Residential Property for Maximum Cash Flow and Resale Value* for more information on how to manage property.)

Depending on your state law, you may be stuck with that explanation. In California, for example, the guy who buys at a foreclosure auction has to the refund security deposits (upon move out less damage and ether authorized costs) of tenants who were there from before the foreclosure regardless of the fact that no security deposits were transferred by the previous owner to the foreclosure buyer. The law says the foreclosure buyer can get the rent from the previous owner through a lawsuit against the previous owner, but that he is liable to the tenants regardless of whether he is successful in getting the previous owner to pay up.

Tough to get new rents and security deposits

As a practical, matter, you probably will have great difficulty getting the tenants to put up another security deposit and pay the rent a second time after a foreclosure. I bought a 32-unit apartment building from a man who had bought it as an OREO. The security deposits of the tenants who were there at the time of the foreclosure were stolen by the owner who got foreclosed. The seller told me which tenants those were.

Before closing, I sent a letter to each tenant stating their rent and security deposit and so forth. And I told them to contact me if it was inaccurate. The tenants whose security deposits were outraged—at me. I told them I didn't have a damn thing to do with the disappearance of their money and I sure as hell wasn't going to make it up out of my pocket. My pointing out that I had never laid eyes on their security deposits or even the man who stole them meant nothing to the outraged tenants. I was the messenger bringing the bad news and they called me the thief.

I also had demanded the leases as part of my pre-purchase investigation of the property. I discovered that the managers had reinstated the lost security deposits by entering them into the leases which they had the tenants sign every six months (in spite of the fact that each lease contained an automatic renewal clause making signing new leases an unnecessary expense and hassle).

I told the seller I would not buy the property unless I got all the security deposits which the leases said currently existed—in other words—the original security deposit each tenant had put up regardless of whether it had been stolen by the foreclosed owner. The seller then turned to the Realtor® who was selling the property **and** whose company had managed the property since the foreclosure and said, "You were supervising that manager. **You** pay the lost security deposits." And the Realtor® did.

If it appears a building you are buying in foreclosure has tenants, expect no security deposits or rent for the month in which you buy.

For more information:

Get John Beck's *Forced Sale Workbook* and *Foreclosure Superbargains in California* from John Beck Publishing, 1024 Regent Street, Alameda, CA 94501 510-523-6115. They also sell Barry Adams' book *How to Research Title* [in California]. Get the books even if you are not in California. There are no such books for other states as far as I know. So these are all there is.

7

Conventional OREOs

OREOs stands for Other Real Estate Owned by lending institutions as a result of being the high bidder at foreclosure auctions or trustee sales on loans previously made by the lender in question. In other words, when a lender forecloses on a property and becomes the owner because no one bid as high as the lender did, the property is turned over to their OREO department.

Real estate investors often mistakenly call this type of property REO. REO stands for Real Estate Owned—which refers to real estate used for bank business like the bank's branch offices and office buildings occupied by bank employees.

Many kinds of OREOs

The differences between types are so great that some categories of OREOs have almost nothing in common with other categories of OREOs. For a real estate investor to say, "I specialize in OREOs" is like a doctor saying he specializes in diseases affecting the upper half of the body.

OREO owners include:

- FHA and VA
- State veterans agencies
- FmHA
- Small Business Administration
- Mortgage-insurance companies
- Federal deposit insurance agencies or the federal disposition agency of the year (RTC at present)
- Insurance companies
- Conventional mortgage lenders like banks and s&ls

- Individuals who invest in mortgages or trust deeds
- Consumer-finance companies
- Sellers who took back mortgages then had to foreclose

The widely-believed theory is that OREOs are bargains because, "Those lenders don't care what the property sells for as long as they get their money out of it." While there is some truth to that, the actual reason bargains can be obtained in the OREO market is more complex than that. And, in many of the bargains, the lenders do **not** get their money out of the property.

How it works

You contact the lender official who has the power to sell property which the lender has taken back in foreclosures and offer to buy the property in question at a discount below market. In a small percentage of cases, the officer agrees.

Why it works

Lenders do not like to manage tenant-occupied property because they are not very good at it and do not wish to become good at it. If the property in question has **no** tenant who is paying rent, they are very eager to get rid of the carrying costs of having their money tied up in a vacant property.

In general, they are willing to sell for quick-sale value which is about 10% to 15% below market value. That's because they want to sell quickly in order to get rid of management responsibility and carrying costs quickly. Quick-sale value is not good enough for this book. But a small percentage of OREO properties don't sell even for quick-sale value. They may need work which the lender is unwilling to have done. Or the asking price may be too high. In general, it is not good to have people in charge of selling real estate in which they have no equity. OREO officers generally list the property with a Realtor® which is smart. But a Realtor® working with a corporate bureaucrat who works bankers' hours is not as effective a team as a Realtor® working with a motivated owner who has equity in the property being sold.

The bargain prices stem from:

- the lender's need to get rid of vacant property quickly to avoid carrying costs, opportunity costs, and vandalism risk
- incompetence on the part of the lender
- lack of motivation on the part of the lender
- accounting rules

Price or terms

As with most acquisitions, you can get good price or good terms from an OREO seller. Although, because of accounting rules and the fact that they are lenders, OREO sellers often give exceptionally good terms.

The reason you sometimes get super financing from OREO sellers is that lenders have to acknowledge the loss in their income statement if they sell cheap. But they can **hide** the loss if it's in the form of much-better-than-market financing.

John Beck got several good deals from Oakland's Fidelity Savings and Loan just before it was taken over by government regulators. Fidelity sold the properties for less than market, asked for only ten percent down, and financed the deals with fixed-rate, fully assumable, self-amortizing mortgages and interest rates which were 1/2% to 1 1/4% below market rates.

Accounting rules cause institutional lenders sometimes to behave in ways almost completely foreign to real estate investors. For example, institutions are usually trying to make this quarter's or this year's financial results look as good as possible. As a result, they often will give a better deal to a guy who is willing to either close quickly or wait to close so as to put the best light on the accounting period the institution is most concerned about. Ernie Kessler, owner of Foreclosure Research of America™ (301-294-2274), got a good deal on one OREO because he said yes to a lender who asked near the end of the year, "Can you close before the end of the year?"

Basic principles

To succeed at OREO investing, you must get to the decision maker. In general, banks do not publicize who their OREO people are. Secretaries are told to fend off would-be OREO buyers. Most OREOs will **not** be sold cheaply enough to give you a 20% or greater discount. You have to pursue many to get the few bargain purchases. In the case of FHA and VA, you have to make many bids for every one which is accepted.

Tax Ramifications

There is only one tax ramification: the **at-risk rules**. If you buy from a lender who is not the government (local, state, or federal) or an instrumentality of the government or guaranteed by the government [IRC § 465(b)(6)(B)(ii)], and who gives you a **nonrecourse** mortgage, the at-risk rules apply [IRC § 465(b)(6)(D)(i) and 49(a)(1)(D)(iv)(II)]. That generally means your cumulative loss deductions on the property may not exceed your down payment. In a high-leverage deal, that means you will quickly lose your ability to deduct losses.

The rolling–recourse mortgage

I suggest the "rolling-recourse" mortgage as a solution to the at-risk limits in nonrecourse seller financing. In a rolling-recourse mortgage, you would agree to become personally liable on as much of the loan balance as you needed in order to deduct the losses currently. The amount for which you agree to be personally liable would increase each year until the property's net income was large enough to absorb its depreciation deductions.

It would be best to agree to the rolling-recourse schedule up front so you avoid the following possible conversation:

Borrower: Mr. Lender, before the end of the year, could I change the mortgage so as to make me personally liable for $11,314?
Lender: What's it worth to you?

Of course, that upside-down conversation could only happen in the through-the-looking-glass world of the Internal Revenue Code. But it **could** happen. The ideal thing would be for you to have the option to increase the amount for which you are personally liable each year.

The big picture

But let's not lose sight of the big picture. Nonrecourse mortgages are nice to have when you can get them. So you ought not give them up partially or completely without considerable thought.

One subscriber recently told me he turned down a nonrecourse seller mortgage and insisted on personal liability—as the borrower! Because of the at-risk rule.

I pointed out to him that he had to clear **two** hurdles, not just one, to deduct rental property losses: the at-risk rule **and** the passive loss limits. It would be sad indeed to agree to personal liability on a mortgage only to find out that although you had eliminated the at-risk limit, you **still** could not deduct your losses because you are up against the passive loss limits.

Furthermore, the losses which you cannot deduct currently because of the at-risk rules **can** be deducted from the resale gain, if any, when you sell. Requesting personal liability, which can have disastrous consequences, only lets you claim the deductions **sooner.** **That's** a large increase in risk for very little reward.

Toxic liability considerations

You can inspect OREO property before you buy it. Either the lender or their real estate agent will make the arrangements.

Need for secrecy

You do need to keep your OREO buying secret. One of the main reasons for the big bargain is lack of advertising. You should also work quickly to commit the deal to binding written form as soon as you agree on price and terms.

Unique risks

There are no special risks to OREO buying unless the lender asks you to assume risks not usually assumed by a buyer in a one-sided purchase and sale agreement drawn up by an overzealous in-house lawyer.

The Kessler System

Kessler has an OREO system. When a foreclosure is sold to the lender, he contacts the attorney for the lender **immediately.** He asks for the name and phone number of the bank officer in charge of the property and calls that person **immediately.** He tells the officer up front he is interested in buying the property for cash or terms immediately if the bank is willing to sell it to him for a "substantial discount."

If the officer won't sell him **that** one for the discount he wants (at least 20% below market), he asks if the bank has any **other** properties they'd be willing to sell. If not, he thanks the person and says good-bye.

Kessler then enters the officer's name and phone number into his tickler system. He will continue calling that officer about that property **once a week** until the property is sold **and closed**.

Actual case history

In one case in 1987, five "gorgeous" townhouses in the DC area became OREOs when an investor went bust. Kessler called the bank officer immediately and offered $85,000 each. The loan officer laughed and said they were confident they would sell them for full retail value of about $105,000 each.

Persistence was key

But Kessler kept calling every week. And every week, the loan officer laughed at him. But as the months wore on, the officer laughed less. The lender **did** sell the properties, but three of the deals fell through.

Kessler kept calling even after the deals were signed. Finally, the lender agreed to sell Kessler the three townhouses for $92,000 each. Kessler found buyers in five to ten days and assigned the purchase agreements to them.

He made $20,000 profit overall (about $6,700 per property) and never even had to put up cash earnest money. (The consideration for the three deals was a single unsecured 30-day note for $4,000.) In other words, he acquired the right to buy real estate costing 3 x $92,000 = $276,000 with no cash down and resold it within days for $296,000.

Special expertise required

Kessler likens his system to selling insurance. The keys are:

• Get past the secretarial barricade to the decision maker

- Ask for the "order" (bargain deal)
- Be persistent

Another key which is not generally a factor with insurance sales is **speed**. In real estate, you need to get to the seller early and often.

Kill ratio
Kessler says that if he makes a deal, it comes on the 3.7th call on average. He also says that he pursues about 25 OREOs for every one he ultimately buys. His minimum deal is 20% below market value. Although he will agree to buy for just 10% below market value if he gets generous terms like a below-market interest rate, 10% or less down, and one-time assumability.

How you find them
The standard advice is that you should send letters to all the financial institutions in your area telling them of your interest in OREOs. I did that once early in my career. I got zero response.

Ernie Kessler says he uses the general letter but it is his **least productive** method. And he does it a little more carefully than the typical seminar speaker advises. First he takes pains to find out the name and address of the person who actually is in charge of disposing of OREOs. Then he sends them not just one letter, but **a letter every week to ten days**. And he calls after the third letter.

Small, out-of-state institutions
Furthermore, he says he's generally found success buying OREOs at bargain prices from **small** lending institutions. Institutions **too** small to have an OREO department. In those small institutions, the OREO is generally handled by a loan officer—typically the loan officer who made the bad mortgage loan to begin with. The property is an embarrassment to him and a reminder of his screw-up. He wants to get rid of it as soon as possible.

I have also heard that **out-of-state** lenders (not in the same state as the property in question) are more likely to give bargains than local lenders and that lenders with **few** OREO are more likely to give bargains than those with many. And I've heard from columnist Bob Bruss and real estate educator Ron Starr that OREO sellers tend to be **far less concerned about your credit history** than when they are making a normal mortgage loan (not that either Bruss or Starr need lower standards to get a loan).

Some selectivity
Kessler mainly pursues properties where the market value is higher than the balance of the foreclosed loan. In general, he only pursues foreclosures of loans which are at least six years old. He never pursues FHA or VA repos (see the next chapter) or properties repossessed by sophisticated **individual** mortgage investors.

Full-time or part-time possible
Kessler does this **part-time**. He invests in foreclosures and runs his publishing and seminar businesses in addition to buying OREOs. Even the "full-time" investors like Paul Thompson rarely work a 40-hour week.

REO services
There are a number of services which claim to provide REO [sic] information. In general, I'm dubious of them. They strike me as being more in the business of making a buck off the public's notion that OREOs are bargains rather than providing valuable information. In the April 1988 *Distress Sales Report,* editor John Beck says subscribers to

the REO services complain that the property in question is already sold when they promptly call about properties listed in the services.

Also, there's a flaky aspect to the OREO information industry. If you call the *REO Realty Registry* number listed in Beck's April 1988 newsletter, you get a recording saying that the number has been **disconnected** and that no further information is available.

The *REO Guide* number is answered grandly as, "Financial Services of America." When I identified myself and asked for information on the *REO Guide*, I was switched to Dante Perano, a longtime associate of late-night book-and-tape guru, **Dave Del Dotto**. While on hold, I was subjected to a continuously running cassette of the kind of sale pitch you hear on the off-hours, cable-TV, real estate "infomercials." Although, I must note that Bob Bruss says he bought a bargain property he saw in Perano's *REO Guide* during a trial subscription.

When I called *The Property Acquisition Guide* in Portland, OR, someone picked up the phone, played "**Mary Had A Little Lamb**" on the touch tones, and hung up. I swear.

REO Registry promised to call me back in a half hour. I never heard from them.

The only publisher I recognized in Beck's list was Alan Crittenden. Unfortunately, Crittenden decided to stop publishing his *Crittenden Foreclosures For Sale*. Crittenden feels there are, indeed, bargain opportunities in the OREO market. But he got the impression that after his subscribers found one deal, they were tapped out for several years and therefore not interested in renewing.

The publisher of *REO Registry* said the only real benefit some subscribers got from OREO-information services was the names and phone numbers of the bank officers in charge of them. And that developing "relationships" with such people was one of the keys to getting OREO bargains.

How to find OREO services

To find REO services in your area, John Beck and Ron Starr recommend the following in their book, *Take This House, Please! The complete guide to buying real estate owned by lenders*. Ask:

• Other buyers at foreclosure auctions
• Auctioneers at foreclosure auctions
• Local real estate brokers
• Local legal newspapers (See *Yellow Pages* under "Newspapers")
• Other persons researching mortgage or trust deed records at the county recorders office
• Fellow real estate investors at investor association meetings
• Classified section of main newspaper
• OREO departments of local lenders

If you cannot find an adequate published source of information on OREOs in your area, you'll have to create your own from county courthouse records.

Who you know

I, too, had previously concluded that "relationships" are necessary in the OREO market. The first OREO bargain I ever heard of involved a long-time bank customer who got a call from his bank when they foreclosed on and acquired an apartment building. Apparently, the property was never offered to the public. The bank officer in charge just made a call or two to apartment-owner bank customers who were in his Rolodex.

Ethical questions

The relationship aspect of the OREO market bothers me. All sellers should try to sell their property for market value. If the property is **vacant**, it makes sense to sell for **quick-sale** value. But OREO buyers want to buy for **less** than quick-sale value

Many laymen seem to think that financial institutions operate under some strange rules which say getting the maximum price doesn't matter. That's nonsense. It matters the same to institutions as it does to individuals.

Bureaucrats

Institutions are bureaucracies. Incompetent and/or inadequately-motivated people abound in bureaucracies. When a better-than-quick-sale bargain comes out of a lending institution's OREO department, it's because somebody deliberately or accidentally **screwed up**. **Not** because the banks don't care what their OREOs sell for.

There's nothing wrong with your buying a property for less than it's worth as a result of a bank officer's screw-up as long as you did not **bribe** him to deliberately screw up—or mislead him into thinking he was getting quick-sale value or better. That's where my problem with "relationships" comes in.

"Relationship" is one of those words which is often a euphemism for something less benign. When Congressmen get caught committing adultery or sodomy, their contrite public statement invariably acknowledges only that they had a "relationship" with the adulteree or sodomee in question.

Fiduciary relationship

Officers of financial institutions have a relationship with their **employer**. It is a fiduciary relationship. They are permitted to have relationships with other persons or entities—like relatives, friends, church, clubs, etc.—as long as those relationships do not **conflict** with their fiduciary duty to their employer.

But when a would-be bargain buyer seeks to establish a "relationship" with an OREO officer, he or she is probably trying to establish a **friendship** in the hope that the officer will give them a chance to buy OREOs at bargain prices before they are exposed to a wider market. In other words, to act **against** the interest of the institution to which the officer has a fiduciary relationship—to **violate** fiduciary duty.

Not the only way

Does that work? I believe it does. Should you do it? **No.** It's wrong. You should not try to establish friendships with OREO officers for the purpose of getting bargains.

Does that mean you should not be friendly toward OREO officers, learn their first names, get their direct number in your Rolodex? Of course not. Those are perfectly legitimate ways of establishing good will and efficiency.

It is when you start taking OREO officers to lunch or buying them gifts or golfing with them that you are getting into a gray area. One test of propriety is whether what you are doing with the officer—and your interest in the institution's OREOs—could be told to all of the persons in the financial institution's chain of command **above** the OREO officer. If such full disclosure would make the officer uncomfortable, your relationship is improper.

Incidence of this opportunity

According to a July 10, 1992 Veribanc, Inc. (617-245-8370), the following was the total OREOs in the U.S. by category:

Undeveloped land and buildings under construction	$7.786 billion
Farmland	$501.9 million
1-4 family homes	$3.648 billion
Apartments	$2.840 billion
Commercial	$15.558 billion
Total	$30.333 billion

8

FHA and VA repos

With FHA and VA, you submit bids in accordance with HUD and VA rules. The highest bidder gets the property.

Why HUD and VA sell cheap

In the case of HUD and VA properties, they sell cheap because of neglect or vandalism and the fact that they are often boarded up which makes them show badly to prospective purchasers. And again, you have bureaucrats—this time the government variety—working with Realtors®. It has been said that the answer to the question, "How many people work for the government?" is "About half of them." There is considerable truth to that joke.

John Beck attributes the existence of HUD bargains to the fact that HUD pays too little for the appraisals they use to set sale prices. And to lack of interest by real estate agents especially in outlying areas where HUD foreclosures come on the market infrequently.

FHA OREO case history

On September 1st, 1988, Larry Kaplan bought a two-bedroom house in a Chicago suburb for $43,370. After $5,000 of needed fix-up, he figured it was worth $60,000 and rented for $675. Carrying costs were about $500 a month leaving $675 - $500 = $175 a month positive cash flow.

HUD foreclosures

Kaplan buys Department of Housing And Urban Development (HUD) foreclosures. He has to use a flashlight—even in broad daylight—because many of them are boarded up, winterized, and have the utilities turned off.

How to find them

Finding HUD foreclosures is straightforward. There is generally a big HUD ad in your local major metropolitan area paper each week. Real estate agents can get on a HUD mailing list. You inspect the properties by calling an agent. (HUD compares **net** bids after commissions so it behooves you to find an agent who will take a smaller commission if possible. Although you should know that HUD discourages non-agent bids because a high percentage of them fall through.) Kaplan says there's generally one agent who's willing to work on HUD foreclosures in each major real estate brokerage firm.

Kill ratio

He restricts his efforts to one lower-middle-class community with a population of about 25,000. About 100 HUD foreclosures came on the market there in 1988 (but only 40-50 in 1991). He made offers (by sealed bid in accordance with HUD procedure) on about 75 of those. And won two.

Full-time or part-time possible

Kaplan had a full-time, **non**-real estate job at the time.

Screening

He does not **bid** on the **other** 25 properties because they have poor location or the repairs required are too great to allow enough profit at HUD's probable sale price. He does not **get** 73 of the 75 properties he bids on because other bidders—who are incompetent at estimating fix-up costs—or who have lower profit requirements—outbid him.

Condition

HUD foreclosures generally need thousands of dollars worth of work including new appliances. In the example above, Kaplan needed:

• paint inside and out
• new kitchen floor
• steam cleaning of carpet
• re-caulk tub tile
• new refrigerator.

In addition, the basement had four inches of water in it—which Kaplan says is probably the reason he was not outbid on this particular property. He eliminated the water by installing a $65 sump pump. Fixing the damage done by the water will require replacing the basement floor tiles and a molding, wainscoting, or paint job to correct the stain on the bottom four inches of the wall paneling.

The house is a detached single-family with a pitched roof. Kaplan plans to add a wall in the basement to increase the number of bedrooms to three.

Financing

You finance HUD foreclosures like a regular purchase. HUD gives you 60 days to get a loan. Kaplan does not move into these properties, so he has to pay a non-owner-occupant "penalty" in terms of higher interest rates, stiffer qualifying requirements, etc.

In this case, he expected either to get an 80% first mortgage of 80% x $43,370 = $36,700—or to pay all cash, then refinance after fix-up. In **theory**, refi after fix-up would enable him to get 80% of $60,000 = $48,000—which is about **all** of his purchase and fix-up costs. But in the event, he found a lender who appraised the property at $59,000. They loaned him 80% x $59,000 = $47,200. He had to pay the non-owner-occupied interest rate of 11.75% rather than the owner-occupied rate of 10.75%.

With a $47,200 rather than $36,700 mortgage, this was a nothing-down deal with about breakeven before-tax cash flow. Most nothing-down deals have large negative cash flow.

Criteria

Kaplan says his approach does **not** work in **other than** lower-middle-class communities. In **better** areas, fewer HUD foreclosures are available and those houses sell for prices too close to the market value after fix-up to allow a resale profit or positive cash flow. In **lower** class areas, crime, lack of buyer or renter interest in the fixed-up house, and rent-collection problems increase hassles.

Regional variations

California foreclosure expert, John Beck (510-523-6115) says in his state you generally have to go to outlying or inner city areas to find profitable HUD foreclosures—and that the incidence of profit opportunities in HUD foreclosures is **cyclical**. The more properties they have, the better deals they give. He also says profits can be made in the lower-income areas if you can handle the extra hassle.

Incidence of this opportunity

In 1987, HUD sold 52,000 houses nationwide. They anticipated selling 80,000 in 1988. But the Berserkeley, California-based National Housing Law Project (NHLP) sued under the McKinney Homeless Assistance Act of 1987 to stop a nationwide HUD Sales Weekend. NHLP claimed the McKinney Act requires HUD to use its foreclosed houses for the homeless. NHLP subsequently got a temporary restraining order from Judge Harold Greene of the U.S. District Court for the District of Columbia which banned all HUD foreclosure sales nationwide.

HUD spokesman Bill Glavin said the HUD reserve fund contained about $6,000,000,000 at the time. Since HUD got about $37,500 per house from foreclosure sales in 1988, the fund would have gone bankrupt in about two years if the sales had not resumed. The restraining order was lifted.

If the restraining order had become **permanent**, the way to profit from HUD foreclosures would be to get rid of your house—thereby joining the ranks of the homeless. Then prostrate yourself on the steps of the local HUD office. Say, "I'm homeless." Whereupon a HUD guy will say, "Not anymore. Here's the deed to a $37,500 U.S. taxpayer-owned house." As Soviet defector and comedian Yakov Smirnov would say, "What a country!"

VA

The Veterans Administration has a similar program of selling its foreclosures. But Kaplan says VA houses in his area generally sell for only about $2,000 less than market—while needing much the same fix-up as HUD foreclosures—and there are fewer VA foreclosures. One reason for the higher prices may be that the VA gives buyers of its repos mortgages similar to those it gives to veterans, i.e., fixed-rate and little or nothing down. VA will do this even if you're not a veteran.

The investor who went out in the cold

Although he had never been winning bidder on a VA foreclosure, Larry Kaplan kept trying. In the winter of 1988-89, one VA auction fell on a windy, ten-degree, snowy day in the Chicago area. Kaplan almost stayed home because of the weather. The folks who usually outbid him apparently **did** decide to stay home. That was their loss; Kaplan's gain.

He made his usual low bids on two properties—but this time, he **won** one. He got a house for $55,000, $2,500 down and a 10 1/8% 30-year mortgage for the balance. After

$2,000 work, Kaplan figured it would be worth $65,000. Plus, it came with an additional lot worth $6,000.

The moral of the story: the more miserable the weather, the better day it is to bid at auctions. This applies to all types of auctions where the decision makers are **bureaucrats**, not just FHA and VA.

Private auctions

Where the auction seller is a **private party** and any low sale prices come out of his hide, bad weather auctions with poor turnouts are more likely to be **canceled** than to produce bargains. (Such sellers have one incentive **not** to cancel: re-scheduling the auction will force them to pay the substantial cost of promoting the auction a second time.)

If the auction is advertised as an "**absolute**" auction (no minimum bid), the show **must** go on. If you come across a bad weather, absolute auction, by all means go—and take a witness.

The bad-weather principle doesn't always work. Jim Zimmerman of Carrigan & Associates, a firm that used to do auctions, says he sold some Florida land in a torrential rain that flooded the auction tent to ankle depth. Local brokers said the land would sell for no more than $5,000 an acre. Zimmerman got $11,000.

On another occasion, he sold $3,000,000 worth of Oklahoma condos to a standing-room-only crowd in near-blizzard conditions. Zimmerman has also seen bad weather adversely affect the turnout to the point of reducing the sale price. In general, the bigger the deal, the less likely weather is to affect the turnout.

Special expertise required

You have to make a good inspection of the home when its utilities are turned off. This is tricky because it's hard to check the plumbing and electrical systems when they are not connected.

You can turn the electric on by setting up a gas-powered generator and plugging it into an outlet in the house. One investor uses a four kilowatt portable generator. Turn off all the circuit breakers in the house first. Then just turn on the one circuit breaker you want to check at a time.

In this case, you will pumping electricity **in**to the outlet rather than the usual taking it **out** of the outlet. You can also take a long extension cord with two male ends and plug one end into the house you are inspecting and the other into a neighbor's electric if they will let you. Paying them $5 or $10 may be necessary.

Some investor's, like Larry Kaplan, just take a powerful battery-operated flashlight when they inspect boarded-up HUD houses. That will enable you to see better. But it does not tell you whether the electrical equipment like heater, air-conditioner, or other appliances work.

You also need to know the current FHA and VA bidding procedures.

Ethical considerations

There are no ethical considerations in FHA and VA repo buying except to resist the temptation to tell the HUD that you are going to owner occupy the property if you are not.

Sequence

The sequence in HUD and VA purchases is the same as normal non-bargain purchases: You inspect the property and make an offer. If your offer is accepted, you seek financing.

Toxic liability considerations

You can probably successfully sue a conventional lender who sells you a contaminated property. But you probably can**not** successfully sue HUD or VA for selling you a contaminated property.

Need for secrecy

There is no need for secrecy because the knowledge of the deal is public until the winning bidder is announced.

Unique risks

In colder climates, it is common for the pipes in houses owned by HUD during freezing weather to have burst. It is impossible to ascertain this when you inspect because the water has been turned off.

9

Builder auctions

Why it works

Some builders often build homes which they can't sell at the prices they hoped. Since builders' unsold homes are typically vacant, they have huge carrying costs and produce no income. That puts the builders under tremendous pressure to sell the homes quickly. Often, the builder or his lender or the federal agency which takes over the lender turns to **private auctions**—as opposed to foreclosure auctions—to move the houses quickly. Sometimes you can get bargains at those auctions.

Actual case histories

In 1991, Paul Thompson told me he bought two houses at 80% of current market value at a **builder's** auction, rather than a foreclosure auction. One had three bedrooms, 2 1/2 baths, and 2,200 square feet and cost Thompson $141,000; the other had four bedrooms, 2 1/2 baths, and 2,400 square feet and cost $150,000. Both were brand new, detached, single-family homes with three-car garages.

It's possible for **new** housing developments to be **bad** neighborhoods. That happened in Houston. But Thompson's purchases were in good neighborhoods.

He figured the first house was worth $180,000. It appraised at $170,000 by a bank which knew he just bought it for $141,000 at a builder auction.

He thought the second house was worth $185,000 to $190,000 but again the bank appraiser came in low at $180,000 knowing that Thompson had just paid $150,000.

The second house rented for $900 a month, says Thompson. He normally lease options such properties and got monthly lease option payments of $1,100.

At 25% down, the mortgage on the second house would be $150,000 x 75% = $112,500. At 9.25%, the monthly payments on a fixed-rate, 30-year mortgage would be $925.51. That's not enough of a bargain to produce positive cash flow. But in parts of the country where the gross rent multiplier is lower than the $180,000 ÷ $900 = 200 in this example, a 20% discount ought to be enough to enable you to get positive cash flow on a straight rental (not lease option).

$10,000 in 45 days

Thompson assigned (sold) the purchase agreement on the first house for a $10,000 profit within 45 days of buying it. The buyers were referred to him by his accountant and they just happened to call at the time he bought the property.

How it works

Most of the time, there is a trick to buying at bargain prices. That appears **not** to be the case with builder auctions. You simply attend all the auctions after you inspect the homes. You inspect by visiting the models or the actual houses, then decide on their value, and knock off the discount you want. Bid until the bidding reaches that amount or you get the property, whichever comes sooner.

Registration

To become a qualified bidder, you have to pre-register and pay some sort of deposit.

How to find them

Private auctions are heavily advertised in regular newspaper real estate sections.

Regional variations

In some depressed parts of the country like Houston and New England, there have been whole auction sections in the newspaper in recent years.

Incidence of this opportunity

Buying bargains at private auctions is a **cyclical** opportunity. When values increase, virtually no builders have such problems. So there may be no builder auctions for years in a given area. Then, there's a deluge.

Not like government-regulated auctions

When you buy your bargains at government-regulated auctions like foreclosures, trustee sales, sheriff's sales, and the like, you get a clinic on how **not** to sell real estate. They demand **all cash**, won't let you **inspect** the property, give you an **unwanted tenant** in many cases, **won't guarantee title**, etc.

With **builder** auctions, you get none of that. You can **finance** with your own lender or, in many cases, the owners of the homes being auctioned offer attractive financing. At some auctions, local lenders not involved in the homes being sold set up booths in the hopes of getting your business.

You get **title insurance**. You get to **inspect** the same as anyone who buys from a builder. That is, you stroll through the builder's accessorized, well-lit, cleaned-daily model homes, peruse their brochures, question their well-groomed sales staff, and examine their jazzy maps or scale models.

The homes are **empty**. You don't have to evict the previous owner as Thompson has to do about half the time when he buys at foreclosure auctions.

Kill ratio

One thing that's typical of other bargain purchase techniques is also true of builder inventory auctions: The ratio of good deals to all deals is quite low. Thompson says it's about one in a hundred in his experience with builder auctions in central California.

Attendance key

Thompson's impression is that the **number of people who attend** the auction is the main factor in determining whether you will get a bargain at that auction. He has attended seven builder auctions but only bought at one. Thompson says if the ratio of people at the auction to properties available is **five to one or less**, you can probably make a bargain purchase. Some auctioneers will give you an idea in advance of what the attendance will be if you call and ask.

Several factors can affect attendance: **advertising**; **location** of the auction; **weather** on auction day; **major news stories** like the recent Gulf War; **major sports events** like a college football game between top-rated teams; whether the auction is "absolute" (no minimum bids); and so forth. You **most** want to attend those auctions which are likely to be **poorly attended**, that is, those with poor advertising, out-of-the-way location, terrible weather, or competing with major news stories or sporting events.

Basic principles

No joke, the atmosphere at private auctions is extreme high pressure. As experienced as Thompson is at buying at foreclosure auctions, he still had to struggle to resist the "bid higher" demands of the high-pressure salesmen who run up and down the aisles of private auctions and "get in the face" of the bidders.

Come with a written bid ceiling on each property in your pocket and steadfastly resist the temptation to bid above it. Private auction buying is a game which requires **iron discipline** on your part. You must go in with the attitude, "If I can buy right, I'll buy. Otherwise, I'll keep my money."

Unique risks

The auctioneers involved in Thompson's purchases were **so** pushy and obnoxious they appear to have fouled up an exchange Thompson hoped to do into the second auction purchase. Unbeknownst to Thompson, the auctioneer apparently called the lender who was considering making a loan to the buyer of Thompson's old property, left the impression they were representing Thompson, and pressured her.

So obnoxious were they about it that the loan officer stopped returning Thompson's phone calls. When he finally got through, she blasted him.

Criteria

Thompson says the middle of the auction usually offers the best buys. At the outset, people are afraid they'll miss out so they are a bit frenzied—properties sell at a rate of about one a minute. Then as the auction draws to a close, they again become afraid they'll miss out. "The girls all get prettier at closing time" syndrome sets in as people begin to compare the remaining properties to leaving empty handed instead of comparing the prices to market values.

Beware unfinished houses

Sometimes the houses being auctioned are not finished. Thompson says the auctioneers will **verbally** promise to complete the houses after you, buy but they will **refuse** to put it in writing. So ignore the verbal promise and only bid what the house is worth in its unfinished condition.

Refinancing ramifications

If you try to fully refinance based on fair market value within six months, you'll have trouble. That's because the appraiser will go back that far looking for comps and find your purchase. But **after** six months, you are more likely to get an appraisal which is unbiased by your purchase price. Thompson says there is no such "cooling-off" period in regular foreclosures. Banks and appraisers **believe** those are bargains and give you a true fair market value appraisal on the house you bought at a foreclosure auction even if you request the appraisal immediately after you buy the property.

Full-time or part-time possible

Buying at private builder auctions is an ideal investment strategy for those who work full-time at other jobs. The auctions are invariably held on **weekends**—instead of the nine a.m. weekday sales typical of foreclosure and other government-regulated auctions. You may inspect the homes at your leisure, generally with**out** an appointment, evenings and/or weekends. Buying selectively at private auctions is about as clean and easy as bargain purchases come.

Tax ramifications

As with other OREOs, builder auction purchases may trigger the at-risk rules if the seller takes back nonrecourse financing.

Ethical considerations

Because the purchase is made at a public auction, there are no ethical considerations. You bid—and if you win—you pay.

Toxic liability considerations

You can inspect the property before you buy it, so you have a good chance to identify toxic contamination before you commit to buy. On the other hand, there is a bit of a **bum's rush** aspect to private auctions. You may feel you need more opportunity to inspect than the people running the auction are willing to give. If you cannot assure yourself that the property is contamination-free—and the sellers prevent you from making adequate inspections, pass on the property.

10

Builder leftovers

Why it works

Mike Crenshaw (not his real name) buys home-builder leftovers. He's done it long enough that he now owns over 300 Northern California houses. When home builders put up a housing development, they almost invariably end up with a handful of hard-to-sell houses. The houses in question may be on the **worst lots** in the development. Or the developer took them back to settle a **construction-defects lawsuit**.

Such taken-back houses back in phase **one** stand out suspiciously when phase **three** is the one currently being sold. In some cases, the leftover houses may just be the **last** unsold ones. At that point, the developer can no longer justify the same advertising and sales staff budget as when he had dozens of houses to sell.

Builders build. When they finish one development they feel they have to go start another. Frequently they have land that is burning a hole in their pockets. Just as frequently, their lender insists that they finish the sales of the old development before they begin development of the new one.

All of which pressures the builder to sell the last houses in the old development fast.

Premiums but no discounts

The sensible response to hard-to-sell real estate is to lower the price. New housing developers have a particular problem with that.

When I bought the lot on which we had our home built, I noted that our developer's project map showed a cluster of sold lots around ours. The reason was a proverbial "babbling brook" with huge oak trees next to those lots and lot prices that were only slightly higher than lots with no babbling brook or oak trees.

I locked in the price of my lot. Then I told the builder what I said in my *How to Manage Residential Property for Maximum Cash Flow and Resale Value* book. There should be **no pattern** to the sales or vacancies in a housing development or apartment complex. The "sold" pins should be randomly distributed around the development. If there **is** a pattern, it means the pricing is incorrect. In the case of my home lot, the developer priced it too low or he priced the less desirable lots too high.

I asked Crenshaw why the builders don't wise up and price the lots so that they all sell. He said they never offer a discount for a lousy lot. They always have a standard lot price and charge premiums for more desirable lots. In other words, all builder lots range from "desirable" to "really desirable" and the pricing matches that fantasy.

Not big on agents

Another standard approach to selling hard-to-sell property is list it with a real estate agent. After all, builders are essentially for-sale-by-owners.

Builders rarely use real estate agents. Builders typically sell houses with a one-year warranty these days. And there are increasingly draconian laws and court decisions about disclosures in home sales. Builders fear independent real estate agents may say things to buyers which would create legal liabilities that would not arise out of the sales pitches of the builder's in-house salespeople. Independent agents also tend to have less loyalty to the builder. Agents bread is generally buttered on the buyer side in that the buyer represents a potential future listing if the agent makes a favorable impression. So if there are any disputes about the sale, the agent is tempted to side with the buyer rather than the builder. Builders' in-house salespeople are less likely to do that.

Shhhhh

Once the lot-premiums-only stupidity starts in a particular development, it's locked in. That dozens or hundreds of consumers have paid a certain range of prices to buy in the development makes it extremely impolitic for the developer to sell any houses at cut-rate prices. In many markets, local newspapers report publicly-recorded sale prices. Appraisers can frequently find out about low sale prices even in areas where the local paper does not carry them.

If recent home buyers learn that the builder sold some houses for significantly less than they paid, they go ape. During the one-year warranty period, angry buyers drive the builder nuts with nit-picky demands for warranty work to punish him for selling cheaper.

Special expertise required

In California, you can request that the amount of transfer tax due be shown only on a separate paper which is attached to the deed **after** it is recorded in the public records. (Revenue & Taxation Code §11932) This keeps the sale price secret from all but the most diligent researchers. In some California counties, the recorder will not let anyone see those separate papers. That's probably a violation of the Freedom of Information Act. But until a successful suit, the policy will stand. Crenshaw keeps his prices secret by invoking R&T §11932.

Case history

In April of 1992, Crenshaw closed a deal in which he bought five leftovers and the builder's model home. The subdivision was in an average area which had been over built. The houses in question were all the same 2,600-square-foot model and had been sold for as much as $225,000. Crenshaw got them for $160,000 each. Except for no floor covering in one, they were finished including appliances. If they were worth $200,000 or more, he got the 20% discount which I regard as the minimum.

Financing ramifications

Crenshaw pays all cash. The builders want an 8- to 12-day closing with no contingencies.

After he buys, Crenshaw refinances immediately—often getting back 100% of his purchase price. There is a four-mortgages-per-person limit on FNMA mortgages. That could limit your ability to own very many of these houses at a time. I asked Crenshaw how he gets around the four-houses-per-borrower limit. He said he got a new blanket mortgage from one of the biggest California banks just before the April '92 deal. The total mortgage was $4 or $5 million. When you own 300 properties, lenders don't worry about FNMA limits. Crenshaw says the banks hold such nonstandard loans in their portfolio and/or sell them in a less-well-known secondary market made up of pension funds and other private investors.

The four-mortgages-per-person limit does **not** apply to adjustable rate mortgages.

Lewis Goodkin is editor of the *Goodkin Real Estate Report/Florida* (305-493-5011) a newsletter that covers real estate development. He says the builder's lender will finance the sales of leftovers in many cases.

Selective buying

You can buy home-builder leftovers for 80% of current market value in a small percentage of cases. In the April 1992 deal, Crenshaw turned down another 16 houses. However, this is not an area that requires sophisticated screening procedures or special sequencing. The numbers of deal s available simply are not high enough.

Goodkin confirms that developers often sell the last half dozen or so houses or condos for below cost to shut down the marketing expense on that project. Below cost may sound like a great deal. But Goodkin says the average builder's cost is 89 to 90% of the sale price. So this niche is like most of the others I write about. Even with**in** the niche, the adequate deal is the exception rather than the rule.

Ethics

Buying builder leftovers is perfectly honest work. But the builder's desire to conceal the true prices may raise an ethical, or even legal, issue.

In some cases, the builder writes the sale up at a phony inflated price. Then he rebates the difference between the real and inflated price after closing—or forgives what was always a phony second mortgage. Going along with this can get you in trouble depending on who makes what representations to whom.

If the builder is trying to obtain financing—and uses your purchase documents as parts of his application—those documents should fully disclose **all** terms of the deal. That includes any future rebates or mortgage forgiveness. Obviously, the builder's not going to want to disclose if there are any shenanigans. Don't do those deals.

You might use a **lease option** that is, in substance, a sale, but which the newspaper does not report that way because of the form of the transaction. Report that it is in substance a sale to tax assessors, IRS, etc. With lenders, the builder would simply make full disclosure but not go into substance-over-form issues. For more on lease options see my *Special Report on Single-family Lease Options*.

How to find them

It's easy to find home builders. They advertise a lot and have model home sales offices. Crenshaw said he works for home builders as a subcontractor. That's how **he** contacts them. Now, he has bought so many houses from so many builders that he gets word-of-mouth calls from builders he has never met.

I doubt you need to become a subcontractor to pursue this niche. Just contact the builder and tell him you want to buy leftover houses at good prices. Do not communicate your interest in leftovers to the sales staff. Go direct to the builder himself. Don't file nit-picky warranty claims if you want to buy future builder leftovers from the builder in question or his friends.

Shades of EPIC?

In the '80s, there was a syndicator that specialized in investing in builder model homes and builder leftovers. That company was EPIC. EPIC defaulted on its mortgages in the fall of 1985. EPIC was a typical syndicator in most respects other than its propensity to buy builder leftovers.

That EPIC did so many deals indicates that there truly are deals available in the builder-leftover market niche. That EPIC went bankrupt is generally **irrelevant** to the technique. Most syndicators went bankrupt. Their trade association shut down.

EPIC's failure should not dissuade anyone from the home-builder leftover market niche.

Tax Ramifications

If you resell the homes regularly, you will almost certainly be a **dealer** for tax purposes. If you acquire the homes through lease options, the income tax ramifications can be very extensive and complex. Again, I refer you to my Special Report on *Single-Family Lease Options* for more information.

Full-time or part-time possible

Crenshaw does this on a part-time basis. Anyone else could, too. The secrecy builders require prevents buyers from stampeding toward these deals. That means you do not need to be ready to buy on a moment's notice which would require full-time effort.

Regional variations

As far as I can tell, this is a **nationwide** opportunity. Virtually all home builders end up with white elephants that they are unable to sell efficiently because of the unique facts about builders that are described above. Furthermore, this is not a cyclical phenomenon. It happens whenever builders build, wherever builders build.

Environmental liability considerations

Builder property generally has been scrutinized by **institutional lenders** in connection with the construction loans made to finance the houses. The same is true of the permanent loans obtained by the individual home buyers. Those institutional lenders usually inquire into environmental liability these days. So it would be surprising to find a new home with environmental problems.

On the other hand, you cannot assume no new homes have environmental liability problems. In some cases, there may be no construction lender. In other cases, the environmental expert may have overlooked or lied about environmental problems on the property.

Unique risks

These days, many, if not most, new home developments have a **home owners association**. Home owners associations are a pain in the butt. They file so many lawsuits against builders and other construction-related parties that many firms now refuse to have any thing to do with construction of home owner association property. Home owners associations are also more likely to **be** sued by individuals than individual home owners are. To the extent that you helped a builder conceal lower prices, they might even sue you as some sort of co-conspirator.

Home owners associations can have problems with **title**. When they do, all homes in the association are generally affected rather than just the homes which directly relate to the problem.

Budget problems like not setting aside enough for capital replacement items can also adversely affect all homes in the association. Lenders have been known to redline associations that do not meet state guidelines in the amounts they have in reserve. If your buyer cannot get financing, you probably cannot sell. Or at least you cannot sell for normal market value.

11

Resolution Trust Corporation properties

In 1989, the Pensacola, FL house John Lewis rented had been listed by the bank that owned it for $35,000. Lewis couldn't afford that. He offered $22,000, which the bank rejected. But when the bank was taken over by RTC, the house was auctioned off and bought by the Lewises—for just $11,500. RTC only required a $500 down payment.

That account appears in *Profiting From the Bank and Savings and Loan Crisis* by Stephen Pizzo and Paul Muolo, a decent guidebook to the inner workings of the RTC.

Why it works

You can get some bargains from the RTC because many RTC people are incompetent and/or lazy. They neglect properties and make it extremely difficult to buy. The very name RTC turns a great many potential buyers totally off thereby leaving less competition for the few who persevere through the RTC bureaucracy.

Tax Ramifications

The only tax ramification of buying RTC property is the same at-risk rule caution that applies to all seller financed OREOs. There is a possible future unique tax ramification of RTC property. There has been talk of treating property bought from the RTC differently than other property for tax purposes. That is, they might reinstate some of the tax benefits taken away by the Tax Reform Act of 1986—but only for properties bought from the RTC. Keep an eye out for such legislation.

Regional variations

RTC properties are primarily in the Oil Patch and New England. Although virtually every region has some. Call RTC at 800-782-3006 for information about your area.

Ethical considerations

The ethical considerations in dealing with RTC are the same as dealing with conventional OREO lenders.

Toxic liability considerations

You generally get ample opportunity to inspect RTC property before you commit to buying it. However, the contract from the RTC is far more anti-buyer than you would normally see. And since the RTC is the federal government, they can enforce onerous provisions which would be unenforceable if private parties tried to use them. In short, when you buy from the federal government—especially the RTC—you are back in the "Buyer beware" land of old. When it comes to toxic contamination, there is more to beware of.

Incidence of this opportunity

At the beginning of 1992, RTC had $27 billion in real estate.

Unique risks

There's a problem with RTC giving buyers bargains: the **taxpayers** are at the other end of the bargain. The politicians who set up the RTC required the RTC to sell for market value or very close to it. The RTC bureaucrats responded with red tape designed to **prevent** bargains. Predictably, they prevented not only bargains but also sales.

RTC is also a new bureaucracy. Instant red tape, it turns out, is even worse than the kind that develops over years. Virtually everyone who has tried to do business with RTC has found it next to impossible. No one seems to be in charge or have the power to make any decisions. Actually some people **can** make decisions, but finding them requires you to make a heroically persistent trek through a Kafkaesque bureaucratic maze.

Some salted peanut company had the slogan, "Betcha can't eat just one." When it comes to the RTC, "Betcha can't do just one deal" is an apt slogan. I have spoken to a number of people who have tried to do one deal with the RTC. They are **livid**.

RTC bounces you around far more than other bureaucracies. You call the guy who's supposed to be in charge of a particular property and he refers you to a real estate agent. The agent never heard of the property. He refers you back to RTC and so on.

RTC reneges on promises made by S&Ls it took over and it reneges on its own promises. One bank which held a delinquent mortgage on a property owned by RTC said RTC was so screwed up they preferred to let the property go to foreclosure rather than try to work something out with the RTC even though RTC obviously had the money to reinstate the delinquent mortgage.

One investor complained to her Congressman about RTC but got the impression the Congressman was afraid to say anything to the RTC no matter how screwed up it was because he was afraid of Keating Five Syndrome.

RTC property is neglected and deteriorates by the day. Lawn and pool are not touched for months. The front door is left unlocked and often wide open. If the roof starts leaking it's allowed to continue. What you start to buy will typically be in much worse condition by the time you take title. On one $1,000,000 house, the agent involved said the RTC literally threw away $200,000 of the value by dragging their feet on the decision and letting the house deteriorate.

RTC's contract to sell a single-family house was a "40-page horror story...totally one-sided" in the words of one would-be buyer. Everything is as is, no recourse to the government, none of the many protections you get when you buy from someone other than the RTC. After delaying responding interminably, the RTC had the nerve to ask the buyer to close in ten days.

Subcontractors working for RTC complain the agency doesn't pay its bills on time. If someone wants to buy RTC property at an auction, they must read and comply with 239 pages of specifications.

The Wall Street Journal (3/28/91) quoted a survey in which 2,000 real estate investors all said they were unsatisfied with their dealings with RTC and 65% said they would never deal with RTC again. The *Journal* reported Chase Manhattan Bank was interested in locating a credit-card processing center on a parcel of Arizona land until they learned the RTC was involved. They backed off as soon as they found out the RTC was involved and went elsewhere.

Actual case histories

San Francisco Examiner writer Corrie Anders spotted a successful RTC bargain purchaser: Joseph Smith of Sacramento (916-922-0307). He has bought over 50 houses and duplexes for all-cash from the RTC. He paid from $500 to $4,000 each for the properties, mostly located in the Polytechnic section of Fort Worth, others are in Kansas and Florida. He fixed up two for $500 each and is offering them at $270 a month. The worst need $2,000 to $3,000 in renovation.

Basic principles

Smith found the RTC a "mixed-up mess." But he used the age-old key to success with bureaucracies: **persistence**. He kept his cool and made literally hundreds of calls until he finally found someone who could accept or reject his offer. He offered $1,700, sight unseen for a house listed by the RTC at $10,000. They accepted. Turned out to be a two-bedroom in decent shape.

Smith says the properties are in low-income neighborhoods where houses sell for about $35,000. He expects to rent them for about $225 per month. Smith resold one duplex he bought from an S&L ten days after he bought it. The purchase price was $4,040; resale price, $11,000.

Smith says he would have been better off spending the same amount of time working at Burger King if he had only done **one** deal. But finding **the right people** to deal with **was** worthwhile considering all the deals he's done **since** the first one.

Need for secrecy

He would not name the right people. The identity of the people at RTC who can and actually will sell property is a precious commodity. If you find out who they are, keep it a top secret like Smith.

It should get better

It is impossible for RTC to be such a pain in the neck to deal with and still get people to pay the same prices which they pay sellers who are not a pain in the neck. So eventually, RTC will be forced to sell cheap. When that happens, there may be legitimate bargains. But I would not hazard a guess as to when that may be. Furthermore, dealing with them at present seems so enormously time-consuming and unrewarding that it's hard to justify any monitoring effort to make sure you are ready to move when RTC starts selling bargains.

Right now, RTC is a Kafkaesque nightmare. You'd better stay away unless you are willing to buy lots of properties only after heroic persistence and the patience of Job.

Full-time or part-time possible

Because it is so difficult to find someone to do business with in RTC, buying from them is probably a full-time job—at least until you get the right names and numbers in your Rolodex.

12

Tenant-in-common interests

How it works

Owners of real estate sometimes split the ownership of their property among several people. Each owns an **undivided interest**. That is, you cannot say one guy owns one bedroom and another guy owns another bedroom. Everybody owns a percentage of every part of the property.

Tenant-in-common interests most commonly arise out of **inheritances**. The parents die and leave each child an equal portion of their estate. If they have four children, each gets a 25% tenant-in-common interest in each piece of real estate owned by the deceased.

They also are common in **divorce** settlements or judgments. That's because one spouse frequently wants to remain in the family home but cannot afford to buy the other spouse out. So the judge divides the house in Solomonic halves awarding one to each spouse. The theory is that the spouse who remains can later buy the other spouse out through a refinancing or can sell the house and split the proceeds.

Sometimes, the owners of tenant-in-common interests **want** to sell or are **forced** to sell. If you buy a tenant-in-common interest, then just try to resell it as is, you'll run into the same lack of buyers that created your bargain to begin with.

If the other owners of the property in question won't buy them out, they must either sell their tenant-in-common interest on the open market or **sue** the other owners for **partition** of the property.

Partition means the court either divides the property up and deeds each heir his section—or the court orders the property sold and gives each heir his share of the sale proceeds. Actual dividing up of the property generally only takes place when the property is raw land and its value is not adversely affected by subdividing it.

You profit by buying the interest at pennies on the dollar then you:

- Sell your interest to the other owners at a profit
- Buy the other parties out for fair market value or less
- Sue the other owners for partition
- Wait until the other owners want to refinance or sell.

Why it works

There is **no market** for tenant-in-common interests in real estate. As a result, such interests sell for pennies on the dollar—if they even sell at all. Owners of tenant-in-common interests may learn that they could sue for partition, but they are typically reluctant to sue their brothers and sisters.

Siblings who refused to buy out their relative may be shocked upon learning that you, a total stranger, now own part of their property. The shock may get them to agree to buy you out to get rid of you. If you just wait, they will eventually be forced to buy you out when they sell the property or refinance it.

Over the years, a number of property owners have asked Seattle income property broker, Mike Scott (206-285-7100) to help them sell a tenant-in-common interest in a property. Invariably, he politely told them he knew of no buyers for such interests. As the **inquiries** he receives indicate, some people who own such interests do want to sell them.

When **no one** is interested, you can get a bargain.

Basic principles

In the Fall/Winter 1988 edition of *Real Estate Issues*, author Peter J. Patchin, who is an appraiser, says that tenant-in-common interests "are not all that rare" but that sales of such interests are "comparatively rare." Great! That's exactly what we want: many prospective sellers and few prospective buyers.

In two studies of 24 sales of tenant-in-common interests in farm land, discounts ranged from 15.2% to 79%. The average discounts were 56.0% and 32.1%.

In two other studies of sales of limited partnership interests, **not** tenancies in common, the discounts ranged from 0% to 82.4% with averages of 44.6% and 14.6%. However, I don't see how you would profit from buying limited partnership interests even at such discounts.

In a tenancy in common, you can usually file a **partition suit** to force sale of the property. You generally can**not** do that in a limited partnership. So you'd have to wait until the entire property were sold. That wait is precisely the **cause** of the discount. In order to **profit** from a tenant-in-common interest, you must be able to buy at a discount then **eliminate** the cause of the discount. Also, in tenancies in common, the wait is generally shorter than the wait in limited partnerships. Indeed, there is a question as to whether limited partners will **ever** get anything out of their investment.

Financing ramifications

Few, if any, institutional lenders will **knowingly** make loans on tenant-in-common interests. Some lenders have **un**knowingly made such loans when they mistakenly thought the borrower was the only owner of the property.

Non-institutional lenders, on the other hand, do occasionally make such loans. Hard-money lenders would probably be extremely rare. A hard money lender is one who writes a check to make the loan rather than taking back a mortgage on a property he is selling. You might find a note investor who prides himself on looking at "any deal that makes sense."

Soft-money lenders, better known as **sellers**, may take back a mortgage when they sell you a tenant-in-common interest. That might be one way to protect yourself against undisclosed anti-partition agreements. You could pay the seller so much in cash now and put the rest of the price in the form of a note which says the balance is forgiven if an express or implied anti-partition agreement is found to cover the property.

In general, however, the business of buying partial interests is probably all-cash. But in view of the low prices, that should not be a problem.

Kill ratio

I know of no professional tenancy-in-common investors so I have no data on what your kill ratio would be contacting cotenants systematically. I **do** know that you would be virtually the entire market for such interests. And that bodes well for your kill ratio as well as your profit margins.

Full-time or part-time possible

Since you are virtually the entire market, you should not have to hustle to beat out other buyers (other than the other tenants in common who own the rest of the property in question) the way you do in most bargain-purchase techniques.

Regional variations

State laws regarding tenancy in common and partition suits vary. So the details may vary. But the basic principles apply and the profit opportunities exist in every state. In some states, you cannot use a partition suit to force someone out of their **home**. In other states, inherited tenant-in-common interests are governed by different partition rules than tenant-in-common interests acquired in other ways.

Some states respond to delinquent property taxes by auctioning off a tenant-in-common interest in the property in question instead of auctioning off the entire property. Presumably, those states offer more opportunities to buy tenant-in-common interests.

Ethical considerations

If you plan to sue for partition, it would probably be prudent to refrain from volunteering that information to the seller before you close—especially where the tenants in common are related. But, if you are asked about your intentions, you must answer honestly or plainly refuse to answer at all. You must not leave the person from whom you are buying the tenant-in-common interest with the impression that you would **not** sue for partition.

You should probably refrain from making any representations about the value of tenant-in-common interests in general or of the particular tenant-in-common interest which you are buying. If you are pressed for a value, refer them to an appraiser or real estate agent.

Screening procedures

Ask the would-be seller what they think the entire property is worth, what liens are on it, and how much they want for their interest. If those answers indicate you can buy very cheap, proceed.

Sequence

Step one, get a viable deal verbally over the phone or by mail. Step two, Ask for written proof of the liens. Step three, get the seller to give you a written option to purchase his or her interest or both of you sign a purchase agreement contingent on the confirmation of the representations made as to value, liens, sale price, and ownership. Once the deal is locked up on paper, make your normal due-diligence investigation. If you are relying on the ability to partition, investigate to make sure that right has not been eliminated by agreement or some other fact.

Environmental liability considerations

Don't let your guard down because you are buying so cheap. It could be the entire group of owners was willing to sell the property but couldn't because of toxic contamination. Then, when one of them got your letter asking if they'd sell, they decided to dump at least part of the property on you and split the proceeds.

You may be able to avoid liability by making "all appropriate inquiry" and by taking title in a corporation which owns nothing else. Environmental laws typically allow the government or other complainant to go after the owner or operator. The operator part of the law allows them to get around most corporate veils. But in a tenant-in-common situation where you have nothing to do with the property and simply wait until it's sold or refinanced, you may be able to claim successfully that you are not now and never were the operator of the property. Check with an environmental attorney on that one.

Criteria

The time value of money is the main hidden factor. You cannot count on the other owners buying you out or selling out to you promptly. You may have to wait years for your profit if you don't file a partition suit. Even if you file a partition suit, you may have to wait years for it to be consummated.

Buying a property for pennies on the dollar is great—unless you have to wait thirty years to get the dollar. So be sure to take into account a possible multi-year wait until you get your profit.

2 1/2 cents on the dollar

The near total absence of a market can lead to some amazing bargains. John Beck once bought a 50% interest in a rental house for 2.5% of its market value! A woman and her former husband owned the free-and-clear house worth $40,000 (circa 1980). Because of animosity, she would not negotiate with the husband. So she sold her 50% interest for $500.

John sold the half interest back to the husband for $10,000.

23.5% average discount

In a study of sales of tenant-in-common interests (large commercial deals only) reported in the July 1988 *Appraisal Journal*, appraiser Martin J. Healy, Jr. found that such interests sold at a discount 61% of the time and that the discounts ranged from 3% to 52% of the market value with an average of 23.5%. In a phone call, he told me he had seen discounts as high as 90% in tenant-in-common interest cases.

St. Louis case history

Dwain Sachs (314-647-0001) is an investor and Realtor® in St. Louis. He didn't do the deal I'm about to describe—in part because he thought it might cause adverse publicity that could hurt his brokerage business. But investors with no such inhibitions could have grabbed this one.

A man owned 49% of a free-and-clear apartment building worth $400,000. His father-in-law owned the other 51% and lived in the building. But the father-in-law refused to manage it. The law allows a tenant in common to live in a property without paying the other tenant(s)-in-common rent.

The man offered to sell his share to Sachs. The terms were only partially discussed before Sachs backed out. Sachs was to pay $15,000 up front and the rest upon resolution of the sale of his interest. The total price was not agreed on but Sachs said it was clearly going to be in the range of at least a 50% overall discount. That is, he'd be buying $200,000 of equity for less than $100,000.

Farm for $500

A real estate agent purchased a 1/37th interest in a farm for $500. He then filed a partition suit against the other owners. The property was sold and the agent was the only bidder at the sale. This was related in an article entitled "Acquiring Property Through Forced Partition Sales: Abuses and Remedies," (27 *BC Law Review* 755-783 July 1986).

Get bought out at a PREMIUM!

Getting bought out by the other owners is the most probable outcome. They may even buy you out at a **premium** over market value. Appraiser Healy's study found that 19% of the tenant-in-common interests sold at premiums ranging from 6% to 35%!

Healy said premiums occurred when:

• The buyer had a **business** on the premises.
• Several **partners** purchased the interest of another for business reasons or to settle an estate.
• Family members purchased an interest in order to maintain **family** ownership.
• The buyer needed the interest to achieve a **controlling** interest position.

Buy from black sheep

A typical buy-at-a-discount,-sell-at-a-premium scenario would involve a family with a black sheep. The black sheep owns part of the family property by inheritance but sells to you rather than to his or her siblings

You then go to the "white sheep" and say buy me out or I'll force partition of the property (court supervised sale). The best negotiating posture might be to simply initiate the suit and negotiate with them to settle it out of court by selling them your interest.

In a business context, the guy you buy from may have had a falling out with his fellow tenants in common. Or perhaps they didn't take his expressed desire to get out seriously. Or maybe he just wants to redeploy his assets and they refuse to cooperate. For friendship or to avoid litigation or whatever reason, he'd rather sell to you at a discount than file a partition suit.

Lock it up quickly

Whenever there is more than one buyer for a property, there is a danger that your offer will be used to prod another buyer to raise his bid to an amount just above yours—or to prod a mildly-interested party into action.

There is a **greater** danger of this in tenant-in-common interest situations because there is always a prime, competing buyer—the other tenant(s) in common. Because of lingering emotional ties, the person wanting out may say to them, *"Look, this guy's willing to pay me $50,000. I'd rather sell to you but you're going to have to match his price."* Owners who shrugged off the odd man's desire to get out may be galvanized into action by his reporting your offer to them. Especially when they hear what a bargain you're getting.

So it behooves you to get the deal in accepted—in writing—with some consideration **as soon as possible**. You can do that by having appropriate forms ready to sign during your initial contact. And/or by setting extremely short deadlines for acceptance.

Buy out others

If the other owners will not buy you out on acceptable terms, you can buy **them** out. In fact, you can afford to pay them **as much as market value** for their interests. You can even afford to pay them a little **more** than market value to avoid the cost and delay of the partition suit. Ideally, of course, you'd buy them out at a discount also. Your argument would be, *"Try to sell your interest to someone else if you don't like my offer."* But, like you, they can wait until the partition suit.

You can afford to pay as much as market value for the other interest(s) because you already have an adequate profit locked into the part you already bought.

Partition suit

A tenant in common can sue to force "partition" of the property. The court can:

• order that each party get part of the property (typical in raw land)
• order the property sold and the cash proceeds be divided according to each's interest.
• order one or more party get property and that money be paid (that's called "owelty")
  between parties to make the final outcome match the respective interests.

In *The Language Of Real Estate*, John Reilly describes partition suits as "lengthy, expensive legal matters." The defendants (parties you are suing to force partition) may claim that you are not **entitled** to partition. The main reason being that all the owners including the one you bought from had agreed explicitly or implicitly to waive their right to partition. Such an agreement can be **oral** and it's still enforceable, in California at least. (*California Real Estate 2d* § 12:17, *Williams v. Williams*, 63 Cal Rptr 354)

In *Schultheis v. Schultheis*, (36 Wash. App. 588, 675 P 2d 634) the court said an agreement to **never** partition was not enforceable but it could be enforceable for a limited period of time. You need to check your state law on the right to partition.

In some cases, the **will** prohibits partition by any heir for a period of years. Such prohibitions are generally binding on you. (*Bank of Ukiah v. Rice*, 76 P 1020) One example of an implied agreement not to partition would be if the parties expected to do something with the property like develop it. That expectation may be considered an implied agreement not to partition until the development had been completed or efforts at development had been abandoned.

In one case, a lender made a loan secured by one cotenant's half interest in a divorce property. The husband/borrower defaulted. The lender foreclosed and was the high bidder at the foreclosure auction. The appeals court said that was fine and that the foreclosing lender had became the owner of half the property and could sue for partition. If the wife did not make the high bid at the partition sale, she would have to move out. [*Kane v. Huntley Financial*, (1983) 146 CA 3d 1092]

Less than fee simple

You can partition even if the interest you own is less than fee simple ownership of the tenant-in-common interest. Lesser interests include life and remainder estates, estates for years, and so forth. For example, let's say you bought a remainder interest in a tenancy in common. You could sue for partition.

In California, when you file a partition suit, you must also file a *lis pendens* which tells the world the title is in question. [Code of Civil Procedure § 872.250(a)] A *lis pendens* clouds the title even further than your owning the tenancy-in-common and may put additional pressure on the other owners to settle with you.

Defendants may also claim that they are owed money for work they've done on the property—money which should be paid out of your share of the property—a sort of invisible lien. In some cases, courts have said that such liens can be offset by the rental value of the non-occupant's interest where no rent has been paid. (*Hunter v. Schulz*, 49 Cal Rptr 315) A defendant in a partition suit must state any claims he has against the other tenants in common in his answer to the partition complaint—so if there are such problems, you find out about them very soon after filing your suit. Otherwise, an occupant cotenant has no obligation to pay rent to a non-occupant cotenant.

Partition sale procedure

To subdivide or sell the property, the court appoints a referee. He or she gets appraisals and such to see what's the best way to go. All parties with an interest in the property are notified of the pending sale. The property is publicly offered for sale. Any bids received must be confirmed by the court in a public hearing where new bidders can overbid the previous winning bid. Then the sale can go through.

Partition in kind

The defendants may gum up the partition suit by insisting on partition **in kind** rather than sale and splitting of the proceeds. Partition in kind means each tenant in common gets a piece of the real estate. Then they argue over what's a fair division the property.

Although judges pay lip service to the historical legal doctrine that partition in kind is **preferable** to sale of the property, they actually favor **sale** of the property. Courts are not supposed to partition in kind if splitting up the property would diminish its value. So you really shouldn't care much whether you got a piece of the property or cash. Either way, you got a heck of a deal.

You can minimize the litigation probability by doing deals so small that the other owners won't want to incur legal fees—or by avoiding **seasoned** undivided interests. If the various owners just became owners, there's less chance that they have entered into anti-partition agreements or did work on the property in question. On the other hand, seasoned tenancies in common are the ones most likely to result in the sales at a premium described above. Where a will is involved, you must read it to make sure it contains no anti-partition language.

Special expertise required

An intelligent layman could act as his own attorney in partition actions if he read the pertinent law books, started small, and consulted with a local real estate attorney as needed. In general, I'm a little leery of the partition suit approach. I'd try one or two. But I would not be surprised if the courts supported cotenants who vigorously resisted partition. The fact that you bought your interest for pennies on the dollar and were just trying to make a killing would go against you in most judges' minds. The law may be on your side. But the judge will find a way to decide in the other party's favor.

As long as there were no big legal fees, a failed partition suit wouldn't mean much. You'd still own an interest in the property which you bought real cheap. And you'd still get your share of the proceeds when the property was sold or refinanced. Losing the partition suit would mean you'd have to **wait**. That diminishes the present value of your original profit. But it also puts you in the position of one who speculates on the value of the property. While you're waiting, the value of the property could go up thereby giving you additional profit.

Filing a partition suit does not necessarily mean you'll ever get a court verdict either. Most suits are settled out of court. The partition suit and its uncertainty would inspire many cotenants to buy you out just to be done with you and the partition suit. They can't be **sure** the judge will decide in their favor.

Waiting case history

Ron Starr bought a half interest in a house at an IRS auction. He paid $17,400 for equity which he believes was worth $40,000 at the time. He's waiting for the owner of the other half—who is occupying the property and paying the **entire** mortgage payment but no rent to Starr—to come to him. If and when the other owner wants to refinance or sell, he will need Starr's signature to do so. Starr will insist on all or at least part of his profit at that time in return.

Starr previously waited **two years** to make $5,000 profit on a 1/4 interest in a house he bought for $475. The owners of the other 3/4 decided to sell and needed his signature.

IRS auction case history

A man and wife got divorced. The divorce court gave each a tenant-in-common half interest. The man remained in their home. The wife moved out. In 1985, the wife suddenly began getting calls from men who wanted to buy her half of the home for $500 or so. The callers explained that the husband's half interest in the home had been seized by the IRS and was about to be auctioned off. The callers wanted to buy the wife's half interest so that they would own 100% if they bought at the auction. She called Dan Kinter (916-965-6716), an attorney friend for advice.

Kinter investigated and found that the property was worth about $100,000 and had a first mortgage of about $41,000. The IRS minimum bid was $5,000 for the $100,000 - $41,000 = $59,000 equity in the property.

The auction procedure called for sealed bids. One thing you should keep in mind whenever you bid in a sealed bid auction is to **avoid round numbers**. That's because in the event of a tie, they usually flip a coin or draw lots to decide who wins. There were a lot of people at the auction, so Kinter decided he'd better go higher than the $5,100 bid he originally intended to make. He decided to bid $6,000 and added an extra $75 because he knew about avoiding round numbers.

Turned out most of the crowd was there to bid on **another** property—not the half interest. Only one other party bid on the half interest. And they bid exactly what Kinter wanted to bid before he changed to avoid a round number: $6,000. That round-number bid was $75 too low. Kinter won.

He and the former wife, who did not have the money to bid herself, then spent $5,000 fixing the place up. The house was vacant after the sale so they did not have to evict the husband. They tried to sell at $99,000 with no luck. Then they lease-optioned the property for $850 a month for three years with a sale price of $96,000. The fair market rental value was $550 a month. The mortgage payment on the first mortgage was $475. So they had positive cash flow of $850 - $475 = $375 per month. They gave the lessee-optionee a credit of $150 per month toward the purchase price. After 30 months, he had built up a cumulative credit of 30 x $150 = $4,500. He exercised the option and bought the property for $96,000 - $4,500 = $91,500 in the spring of 1988. (See my *Special Report on Single-family Lease Options* before you do a deal like this.)

No title insurance

When it came time to sell, Kinter had a problem. The title insurance companies all turned him down because he had bought his interest at an IRS-seized-property sale. It seems all had been burned in the past when they wrote title insurance on such sales. People who lost property through such sales sometimes sued alleging the sale had been improper in that IRS had failed to dot an "i" or cross a "t." And they won. That caused a loss to the title company.

Kinter located the husband and said, "If you will quitclaim deed the house to me, I'll give you $100." The husband protested that he no longer owned it so how could he deed it. Kinter explained that the title company was nervous about precisely the issue of whether he owned it anymore and that the quitclaim deed would eliminate the uncertainty. The husband signed the quitclaim deed. A title company issued insurance and Kinter and the wife each walked away from the deal with $25,000. The $5,000 improvement loan had been paid off quickly with the $375 positive cash flow.

Unique risks

Waiting can be dangerous. The property value may **decline** because of external factors or because of the behavior of the other tenants in common. Also, tenants in common have **unlimited liability** in the event of a lawsuit. If the other tenants in common did not pay their share of the property's bills, the equity could be reduced and possibly wiped out. (Judgment liens, like IRS liens or alimony liens, but not mechanics or materialmens liens, against other owners, would **not** attach to your interest in the property.)

In properties requiring management, lack of leadership or cooperation would likely result in management problems. If the property was rented at fair-market-rental value and had negative cash flow, each tenant in common would owe a prorata share of the negative although the person who only bought a tenant in common interest and did not sign any mortgage documents would presumably not be personally liable for the debt.

Also, you should not buy a property which has negative cash flow, even in a tenant-in-common deal. You are only buying the equity of the seller. In order for him to sell to you for pennies on the dollar or 50¢ on the dollar or whatever, he must have substantial equity and that would generally imply positive cash flow.

Due-on-sale clause

The purchase of a tenant-in-common interest in a mortgaged property could, and probably would, trigger a due-on-sale clause in the mortgage. Whether the purchase of a tenant-in-common interest triggers a due-on-sale clause depends on whether there is a due-on-sale clause in the mortgage in question, how it's worded, and possibly on state and/or federal law. Here's the due-on-sale clause in the trust deed I signed when I refinanced our home in 1987:

> **17. Transfer of the Property or a Beneficial Interest in Borrower**. If all or any part of the Property or any interest in it is sold or transferred (or if a beneficial interest in Borrower is sold or transferred and Borrower is not a natural person) without Lender's prior written consent, Lender may, at its option, require immediate payment in full of all sums secured by this Security Instrument. However, this option shall not be exercised by Lender if exercise is prohibited by federal law as of the date of this Security Instrument.

Our home mortgage was the standard kind, namely "Form 3005 12/83 California—Single Family—FNMA/FHLMC Uniform Instrument." The vast majority of home mortgages in the U.S. use their state's version of this form. Clearly the sale of a tenant-in-common interest, no matter how small, would trigger this due-on-sale clause. As a practical matter, I doubt a lender who found out would accelerate the loan if a minority interest were sold unless there were some additional motivation like the mortgage interest rate was significantly below the current market interest rate.

Even if the due-on-sale clause were triggered and the lender exercised their option to accelerate, what do you care? In fact, you might **deliberately** contact the lender and tell them. It would accomplish the same thing as a partition suit—only much faster and cheaper. Telling the lender that the due-on-sale clause had been triggered would be a sort of poor man's partition suit.

Check with a local real estate attorney before you do that, however. Acting against the interest of fellow owners might violate some state law. Of course, an argument could be made that telling the lender was **in** the interest of the other owners in that it would clarify what would otherwise be a due-on-sale Sword of Damocles hanging over the property.

If the lender accelerated the mortgage, that would put pressure on the other tenants in common to buy you out. And if they refused, the property would be sold at a foreclosure auction and you would get your prorata share of the sale proceeds. Actually, you would also be entitled to some of the **other** owners' share of the proceeds if they had failed to send you your prorata share of the property's cash flow on a periodic basis before the property was sold.

Don't extort

You may be tempted to tell the other owners, "Your brother sold me his interest in the property. That triggers the due-on-sale clause. If you don't buy me out for X dollars, I'm going to tell the lender about the sale."

That is arguably extortion and may violate **criminal** laws. Just ask the others to buy you out without mentioning the due-on-sale clause. Then, if your attorney approves, tell the lender if the other owners do not respond satisfactorily to your offer to sell. And send a carbon copy of the letter to the other tenant-in-common owners of the property.

Black's Law Dictionary defines extortion as follows:

> *The obtaining of property from another induced by wrongful use of actual or threatened force, violence, or fear, or under color of official right 18 USCA § 871 et seq; § 1951*
>
> *A person is guilty of theft by extortion if he purposely obtains property of another by threatening to:*
>
> *(3) expose any secret tending to subject any person to hatred, contempt, or ridicule, or to impair his credit or business repute; or (7) inflict any other harm which would not benefit the actor.* Model Penal Code § 223.4

How to find tenant-in-common interests

Look at

- probate files
- recorded deeds
- IRS seized property auctions
- partition suit in progress
- divorce suits
- in some states, tenant-in-common interests are sold at delinquent property tax auctions
- tell managers of local real estate brokerage firms to keep your name and number so they can help the occasional tenant-in-common interest owner who wants to list his interest for sale.

Contact the owners and brokers by mail offering to buy. Emphasize **quick cash**—which especially appeals to **heirs** waiting for probate to finish—and no real estate commission (don't mention that in the post cards to the brokers). Make no representations as to the market value of the property or of the interest and never even suggest that you are working on behalf of the party you are trying to buy from. Just offer to buy, period.

Insurance

My insurance agent says you **can** insure your tenant-in-common interest. If the total insurance coverage by all parties exceeds the insurable value of the property, the various insurance companies would work out sharing a loss in accordance with state law so that the total payout to all parties did not exceed the loss.

You would only buy a separate policy if the other owners refused to let you be named as an additional insured on **their** policy in return for your paying your share of the premium. Buying your own separate insurance would be a waste of money in that the total insurance premiums paid by all owners of the property for their separate policies would exceed what they would pay if they all used the same policy. On the other hand, you must have insurance. So if hostile other owners refuse to let you share their policy, buy your own. You might be able to persuade the court to make the other owners reimburse you for the wasted premium on the grounds that their refusal to share insurance with you was capricious and malicious.

$45,000 for $20,000

Investor Stephen Kapit bought a son's half interest for $10,000 now and $10,000 upon distribution of the estate which was still in probate. This was spelled out in an "assignment-of-distributive-share" agreement drawn up by one of the top probate attorneys in the Los Angeles area.

Among other safeguards, the **cash** due the son in the estate was pledged as security for the return of Kapit's initial $10,000 if Kapit didn't get clear title or if new liens popped up. The property had a quick-sale value of about $90,000. The granddaughter and some associates tried mightily to prevent the son from selling to Kapit. The son disliked the granddaughter intensely as a result.

Kapit's plan was to allow the granddaughter to refinance the free-and-clear property— as long as he got about $53,000 of the refinance proceeds. Because of the granddaughter's emotional attachment to the house, Kapit expected she might pay a **premium** above the approximately $45,000 equity he owned rather than lose it through a partition sale. He did, in fact get $52,700.

He found this deal by systematically checking probate files in the courthouse and contacting the heirs by direct mail (Kapit uses a computer database program which generates custom letters). As with any other real estate deal, he then had to accurately appraise the property and identify all pertinent liens.

Kapit tried to **record** the agreement assigning the son's interest to him, but the recorders office refused saying they had never seen such a document before.

Tax ramifications

Undivided interest are generally treated like **separate properties** by the tax law. You claim depreciation on your share. You can deduct your share of the operating expenses if you pay them. A tenant in common cannot deduct the expenses of the other owners even if he pays their share and they do not claim the deductions. The excess is treated as a **loan** to the cotenants. (*Boyd Estate*, 28 TC 564)

You can **exchange** into or out of a tenant-in-common interest. In contrast, exchanges of partnership interests are forbidden. But IRS regulation § 31.7701-3(a) says the IRS **may** treat a tenancy in common as a partnership for tax purposes if it bears too much resemblance to a partnership.

One of the disadvantages of buying real estate so cheap is that the tax benefits from depreciation are reduced accordingly. For example, in the Starr example above, he paid $475 for residential property worth $5,000 or more. He would have to allocate part of that $475 to land and the rest to real and personal property. The non-land portion would be depreciated over 27.5 and 7 years respectively. If you allocated $75 to land, and ignored the personal property, you'd have $400 depreciated over 27.5 years or $400 ÷ 27.5 = $14.55 per year. Not much of a tax shelter. In fact, you may be tempted to not take it at all. Don't do that. The law requires you to calculate your subsequent gain based on what your basis would be if you had claimed depreciation deductions, whether you actually did or not.

If you buy and sell a lot of these quickly, you may be a **dealer**. Dealers cannot claim depreciation. Dealers also cannot exchange or get installment sale tax treatment.

If you have no involvement with the property and pay none of its bills, and the property has positive tax flow (taxable income), you probably would **not** want to be an accrual basis taxpayer. With hostile tenants in common owning and managing the building, they will not send you your share of the rent income or net operating income on a monthly or even yearly basis. Rather they will make you wait until the property's sold to get your share of the net operating income.

If you are a **cash**-basis taxpayer, you only pay tax on money when you receive it. But accrual-basis taxpayers have to pay tax on money when they earn it, not when they receive it. So an accrual-basis taxpayer who owns a part interest in a rental property with a positive taxable income and who receives none of the net operating income because the other tenants in common won't send it to him, will, nevertheless have to pay tax on that unreceived money in the year it is **earned**.

If you have no involvement with the building because it is occupied and/or operated by hostile tenants in common, you probably are **not an "active participant"** and therefore are **ineligible** for the **$25,000 exemption from the passive loss limits.**

If all you do is buy tenant-in-common interests which you hold as an investor but do not manage, you probably cannot claim a home office because your business is too passive. Although a dealer **would** be able to claim a home office.

Collect rent from the tenants?

As a partial owner, you may be able to collect rent from the tenants in spite of lack of cooperation from the other tenants in common. You could send each tenant a letter along with a copy of your deed. The letter would state that you own such-and-such percentage of the property and that, henceforth, they are to submit that percentage of the rent direct to you. Check with an attorney before you do this. Collecting the rent may obligate you to the tenant to pay your share of the operating expenses. It may also increase the chances of the tenant suing you if some lawsuit opportunity comes along. And the tenant may be able to pay all the rent to **any** owner and thereby avoid eviction. The court's attitude may be that paying any owner is sufficient and that owners who are unhappy with each other should sue each other over the matter, not the tenant.

13

Rights of redemption

In the movie *The Sting*, Robert Redford and Paul Newman set up a phony horse-racing gambling parlor in which they could seemingly place bets **after** the results of the race were known. This was supposedly possible because the bettors had faster communications with the track than the parlor. Nice work if you can get it.

How it works

In fact, you **can** legally do roughly the equivalent in real estate. When property is seized by the government and auctioned off, the former owner often has a right of redemption. That's **always** true in IRS auctions of taxpayer-owned property (IRC §6335). It's also the case in **some** states in foreclosure, sheriff's sale, and/or property tax auctions.

The right of redemption gives the prior owner of the property the right to buy it back from the auction buyer for what the auction buyer paid plus a statutory penalty or interest amount. For example, in Michigan, you have to pay the auction price plus 1 1/4% per month the first year; 50% thereafter, to redeem the property. The IRS redemption interest rate is 20% per annum.

Property often sells at bargain prices at these auctions. In many cases, the bargain is big enough—and/or the appreciation during the redemption period is great enough—that the redemption right has a large equity on or before its expiration.

People who buy property at tax auctions sometimes find that the property sells for **less** than the taxes owed. When that happens, they lose their entire investment. They are betting on the real estate horse **before** the race. But when you play this race at the right-of-redemption window only, you don't have to place your bet until **after** the results of the race (auction) are in.

Wired bet

Ernie Kessler, owner of Foreclosure Research of America™, Inc. (301-294-2274) made a "substantial five-figure profit" on one redemption deal. He saw a property sell at foreclosure auction for a bargain price in a state with a right of redemption. Let's say the redemption price, i.e. the auction buyer's price plus statutory interest, was $100,000 and the property was worth $150,000.

Before the redemption period expired, he located the prior owner and persuaded him to sell Kessler the property for $103,000. Kessler then put the $103,000 into a double escrow.

The prior owner used $100,000 of it to redeem the property and pocketed the other $3,000 for his trouble. In step two, he deeded the property to Kessler. The agreement with the prior owner and the escrow instructions say that the deal must go **all the way** through so that the prior owner ends up with $3,000 and Kessler ends up with the property—or it doesn't go through **at all**. The prior owner is **not** trusted with the $103,000.

Why it works

Most real estate investors have never even thought of this approach. Real estate agents only want easy listings so virtually all of them would turn down a listing of a right of redemption. There is no heading in the classified section or the multiple listing book for rights of redemption. Most rights of redemption have a relatively short fuse. You have to pay all cash to redeem a property. Most owners of rights of redemption are people in financial difficulty. As a result, they typically hide from creditors which makes them hard for others to find—even people who want to give them money—which includes investors who want to buy rights of redemption.

All of these things combine to make it extremely hard for people to redeem or sell their right of redemption. But the right still has value equal to the difference between the redemption price and the market value of the property.

No takers

Distress Sales Report editor (510-523-6115) John Beck was on the other end of a deal in which a substantial profit **could have** been made by the owner of the right of redemption. Beck bought a Lubbock, Texas house at a property tax auction there for $1,350 in 1987. The property was worth about $25,000 to $30,000 then and now.

Under Texas law, it **could have** been redeemed for Beck's cost plus 25% ($1,687.50) during the first year or Beck's cost plus 50% ($2,025) during the second year. Either would have been a heck of a bargain. But the two years expired with no redemption.

Several years ago, Jane Garvey, Marc Goodfriend, and partners bought an Illinois house at foreclosure auction for $20,000 and resold it for $40,000 in three months.

They were only able to sell it that fast because they got the then normal six-month redemption period shortened to three months. They did that through a judicial procedure applicable to properties which had been **abandoned**. The redemption right in that deal would have been worth about $40,000 - $20,000 = $20,000, but was not exercised.

How to find them

You find redemption deals by following auctions where those rights apply. All such auctions are required to be advertised to the public. Call the sheriff or IRS to get the information.

The San Francisco IRS district, for example, has a Seizure-Sale Hotline (415-556-5021) which has a recording of the date and place of upcoming auctions and even a brief description of properties to be sold. On December 4, 1990, for example, the San Francisco IRS office was auctioning a 13% tenant-in-common interest in a 32-acre mobilehome park in Union City, CA with a minimum bid of $220,539.14. They give the name and phone number of the revenue officer to call for further information.

You would have to find out what price the property sold at in the auction and determine whether the redemption price represents a bargain. Then you'd track down the prior owner starting with the information on the pertinent IRS lien and county deed records or private real estate data services.

How to do it

Beck says you could do a redemption deal by simply getting the prior owner to **quitclaim** deed the property to you **after** the auction at which he lost it. Kessler preferred to have the previous owner sign the redemption papers. In the law library, I learned that §729.020 of the California Code of Civil Procedure says that the successor in interest must show either:

• "a certified copy of a recorded conveyance or
• "a copy of an assignment or any other evidence of the interest verified by an affidavit of the successor in interest or of a subscribing witness thereto."

I recommend you check with a local real estate attorney to make **darned sure** that the method you plan to use will do the trick **before** you turn over any money to the prior owner. Also make sure you comply with any disclosure law. California, for example, makes those who buy rights to excess proceeds after tax auctions to disclose, in writing, the value of those proceeds to the prior owner.

You may also need to learn other details of the law where you plan to buy. For example, these auctions generally wipe off liens junior to the lien that triggered the auction. But **redemption** usually **reinstates** those junior liens.

Reattachment of junior liens

Redemption causing junior liens to be reinstated is logical. If they were not reinstated, borrowers would be tempted to deliberately use tax sales or first mortgage defaults to wipe out junior lien holders.

But section 729.080e of the California Code of Civil Procedure says,

> *"Liens extinguished by the sale as provided in §701.630 do not reattach to the property after redemption and the property that was subject to the extinguished lien may not be applied to the satisfaction of the claim or judgment under which the lien was created."*

The theory is that the junior lien holders had their chance to protect their position when the senior lien holder foreclosed as well as during the redemption period. Check your state law to see whether redemption reinstates junior liens before you conclude that a particular redemption right has equity.

Rare and getting rarer

The right of redemption on foreclosures and tax auctions is rare and becoming rarer. Illinois, for example, did away with a foreclosee's right of redemption in 1987. Other states, like Maine and Oregon, have kept the right of redemption but shortened the redemption period.

Investors in **every** state can do this on taxpayer-owned property auctioned by the **IRS**. IRS's redemption period is 180 days.

Finding prior owner

Standard landlord skip-tracing skills applied to locating a hard-to-find prior owner can make all the difference in a deal where the auction is over. Jane Garvey says auction buyers in redemption situations are typically very concerned about redemption and try to tie up such loose ends themselves.

But they cannot always **find** the prior owner. Superior skip tracing may be the key to succeeding as a redemption-right investor.

As you might expect, property sold with a redemption right generally sells for **less** than it would have sold for if there were **no** right of redemption. So bargains are **more** prevalent in those auctions.

Improvements during the redemption period

A foolish auction buyer may even **fix up** the property during the redemption period. That makes your bargain—if you can find the prior owner and buy it from him—even better. At worst, where the law requires you to reimburse the renovating auction buyer his out-of-pocket costs, you get his labor and general contracting services free.

Incidence of this opportunity

The incidence of this opportunity is the same as the incidence of the auctions (foreclosure, trustee sale, delinquent tax, and execution) which create it in the states where rights of redemption arise from those auctions. The incidence of rights of redemption arising out of IRS seized property sales is the same as the incidence of those sales. Each of these types of auctions is discussed in its own chapter of this book.

How to find them

You find rights of redemption the same way you find foreclosures, trustee sales, delinquent tax auctions, and execution sales: from public notices. One twist is that when the right of redemption comes into existence, it often means the individual who owns the right of redemption has moved out of the property in question because of the sale.

To overcome that, you could contact these folks **before** the auction takes place. At that point, you cannot tell them how much you will pay them or even if you will buy their right of redemption at all. But you can tell them that they will have such a right if the sale goes through, that you buy such rights for cash, when the right of redemption expires, and how to get in touch with you. That way, if they move and you cannot find their new address, maybe they'll call you.

If you also buy pre-foreclosures, pre-tax sales, etc., you could add buying rights of redemption to your repertoire and tell the person who's about to lose his property as your parting message.

Financing ramifications

This is fast, all cash, and big bucks. You need a line of credit large enough to acquire the size properties you have in mind.

Tax ramifications

There are no special tax ramifications except that any interest you have to pay the auction buyer may not be deducted as interest. Although he must report it as interest income, to you it's just part of your acquisition cost and must be added to basis.

If you resold quickly, you would generally be considered a dealer.

Kill ratio

I know of no one who is doing this systematically. So I have no data on what the kill ratio would be.

Special expertise required

There are two kinds of special expertise you need:

• skip tracing and
• knowledge of the pertinent rights of redemption laws.

Skip tracing means finding debtors who don't want to be found. As I said earlier, people who lose properties for nonpayment of debts are likely to be avoiding answering the phone or having an address which can be found out from normal sources like phone books.

Full-time or part-time possible

Because this is an oddball property right which no one else is interested in, you can probably pursue them at your leisure without fear of losing the deal for lack of speed—as long as you beat the expiration date.

Ethical considerations

It would be improper to acquire a right of redemption without conveying to the seller that that's what you were buying. For example, if you could acquire a right of redemption by getting a quitclaim deed to the property from the previous owner, it would be improper to tell him you just wanted the quitclaim deed to clear up a title problem."

Sequence

Ask the seller over the phone what the market value and amount of the foreclosing lien were. If that indicates enough equity to make a deal, sign the seller to a contract in which he promises to redeem the property then sell it to you if you provide the money to do so plus his profit within a certain period of time. This should be contingent upon your confirming the market value and auction price. Then confirm the appraisal and auction price. If your investigation reveals a viable deal, close.

Toxic liability considerations

With right of redemption property, you probably have no legal right of access to the property to inspect it. Check with a local attorney to be sure, though.

You could interview the previous owner on the subject. But he is likely to be judgment proof and has a conflict of interest when it comes to honest full disclosure. That is, he is inclined to tell you what you want to hear, namely, that there are no toxics on the property.

Your attorney may be able to draw up a binding contract which enables you to put the property back to the guy who lost it if you find toxics on it after purchase. There probably is no way you can put it back to the guy who was the winning bidder at the forced sale auction.

Need for secrecy

Although hardly anybody has ever heard of the right-of-redemption approach to investing, the benefits of a good deal will become apparent to any experienced investor who learns of a deal you are trying to do. So you'd better keep the deal as secret as possible.

Unique risks

Rights of redemption are not what attorneys call a "well-settled" area of the law. So you need to be careful that you don't pay out too much money before you are sure that you will end up with the property. For example, buying a quitclaim deed from the owner of the right of redemption may transfer the right of redemption to you. Then again, it may not. In *Hieb v. Mitchell*, (No. 18103, June 13, 1990) the Idaho Supreme Court said a quitclaim deed did not transfer a right of redemption because the deed did not assign the note and mortgage on the property.

Better you should pay the money into a double escrow in which the owner of the right of redemption exercises his right of redemption using your money. The escrow instructions would provide that neither the right-of-redemption owner nor anyone else would get any of your money unless you received title to the property in question.

In general, you should make any payment to anyone contingent on your receiving unambiguous title to and possession of the property.

Lien holders also have right of redemption

The previous owner of a property is not the only one who has a right of redemption. In many cases, anyone who has "an interest in the property" can redeem it. That includes junior lien holders whose liens were wiped out by the auction. So you could buy the right of redemption **either** from the previous owner **or** from any junior lien holders who were wiped out.

Sheriff's sale rights of redemption

If someone loses a lawsuit and fails to pay the winner, property they own can be seized and sold by the sheriff. When that happens, many states give the deadbeat a right of redemption. As with property tax and mortgage or trust deed auctions, junior lien holders can often redeem the property, too.

Rights of redemption by state

States not listed below have no redemption rights on either mortgages, trust deeds, or tax sales. I do not have any information on execution sales rights of redemption except to say that there no longer is any such right in my state of California.

State	mortgage redemption@	property tax redemption law*
AL	12 months	3 years, 6% interest
AZ	6 months if mortgage	none
AR	often waived	none
CA	3 months if judicial foreclosure 12 months if deficiency judgment	1-year to challenge sale on certain grounds
CO	75 days	none
CT	none	1 year, 12% interest
DE	none	1-year, 15% interest in New Castle County, 20% elsewhere
GA	none	1-year
HI	1 month to confirm sale	1-year, 12% interest and costs
IA	6-12 months	33 months, penalties and interest
IN	3 months	
KS	6-12 months	none after auction
LA	none	partial interest# sold, 42 months to redeem
ME	12 months	none
MD	1 month to ratify sale	none
MA	none	6 months, 16% interest
MI	6-12 months	partial interest#, 6 months, penalties
MN	6 months	none
MS	none	2-years, can be redeemed for amount of back taxes, penalties, costs∞
MO	12 months if contested	none
MT	4 months if trust deed	none
NH	none	partial interest#, 2-year, 18%
NM	1 month, court can extend to 9 mo.	?
NY	none	6-months to 2-years
NC	none	6-months, can be redeemed for amount of back taxes, 9% int., costs∞
ND	6 months if 10 acres or less	none
OH	none	?
OR	12 months if mortgage	?
PA	none	2-years
PR	30 days	none
RI	none	1-year, penalty and interest
SD	6-12 months	none
TN	none	?
TX	none	2-years, penalty
UT	3 months if mortgage	?
VT	6-12 months	partial interest#, 1-year on certificate equivalent, 12%
WA	12 months if mortgage	none
WV	none	18-months, 12%
WI	none	none
WY	3 months	partial interest#, 4-years, penalty and interest

@ Source: Dennis A. Jankowski
* Source: John Beck's *Forced Sale Workbook*
# Some states do not auction the **entire** property for back taxes. Rather they auction whatever **part** of it the buyer is willing to take. For example, if the delinquent taxes are $10,000 and the free-and-clear property is worth $100,000, the first bidder may bid a 30% interest (meaning he'll pay $10,000 for 30% of the property or $30,000 worth of equity).

The next bidder may offer 29% and so on. The guy willing to take the **smallest** percentage wins the bidding. The tax deed makes him a tenant in common with the delinquent owner. All bids require the same $10,000 payment (in this example).

∞ Redemption price is money owed to government only, **not** the price the new owner paid at auction.

14

Life and remainder estates

Interests in real estate which are less than 100% fee simple often sell at enormous discounts. Tenants in common, which were discussed in an earlier chapter, are one example. Life and remainder estates are another.

The owner of the life estate is called the **life tenant**; the owner of the remainder estate, the **remainderman**. The life tenant gets to do whatever he or she wants with the property as long as they live—except cause "waste." The remainderman gets fee-simple title to the property when the life tenant **dies**. If the property goes back to the **original** owner upon death of the life tenant, it's called a **reversion**.

No market

In theory, either party may sell, lease, or mortgage their interest. As a practical matter, there is **no market** either for mortgages secured by such interests or for purchase of such interests. So say authors, Lowndes, Kramer, and McCord at ¶18.41 of *Federal Estate and Gift Taxes*.

I love it. Whenever there is no market—but there **is** genuine value—you can get a bargain.

How to profit

You can realize the profit inherent in your bargain purchase by doing one of the following:

• Sell out to the other interest owner
• Buy out the other interest owner
• Agree with other owner to sell jointly
• File a partition lawsuit to force the sale of the whole property

• Wait.

As soon as both the life and remainder interests are offered for sale **together**, the property goes back to normal fee simple and the value goes back **up** to normal.

Partition

Partition means to sue to force the sale of all interests in the property. The sale proceeds are then distributed by the court according to each owner's percentage interest. In the case of life/remainder estates, the court uses an **actuarial table** to make that calculation.

There is no right to partition life/remainder estate combinations under **common law** (law handed down from England in colonial times). The right to force the sale of a property in life/remainder situations arises **only** from **statutes** (explicit laws passed by states) or by **agreement** between the life tenant and remainderman.

Partition rights vary widely. For example, California Civil Procedure §872.210 allows **life tenants** to sue for partition. Many other states apparently have similar laws. In Connecticut and Alabama, **remaindermen** can even sue for partition if the life/remainder estates were created by a **will**.

To see what partition rights apply in your state, you and your attorney should check § 1766 of *The Law of Future Interests 2d ed.* by Simes and Smith.

Frequently, when life and remainder estates are created by joint effort of the life tenant and remainderman, they **agree** in writing that one party, usually the life tenant, has the right to partition the property. In effect, that means that if the life tenant wants to sell the property, the remainderman has to go along. Such joint efforts are a common estate-tax-avoidance tactic known as a **split purchase**.

Wait

Instead of suing for partition, you could just **wait**. In the case of your buying a **remainder** interest, you tell the other owner your name, address, and phone number and point out that if they want to refinance or sell the property, they'll need your signature. Or—and this is the ultimate vulture strategy—when you are the remainderman or owner of a reversion, you can just wait until the life tenant **dies**. At which time you own the property in fee simple.

If you are buying a **life estate**, you profit by renting the place out and pocketing the net income. For example, you might buy a life estate based on the life of a 60-year old woman on a free-and-clear house that rents for $900 a month and has $250 a month in operating expenses. Such a life estate produces $900 - $250 = $650 per month income. If you bought the life estate for, say $15,000, you made a heck of an investment.

Why they'd sell

Why would an owner of a life or remainder estate want to sell it before the death of the life tenant? Because of:

- Change in plans
- Need for quick cash
- Emotional, family reasons.

A life tenancy binds you to one property for **the rest of your life**. In many cases, people who **thought** they wanted to spend the rest of their life in one place change their minds. They may find that a warmer climate or location nearer to grandchildren or fewer stairs becomes more important than they figured when they created the life estate.

The need for quick cash can arise from any number of causes from business opportunity to college tuition to medical bills.

Many times, a widow or widower can't bear to remain in the house they previously shared with their deceased spouse. Or a serpent's tooth of a child may wish to sell a remainder interest just to spite parents. There's a lot of craziness in family relations and life and remainder estates usually are family matters.

Profit scenario

In 1985, parents deed remainder estate in home to only son. They retain a life estate. The widow is now 75 and the home is worth $250,000. The son has a chance to get in on the ground floor of a new Computer Fried Chicken franchise. But he needs $85,000 in cash.

His accountant says he needs to liquidate everything he owns, most importantly the remainder interest. Mom refuses to sell: "Where would I go?" She wisely does not accept Junior's answer that when he makes it in the chicken business, he'll buy her a new house. About this time, Junior gets your letter saying you buy remainder interests. He calls you saying, "Let's make a deal."

After at first angrily rejecting your offer of $50,000, he is unable to get any other bids at all. He calls you back and accepts.

You close the deal and inform the life tenant suggesting that she keep your name and address handy should her plans change regarding remaining in the house.

According to actuarial tables (below), the remainder interest you bought for $50,000 is really worth $152,917.50. Plus you will probably get a sort of **double appreciation**. There's the normal market-wide appreciation most investors expect to get as the property value goes up. Plus there's the "appreciation" in your remainder interest which occurs because of the aging of the life tenant.

For example, even if the property value did not increase at all for five years, your remainder interest would increase in value from $152,917.5 to $174,707.50 (see table below) because of the decreasing life expectancy of the life tenant.

Life estate scenario

Remember the life estate example above. You were making $650 a month clear (before hedging costs—more about that below). Now let's imagine how that could be improved upon. You call the two children of the woman from whom you bought the life estate and say, "I know you were unhappy with your Mom's decision to leave the family home and sell her life estate to me. But that's water over the dam now. I am not interested in managing the property until your mother's death. So I suggest the three of us list the property for sale and convert our respective interests to cash. The property's apparently worth $250,000. But neither of us can separately sell our interests for our share of that $250,000 separately. We have to cooperate."

If the nice guy approach does not work, threaten a partition suit if that is possible in your state and situation.

How to find them

The following are involved with life/remainder estates more than most:

• Estate planners
• Charities
• Guardians and conservators.

One efficient way to systematically pursue life/remainder estates might be to make your interest—and willingness to pay cash fast—known to such folks. Although my county tax assessor says the new life estates he sees being recorded appear to be created by **do-it-yourself estate planners**. He rarely sees the name of a law firm on those deeds.

Indeed, estate planning attorney Peter Lippett says in his 1979 book, *Estate Planning*, that life estates are governed by,

> *...hundreds of legal rules...*" which "*...effectively make a pure life estate an unworkable and unrecommended device. Instead, if the life estate concept is what a testator wants, he will almost always be advised to create a trust and to give his heirs life interests and remainder interests in the trust.*

The sure way

One **sure** way to find all the life estates and remainder estates in your area would be to read all the deeds in your county recorder's office. But, that is probably too time-consuming to be profitable—even if you hired low-paid clerical help to do it.

Some jurisdictions separately identify life and remainder estates in the tax assessor's records or in the county recorder's office or in private data services. My county tax assessor, for example, puts an "L" for life tenant and an "R" for remainderman in the county records. You can access them on microfilm or you can buy a computer tape from the county for $1,680. In the typical case, a buyer of the computer tape would have it converted to IBM or Macintosh format then do a search and merge the addresses into a computer letter to those life tenants and remaindermen.

Forced sales

Persons who get in trouble financially sometimes own life estates or remainder estates. When you get in serious trouble financially, your assets are often seized and sold at auction. So, in theory at least, you ought to see an occasional life estate or remainder estate go up for sale at **IRS auctions, foreclosure auctions, property tax auctions,** and **bankruptcy auctions.** Furthermore, owners of remainder estates sometimes die before the life tenant. Such remainder estates ought to be available from estates being **probated.**

Syndicated real estate columnist Bob Bruss says he has received several letters in which the writers said their **neighbor** had a life estate which he wanted to sell so he could move. So there clearly are life and remainder estate owners who want or need to sell for one reason or another.

Valuing life and remainder estates

Here is a table from Peter Lippett's book. It gives you the rough idea of how to value these interests.

The table shows the present value of a life estate and a remainder (multiply value of property by percentage figures listed). The sex and age are those of the life tenant. L stands for life estate; R for remainder estate.

Sex:	Male		Female	
Age	L	R	L	R
10	.94598	.05402	.96365	.02890
15	.93069	.06931	.95314	.04686
20	.91403	.08597	.94021	.05979
25	.98445	.10555	.92375	.07625
30	.86750	.13250	.90259	.09741
35	.83255	.16745	.87593	.12407
40	.78923	.21077	.84281	.15719
45	.73808	.26192	.80269	.19731
50	.67997	.32003	.75476	.24524
55	.61776	.38224	.69859	.30141
60	.55052	.44948	.63226	.36774
65	.48212	.51788	.55803	.44197
70	.41294	.58706	.47540	.52460
75	.34194	.65806	.38833	.61167
80	.27098	.72902	.30177	.69883
85	.21070	.78930	.22441	.77559
90	.15922	.84078	.16241	.83759
95	.12535	.87465	.12535	.87465
100	.10087	.89913	.10087	.89913

Use the **current** value of the property. For example, if the value of the property in question is $250,000 and the life estate is based on a 75-year old female life tenant, according to this table, the values of the life and remainder estates would be:

life estate:
$250,000 x .38833 = $97,082.50
remainder:
$250,000 x .61167 = $152,917.50.

Now these are prices designed to get you some wimpy certificate-of-deposit kind of return. Such returns are **not** what this book is about. In order to do the kind of bargain purchase I have in mind in this chapter, you'd buy for **less than half the actuarial-table value.**

Waste

The life tenant has a duty to the remainderman to neither cause nor permit waste. That is deterioration of the property. But as a practical matter, "...the law of waste does not adequately protect the remainderman," according to §3.17 of *Future Interests and Estate Planning 2d* by Schwartz.

If the life tenant is a senior citizen or couple, there's probably not much you can do to prevent waste. Although you may be able to recoup the cost of repairs from the estate after the last life tenant has died.

Rare

Life estates and remainder interests are much rarer than the typical real estate license course would lead you to believe. Mike Scott of the Seattle apartment-brokerage firm of Cain and Scott has never encountered one. Every sort of oddball interest in real estate is sold at IRS and bankruptcy auctions—including many tenant-in-common interests. But neither John Beck, editor of *Distress Sales Report*, who has been following such auctions for years, nor an IRS spokesman I talked to, has ever seen either a life estate or a remainder interest come up for sale. The tax assessor's office in my county said fewer than 1% of their 285,000 properties are held in life tenant/remainderman fashion.

So if you want to specialize in life/remainder estate deals, you'll have to pursue such interests over a wide geographic area like a dozen counties. Or you could make the pursuit of life/remainder estates say, a third, of your investment program.

Hedging against Methuselah

The value of a remainder estate is the discounted present value of the expected future value of the property in question as of the expected date of death of the person upon whose life the life estate is based. Actuarial tables tell you that date.

But actuarial tables are only accurate for **large numbers** of people. When you own a remainder interest in just **one** property, you have to worry about whether the life tenant might turn out to be a Methuselah.

The solution is to hedge that risk by buying a deferred **annuity** on the life of the life tenant. Ownership of the remainder interest gives you an "insurable interest" in that person's life, thereby letting you buy an annuity on a non-family member's life.

It would not kick in until the expected year of death of the life tenant. For example, the life tenant is a 65-year old, non-smoking woman. The property generates $1,000 per month of net operating income. To hedge, you need an annuity that pays $1,000 per month and starts paying the year she is expected to die, i.e. 2003 according to actuarial tables. Chris Brower of my local Metropolitan Life office says you can get that either by paying a lump sum now of $32,280 or by paying $353.75 per month from now until 2003.

To arrive at the price you'd be willing to pay for the remainder estate, you would discount the future value of the property back to its present value at whatever discount rate you deemed appropriate (at least 25% in my opinion—but you can probably do a lot better with such an oddball interest in real estate because, again, you are the entire market). Then you offer the remainder estate owner that amount **less** the lump needed to hedge.

Do **not** fail to hedge. An investor with only a handful of remainder estates is in no position to act as his own insurance company.

Hedging life estates

With a **life estate**, you have the **opposite** problem. If the life tenant dies **prematurely**, you're hurt. You hedge against premature death with a life estate the same way you hedge against premature death in your own estate planning: **life insurance**.

Buy decreasing-term life insurance on the life of the life tenant. Keep making the monthly payments until the year at which the life tenant's death had been expected or the death, whichever comes first.

The declining amount of insurance you would need for full coverage would be the present value of the net operating income for the expected remaining life of the life tenant. For example, let's say the property has the same life tenant and net operating income as above. According to my financial calculator, the present value of $1,000 to be received for thirteen years is $46,075.64 when discounted at 25%. Let's call it $50,000. The monthly premium on a $50,000 policy on a 65-year-old, nonsmoking woman is $45.50.

If you ran the policy down to $12,500 (the number picked by my Metropolitan man) during the 13 years, the premium would **rise** to $55.42. It rises in spite of the falling policy amount because the aging of the insured overcomes the declining amount of coverage actuarially. So if you hedged, you would get to net $1,000 minus $45.50 = $954.50 per month initially. That would decline by about $10 during the first 13 years. After 2003, you'd let the life insurance lapse. You'd want to pay no more than about $45,000 for that life estate. Less if you could. Any inflation in the rent you could charge would be gravy. As would any years beyond 2003 the life tenant lived.

If the life tenant dies early, you get all the net rent you received **and** you get life insurance proceeds. If she dies on time, you get all 13 years of the rent you expected at the outset but no insurance because you let it lapse at the time you expected she would die. And if she dies **after** she was expected to, you get **more** months of rent than you figured.

Valuing life and remainder estates for income-tax purposes

For **income**-tax purposes, you don't **not** use **market** value. Rather you use IRS tables located at section 20.2031-7(e) of the IRS Regulations (unless death of the life tenant is imminent, Revenue Ruling 80-80, *Miami Beach First National Bank*, 443 F 2d 116). The politically-correct IRS tables do **not** distinguish between males and females. That means they **under**value life estates of female life tenants and remainder interest where the life tenant is male and **over**value life estates of male life tenants and remainder interests where the life tenant is female. Get an accountant to do the calculations because those regulations change constantly due to changing IRS interest rates.

In the event of a joint sale of the property by you and the owner of the other interest, you may want to state in the agreement that the sale proceeds are to be split according to the IRS tables—especially if their unisex nature makes them more favorable to you than real actuarial tables which reflect the greater longevity of females.

Actual case histories

George Rohmeyer is a real estate investor best known for his building-moving deals. He operates in Marshfield, WI, a rural area where prices are quite low.

A government agency had taken back a house. As usual, they wanted to resell it. But they had enormous difficulty because there was a life estate and they could only sell the remainder interest. No buyer was interested.

Rohmeyer tracked down the owner of the life estate to see if she wanted to sell. Turned out she couldn't wait to sell.

Rohmeyer got both the remainder and life estate interests for a total of $12,000. He double escrowed the deal (sold to buyers at the same closing where he bought from the life tenant) selling the fee simple for a quick $20,000 with no renovation whatsoever.

Ethical considerations

As with any bargain-purchase technique, you must not mislead the seller as to the value of their property. A seller of a life estate or remainder interest is likely to press you for assurance he or she is getting a fair price. In fact, there is virtually no market for such interests beyond the owner of the other interest in that property. You can quote the references I quoted in this chapter. And you can suggest they consult a real estate agent (who will invariably show them the door.) Otherwise, you'd better remain mum. Just make your offer or ask what the seller would take. When you hear an adequate bargain price quoted, accept, and sign the contract.

Environmental liability considerations

Once you buy a remainder interest, you, in effect, buy the property. An heir can refuse to take title to a contaminated property. But a remainderman has title upon death of the life estate whether he likes it or not. So you must do your environmental checking **before** you buy the remainder interest. If you buy a life estate and contamination is found, you would likely be jointly liable along with the remainderman. So this is not a technique in which you can ignore environmental liability issues.

15

Existing options

How it works

An option is the right, but not the obligation, to **buy** a property for a specified price during a specified time period. In the stock market, that would be a **call** option. A **put** option is the right to **sell** at a specified price during a specified period of time. But since put options are extremely rare in real estate, the words put and call are not used. The word option means call option in real estate. When used in this chapter, the word option means the call or right-to-buy option.

Sometimes options have equity. That's true when the option price is less than market value but greater than the total liens on the property. On Wall Street, they would say such options are "in the money." Bargain purchasers are only interested in options that have equity.

For example, let's say a property is worth $100,000. It has a mortgage of $65,000 and no other liens. You have an option to buy it for $70,000. That meets the title criterion of this book—you can buy it for at least 20% below market value. In this example, you can buy it for 30% below market. And if you look at just the $35,000 equity, your need to pay just $5,000 ($70,000 - $65,000) represents a discount of $30,000 ÷ $35,000 = 86%.

Options expire every business day—options to buy property for **less than its current market value**. Why? Job loss, divorce, disappointing business performance, etc.

Incidence of this opportunity

You can get a rough idea of how many single-family options there are in your area by seeing how often classified ads in your local paper offer lease options on homes.

Financing ramifications

This is an all-cash business unless you can arrange a private source of financing or an equity line of credit.

Tax Ramifications

Options are a bit odd-ball from a tax standpoint. Here are the answers to relevant questions.

Can you deduct a loss if you does not exercise the option?

Yes, you **can** deduct the loss if you does not exercise the option. For tax purposes, letting an option expire is considered the same as selling it for zero. Your basis in the option is what you paid for it.

If you ended up with a basis of, say, $5,000, and you let the option expire, you'd have a $5,000 loss.

What is the nature of the loss?

Section 1234. Options to buy or sell.
(a) Treatment of gain or loss in the case of the purchaser.
(1) General rule. Gain or loss attributable to the sale...of,...an option to buy...property shall be considered gain...from the sale...of property which has the same character as the property to which the option relates has in the hands of the taxpayer (or would have in the hands of the taxpayer if acquired by him).

So your loss would be a **capital** loss. If you held the option less than one year, it would be a short-term capital loss in the post-1990 tax rules. Capital losses may be deducted from any capital gains you have the same year. But once your capital losses exceed your capital losses for the year, you are limited to $3,000 worth of capital loss deductions per year. Net capital losses above $3,000 must be carried forward to future years. [IRC§1211(b)]

What is your basis in the property if you exercise the option?

Your basis is your cost. That includes what you paid for the option, any debt you took on when you exercised the option, and any cash you paid above and beyond your option price and debt to cover the amount you had to pay for the property. In other words, when you exercise the option, your basis in the property you acquire is your option price plus the cost of the option if you did not get credit for the option consideration toward the purchase price.

What if you assign the option for a profit?

You have a gain under Section 1234 of the Internal Revenue Code. See the above subheading regarding deducting a loss if you do not exercise the option.

Dealer status

If you did a lot of these deals, you would probably have to admit to dealer status. Dealers can't do installment sales, exchange or claim depreciation.

Number-of-deals laws

Some laws subject persons who buy more than, say, two homes a year, to more severe penalties when a particular behavior is engaged in. For example, the federal rent-skimming law (12 USC 1709-2) **only** applies to people who skim at least **two** properties. The California rent-skimming law (CC 890) provides for **more severe penalties** if you rent skim five or more properties within a two-year period. Check with an attorney to make sure no such laws would cover a buyer of existing options in your area.

Full-time or part-time possible

As with any real estate interest which hardly anyone wants to buy, you can take your time with existing options. That means you could pursue this strategy part-time.

Regional variations

I am not aware of any regional variations in the use of options. However, it would not surprise me to learn that more lease options of homes were done in the West. Residents of the western states seem much more receptive to out-of-the-ordinary solutions to real estate problems than other Americans.

Why it works

Where did those options come from? They were created in past years by **home owners** who were having trouble selling. By **investors** who heard that lease options were a way to turn negative-cash-flow rental houses into positive-cash-flow generators. By **nonresidential** landlords eager to fill vacant space. By sellers of **raw land** who retained title to adjacent raw land.

There is virtually no organized market for real estate options. No "options" classified heading in the paper. No options section in the multiple listing book.

I love it. It has the three things that make a near-**ideal** investment:

- Lots of sellers
- No buyers
- Reason for lack of buyers is correctable

You can correct the lack of buyers either by **better marketing** of the option or by **exercising** the option and reselling the property.

Environmental liability, management

If you exercise your option, you will incur whatever environmental liability attaches to the property. Don't let your due diligence guard down just because you're entering ownership through the option door. Once you own a contaminated property, it matters not which door you came through.

Wired profit

If you buy an option to purchase a property for less than its current fair market value, you have made your money the day you bought as the saying goes.

As with pre-foreclosures and other bargain purchases, it's not enough of a bargain unless the margin covers your profit, carrying costs (if any), rehab cost (if any), transaction costs, etc. But if you assign the option, the carrying and rehab costs are zero and the transaction costs can be quite low (mainly title search). Like the rights of redemption I wrote about in the previous chapter, this is like betting on horse races after the race is over.

How to find them

I suspect that sending a letter to likely option holders offering to buy their option, is the most cost effective way to find them. To whom do you send the letter?

- It is wise for the owner of an option to **record** it—or at least a memorandum of the option. So one way to find options is to look for recorded options in the county recorders office. (Recording the **actual** option divulges information you'd like to keep secret from prospective buyers—information like the option price and expiration date.) Some lessor/optionors prohibit recording. That's unreasonable on their part.

- Options to purchase are often included in **nonresidential** leases—especially in the leases of major **lead** tenants or tenants in **single-tenant buildings**. Options to purchase are more common in **industrial** and **retail** leases than in office leases according to Michael Chemodurow, editor of *Leasing Professional* (602-860-0659).
- Many **investors** like to "sell" their properties on lease options. A high percentage of the lessee/optionees fail to exercise the option even when they have significant equity (the excess of the current market value over the option price).

  Richard Gardiner, who has done about 250 lease options as the seller, says from 15% to 50% of his lessee/optionees walk depending on mortgage interest rates. In his five years experience, about 70% of real estate option author, John Schaub's lessee/optionees walked.

  Try to identify the major lessor/optionors in your area. Ask at the real estate investor's association meetings. When you find an investor who does a lot of lease options as the optionor, get the addresses of all his properties from the county recorder's office and contact all his tenants.
- Look for the word "option" in for-sale and for-rent **classified ads** for past years. When you find it, check the **reverse directory** for the year the ad ran to get the property address. Send the letter to the present occupant.
- **Condo** owners often have trouble selling and are likely to try the lease option route. Contacting all condo tenants might work.
- All tenants against whom **eviction** notices are filed.
- Gardiner says **divorce** is a frequent cause of lessee/optionees walking away from options with substantial equity. Try sending letters to all those who file divorce papers and who appear to be tenants in condos or single-family homes.
- Try an **ad** in your local paper or *The Wall Street Journal* saying, "We buy options to purchase real estate."
- Landowners who are selling one of their parcels are often willing to grant long-term options to buy a contiguous parcel as part of the sale of the first parcel.

Assignment of option

Are all options assignable? If they do not explicitly prohibit assignment, they are assignable. But they may be assignable even if they **do** explicitly prohibit assignment.

A Sacramento case (*In Re James Moore* 99 Bankruptcy Reporter 27) said an option to purchase was assignable even though the option terms said assignment was **not** permitted. It seems to me that the optionor ought to be able to prohibit assignment when the terms of the option include the optionor taking back a mortgage—or at least he ought to have the right to make the assignee pass reasonable credit standards. But if it's a **cash** deal, I see no reason why it should be any of the optionor's business whether the optionee assigns the option or not. Certainly the optionee can sell the property to anyone he wants after he owns it. Why make him go to that extra step?

In *Kendall v. Ernest Pestana, Inc.*, (40 Cal. 3d 488 1985) the court said a landlord may **not** refuse to allow assignment of an option even though such assignment was prohibited by the terms of the option.

If your state law allows enforcement of anti-assignment clauses—and the option you are interested in contains such a clause—just have the optionee **exercise** the option then sell it to you.

Typically, the optionee does not have the money to exercise the option. That's why he's letting an option with significant equity expire in the first place. So you give him the money to exercise it. Not directly—but through escrow. You agree with the optionee to pay him some amount for his trouble: $100, $1,000, whatever it takes and whatever the economics of the deal will permit. Then you pay that amount plus the amount needed to exercise the option into escrow. The escrow instructions say the optionee gets his money only if and when he exercises his option to buy the property and sells it to you. If he only does **part** of the deal, all of your money is to be returned to you.

Defaulted lessee/optionees

Lessee/optionees often default on their leases. Ostensibly, that erases the option.

Not so fast. As I have noted just about every time I write about lease options, there is a possibility that they will be construed to be a **sale** and taking back of a mortgage by the lessor/optionor. That construction arises from the legal doctrine of substance over form which says the substance of a transaction determines the legal treatment, not necessarily the form of the transaction. Indeed, the courts have decided that lease options were sale/mortgages on a number of occasions. (See my Special Report *Single-Family Lease Options*.)

If the court so decides, the mortgage in question is called an **equitable mortgage**. That's a mortgage, not a trust deed, even in western states where trust deeds are the norm. As a mortgage, it must be **judicially foreclosed**. And rights of redemption arise in many states.

If you evict someone from a lease option for nonpayment of rent or some other lease violation—they may persuade a court that they were really owner/equitable mortgagors not lessee/optionees and get their equitable mortgage **reinstated**. The basic idea is that mortgagors (borrowers) have certain rights under law and equity in their property and the courts are not going to let some sharpie lender gyp somebody out of those rights and that equity by the simple trick of selling a property and taking a mortgage but calling it a lease option.

The esoteric legal questions may be beside the point. As a practical matter, if you find a former lessee/optionee who was evicted for a lease violation, you may be able to rejuvenate their interest in the property. One way might be to pay them for a quitclaim deed to the property then approach the owner about settling the matter out of court. Another might be to acquire an option from the former lessee/optionee and bankroll the necessary litigation to reestablish the former lessee/optionee's option right. Check with a local real estate and/or litigation attorney before you start this game.

Ask for an option when you rent

Whenever you rent, rent only from an owner who will agree to an option to purchase. Deliberately go around seeking leases then insist on an option. Look for ads which mention willingness to accept option. Frequently increase during down markets. Some newspapers even have lease-option classified ads categories.

Face-to-face negotiations

Real estate agents often fiercely fight lease options or straight options because they don't want their commissions to be delayed. Best not to go through real estate agents because of that. Face-to-face negotiation is best with options.

Reselling the option

To sell the option, you simply sell the property or list the property for sale. You can even list it with a Realtor® although you may have to go through several who are nervous before you find one who'll take it. You put the property up for sale even though you do not yet own it. Your option gives you the legal right to do this.

Showing the property may be a problem the way it sometimes is with rental houses. If you cannot get access to the property and cooperation from occupants, you probably will not be able to sell your option for market value. In that case, you may have to exercise the option then sell the property. Or you could sell the option cheap to someone who is willing to buy in spite of lack of opportunity to inspect the property.

If you succeed, you simply exercise your option and close your sale to the option buyer at the same settlement. Or you could assign your option to the person who wants to buy the property and have them exercise the option at closing. Assigning the option would be better because it would cut down on extra transfer taxes, escrow charges, and document-preparation charges.

Don't overlook the optionor as a potential buyer of your option. It may gall him to buy back his own property. But the economics make sense if your property has equity and you are willing to sell at a discount. Take the example above: an option to buy a $100,000 property with a $65,000 mortgage for $70,000. That option has $30,000 equity. It would be a good deal for anyone, including the optionor, if it could be bought for less than $30,000.

Unique risks: sellers who welsh

As closing day approaches, optionors often find that they made a bad deal. The property is worth more than they agreed to sell it for.

No guarantor

In the options portion of stock and bond markets, the optionor has to eat the losses whether he likes it or not. The various clearing houses guarantee the optionee's profits. And the parties are required to put up cash in advance to cover the possible losses.

Not so in the real estate business. There is no clearinghouse guarantee. No cash or deed is put up in advance. Human nature being what it is, real estate optionors who made bad bargains often simply refuse to sell. This happens far more often than most investors seem to realize. As a result, optionees are often unprepared and lose their profit.

That's the **bad** news. The **good** news is that the needed preparation is straightforward and victims of optionor reneging who sue generally win a lucrative judgment or settlement.

Case history

Bill Carrithers lease optioned a house in Scarsdale, NY (the actual town was in the same region) in December of 1984 from Del Fuller (names changed to protect privacy). Here are the details of the deal:

- Twenty-year old, four-bedroom, three-bath ranch house with a two-car garage.
- Carrithers to occupy the house as his residence.
- One-year lease with option to renew for one more year at $1,800 per month.
- Fair market rental value was $1,800.
- Lease includes fixed-price option to purchase house for $230,000 until December 1986.
- Fair market value of house was about $255,000 in Dec. '84.

No response

The New York area market appreciated rapidly in early '85 and Carrithers told Fuller he wanted to exercise the option in April of 1985. Fuller, who cashed Carrithers' rent checks every month, **did not respond**.

After Fuller ignored numerous demands to set a closing date, Carrithers' attorney sued Fuller for **specific performance** in the Spring of 1986. Carrithers suit also alleged that the optionor had **forged** his mother's signature on the option agreement and named as defendants the real estate agent and firm that had handled the deal and notarized the mother's signature

Carrithers had stopped paying rent in January of 1986. Fuller tried to evict Carrithers for that but Carrithers' attorney was able to prevent it (presumably on grounds that Fuller owed Carrithers far more money in the form of option profits and attorneys fees than Carrithers owed Fuller).

$120,000 profit

Carrithers moved to California in September of 1986 and the case was moved to federal court on "diversity" grounds (parties live in different states and amount in dispute greater than $10,000).

Trial was set for August, 1988. At that time, the house was worth about $350,000 to $400,000. As often happens, the trial's approach triggered serious negotiations and Carrithers settled for $100,000.

His attorney had taken the case on a contingency basis for a 30% fee so Carrithers netted $70,000. Carrithers does not know how the $100,000 was split between the defendants and their errors and omissions insurance carrier, if any.

Another case history

In 1976, a San Francisco Bay Area investor agreed to buy an apartment building there for $1,000,000. The seller signed the purchase agreement then refused to go through with the deal. This was not an option *per se*. But it further illustrates the problem of welshing which is endemic in real estate options.

He had agreed to do an installment sale, then said it would cost him too much in taxes. So the buyer accommodated him by going out and getting a new, institutional mortgage. But the seller **still** refused to perform.

That ticked the buyer off and he sued. He won the trial in 1982 and got the property, which by then had risen in value to $2,800,000. The seller appealed but lost.

The buyer's **attorney fees** were about $500,000. But the court ordered the seller to pay about half that. Plus the buyer received the property's **net income** for the six years that elapsed between 1976 and 1982.

Attorney key

I often proceed in real estate matters without an attorney. A poll I took indicated subscribers to my newsletter do, too. I generally **dis**agree with the most successful advertising slogan of all time: "A man who acts as his own attorney has a fool for a client."

But when it comes to options, I strongly recommend that you have the documents drawn up by an attorney who has special expertise in that area.

That's because of the high incidence of reneging and the critical importance of properly drawn documents and buyer performance in winning a favorable resolution.

Perform on your end

The attorney should also handle the attempt to **close**. A layman or underqualified attorney may feel that there is no point in going to closing if the optionor states unequivocally that he or she will not perform.

But in order to prevail in a specific performance suit, you must prove that you fulfilled your end of the deal including **actually tendering the money**. If you fail to do that, the optionor will win the case easily. (*Goodale v. West*, 5 C 339)

The money need not be set aside after the optionor refuses to take it (except that you will need it again when you win the case if the court orders specific performance).

If the purchase agreement or option has a "time is of the essence" clause and deadlines or windows for closing, you must scrupulously comply with them.

Defenses against you

You must **not** have obtained the option by:

• Misrepresentation

- Concealment
- Circumvention
- Unfair practice

and you must show that you:

- Acted in good faith and
- Had "clean hands."

"Unclean hands" means you have "violated conscience or other equitable principle."

Suing

As a general rule, you can sue **either** for **specific performance** (force the optionor to deed you the property) **or** for **cash** damages. Cash damages would be better where the property had **not appreciated** much—or had gone **down** in value—since the agreed upon closing date.

Furthermore, you are generally entitled to and should seek **additional damages** for the delay and litigation expenses—above and beyond the market value of the property at the time you had the right to buy it.

For example, you would normally be entitled to **rent** or **net income** from the time the optionor illegally refused to sell to you until the time you actually receive the deed as a result of court decree. You can also get **injunctions** to prevent the optionor from taking action that would adversely affect your interest in the property or for failing to take action that would protect it.

Buyers/optionees only

Buyers or optionees who sue for specific performance usually win. Make sure you understand that does **not** apply to **sellers**. To win a specific performance suit, you must prove that there was a valid agreement and that you lived up to your end of it.

For the **buyer or optionee**, that usually means just proving that you offered the money. **Sellers**, on the other hand, would have to prove all sorts of things. A buyer can find endless fault with the property and thereby legally get off the hook.

No one has the **right** to specific performance *per se*. The court has discretion (in California at least) to decide whether specific performance or cash judgment is the appropriate remedy.

Valid contract

An option to purchase must be as **detailed** as a regular purchase agreement. The usual well-drawn lease option is a lease **with an attached purchase agreement**. If it is not detailed enough, it may **not** be enforceable.

A one-sentence option to purchase in a lease is laughably inadequate—unless the lessor/optionor is willing to honor it. In the case history above, Bill Carrithers' lease option, which was drawn up by his attorney, had 37 addendums.

As with purchase agreements, an option must be **in writing** to be enforceable.

Fight back!

I am no fan of tv consumer reporter David Horowitz. But his slogan, "Don't get ripped off. Fight back!" applies in spades to optionors who renege.

Neither am I fond of litigation. But the belief among businesspeople that litigation is "not worth it" generally does **not** apply to suits against reneging optionors where the purchase agreement or option has significant equity (agreed-upon purchase price is less than current market value).

You'll probably win

In the typical business lawsuit for bad debt or breach of contract, the probability of winning is in the neighborhood of 50%. But the probability of winning in the typical buyer/optionee's specific performance suit is **higher**.

The San Francisco area investor above was advised by his attorney at the outset that the probability of victory was 80%. Some litigation pays you well for your time and for your investment in its cost.

16

IRS sales

How it works

When people or organizations don't pay their taxes, IRS can, and often does, seize property the delinquents own and sell it. Those IRS powers and actions offer five different kinds of opportunities for bargain-hunting real estate investors.

More in recessions?

One might expect a recession to be a time of **increased** incidence of nonpayment of taxes thereby increasing the number of IRS-related bargain-purchase opportunities. Maybe not. Real estate educator Ron Starr says the IRS seized property sales seem more a function of local IRS decisions to crack down on taxpayers than of economic conditions or tax delinquency rates.

IRS opportunities

The five ways to get real estate bargains from IRS actions are:

1. buy real estate from an owner who is **about to lose it** to an IRS seized property sale,
2. buy real estate at IRS **seized property sales**,
3. buy real estate **owned by IRS** because no one bid the minimum bid at a previous seized property auction and the IRS elected to become the owner of the property,
4. buy real estate from previous owners or lien holders who have the **right to redeem** properties lost at IRS seized property sales,
5. buy real estate that has gone to a "nonjudicial" sale [trustee sale, delinquent property tax sale, etc. (Reg. §301.7425-2)] but which the **IRS has the right to redeem** because of an IRS lien having been recorded against the previous owner at least thirty days before the nonjudicial sale.

Minimum bid

According to John Beck's *Forced Sale Workbook* (415-523-6115), the *Internal Revenue Manual* says IRS should set their minimum bid at 80% of forced sale value. That's for the **equity** above liens senior to the IRS lien.

Beck further says that forced sale value is "usually estimated to be approximately 75% of the quick sale value." Quick sale value, in turn, is no more than 95% of fair market value.

Putting that all together, we calculate that IRS's minimum bid will be 95% x 75% x 80% = 57% of market value. However, IRS may not set the minimum bid higher than the amount owed the government. So if the amount owed to the IRS plus senior liens is **less** than 57% of market value, the minimum bid will be less than 57% of market.

IRS worksheets

IRS even has two worksheets (Form 4585 Seizure and Sale Worksheet and Form 2433 quick sale value) for doing this calculation. Form 4585 starts with the quick sale value from Form 2433. The IRS officer has the right to reduce the quick sale value by up to 25% to arrive at the forced sale value. Then he can knock off another 20% to get the "IRS sale value" which, less the superior liens, is the IRS minimum bid.

In other words, the IRS couldn't care less if the property sells for **more** than they need. If it sells for **less** than they need, they'll take what they can get and get the rest by selling another property or garnisheeing wages or whatever.

IRS purchases

As with lending institution foreclosures, IRS can be the winning bidder. If no one offers the minimum bid, the government has the right to declare itself the owner [IRC § 6335 (e)(1)(C)]. They will simply give the property back to the owner if they don't see any benefit to the government of keeping the property [IRC § 6335(e)(1)(D)]. The IRS only keeps it when they figure they can try again to sell it and be more successful.

The property becomes owned by the United States after the taxpayer's 180-day redemption period has run out.

Case history

I do not know what the average ratio of sale prices to minimum bids is at these auctions. Beck relates one actual case history in which a 50% tenant-in-common interest in a house on 10.4 acres in Woodland, CA sold for about $4,200.

The house was apparently worth about $70,000 or more. The only lien was a state tax lien for $6,510.78. At a fair market value of $70,000, the house had $70,000 - $6,510.78 = $63,489.22 in equity. Fifty percent of that would be worth $31,744.61—which is a lot more than the $4,200 the winning bidder paid.

True, a half interest would sell for far less than a 100% interest. But there are ways to correct that, namely:

• Buy out the other owner,
• Sell out to the other owner,
• File a partition lawsuit which forces the sale of the whole property,
• Wait until the other owner wants to sell or refinance.

Beck lost out on that deal. He thought the property was raw land only and did not have a big enough cashiers check to bid more when he discovered, on the day of the auction, that there was a desirable house on the property.

Another case history

Steven Hinton and Mark Anthenien once wrote and published a book called *How to buy IRS seized properties*. It's now out of print. In that book, they relate the story of their first IRS deal.

They asked to be on the IRS's mailing list and as a result received notice of sale of a house in Boulder Creek, CA. The minimum bid was $5,000. Total liens superior to the

IRS lien were $7,700 according to the revenue officer. (Neither the IRS nor the revenue officer will stand behind such informal title reports.) Hinton and Anthenien drove by the two-bedroom house and figured it was worth at least $65,000. Upon closer investigation of comparable sales, they concluded it was worth $80,000 to $100,00.

Tension City

As the hour of the auction approached, Anthenien went through sweaty-palmed, pre-purchase buyer's remorse in the coffee shop across the street. While there, he overheard another group of bidders excitedly discussing how they each would spend their profits after they won the bidding.

With fifteen minutes to go, he went to the auction room and found it full of bidders. A revenue officer invited those interested in the Boulder Creek house into an adjoining room for the opening of the sealed bids. Eight people followed her into that room. Anthenien said, "The tension in the room was phenomenal."

As they opened each bid and announced it to the room, the bidders reacted with relief or devastation depending on whether the bid in question was less than or more than theirs. When Anthenien won with a bid of $40,151, he immediately wondered what everyone else knew that he didn't. The other bids had been: $8,500; $25,645; $16,601; $25,000; $34,000.

Don't bid even amounts

You should **never** bid even amounts in a sealed-bid auction because if there is a tie, they decide the winner by **drawing lots** [Reg. § 301.6335-1(c)(5)(ii)(e)]. If you tied for the winning bid and lost the drawing of lots you'd typically lose tens of thousands of dollars in profits. That for the want of a dollar more on your bid.

Hinton and a roommate moved into the vacant house, cleaned, and improved it. After the 180-day redemption period expired and they got the deed, they sold it for $93,000. Their net profit after clean-up and carrying costs was $38,000.

How to find them

Section 6335 of the Internal Revenue Code requires the IRS to publish notice of seized property sales in:

• a newspaper published **in** the county where the property is located or
• a newspaper generally **circulated** in the county where the property is located.

If there is no such paper, they must post it on the bulletin board of the nearest post office and in at least two other public places. They must advertise or post the notice at least ten days before the auction but not more than 40 days before. The notice tells:

• the property to be sold,
• time and place of the auction (must be in the same county as the property in question),
• manner in which the sale will be conducted (auction or sealed bid)
• conditions of sale.

You could respond to the notice either by contacting the delinquent taxpayer and trying to buy the property from him—or by attending the IRS sale. If you miss the sale for some reason, you may want to contact one of the people who owns the right of redemption and arrange for them to redeem the property and sell it to you.

Why it works

IRS sales produce bargains because they use anachronistic marketing methods. In early America, posting notices on the courthouse or post office wall may have been the best way to get the word out that a property was for sale. Now, it's almost a text book example of how not to market property. I've often said that bargains in real estate involve two kinds of properties: those that nobody wants and those that nobody knows are for sale. This is one of the latter.

Mailing lists and hot lines

IRS district directors can have and do have mailing lists. But those directors discontinued many lists when seminar gurus started telling large audiences to get on those mailing lists. Now many IRS offices have hot lines where you can call a recording about **some** of their upcoming sales.

There are many properties which are not mentioned in either the mailed out notices or on the hot line. But IRS must publish **all** in the legal newspapers or post office articles.

Owners' and lien holders' right to redeem

After the sale, you can still contact certain people who have the right to redeem the property and try to buy it from them. The people who have the right to redeem the property are:

- the previous owner,
- their heirs,
- their executors,
- their administrators,
- any person having an interest in the property,
- any person having a lien on the property,
- any person acting on behalf of one of the above.

They have up to 180 days to redeem the property from the successful bidder at the IRS seized property sale. To redeem, they must pay the successful bidder his purchase price plus interest at 20% per annum.

Cannot be assigned

The right to redeem cannot be assigned *per se*. But that's not much of a barrier because you can pay the owner of the right to redeem through escrow to exercise his right to redeem then deed the property to you. (*Cassell Brothers, Inc.* DC 82-1 USTC ¶9189.)

The following is not a right of redemption *per se* but it has similar characteristics. If the IRS takes title to the property, the district director may deed the property back to the taxpayer, his heirs, or other legal representatives during the **two years** starting on the date the IRS acquired the real estate—if the taxes owed plus interest are paid. Of course, this can only happen if IRS did not sell the property to a third party during those two years. [Reg. § 301.7506-1(d)]

IRS's right to redeem

Sometimes other creditors beat the IRS to the auction block. That is, they hold liens that are **superior** to the IRS lien and they foreclose more than 30 days after the IRS records its lien but before the IRS decides to seize and sell the property itself. In that case, the IRS has the right to redeem the property within 120 days [IRC § 7425 (d)(1)].

To find those deals, you'd have to monitor the various nonjudicial sales and the recording of IRS liens. When you saw a nonjudicial sale which created an IRS right to redeem, you'd contact the IRS to offer an agreement to bid.

Agreement to bid

IRS won't redeem a property unless they already have a buyer for it. To make sure they **can** sell it, they get someone like you to sign an "agreement to bid." In that agreement, you promise to bid an agreed amount (the amount owed to the IRS less liens superior to the IRS lien) if IRS offers the property for sale within 90 days.

You have to put up a 20% deposit. If you don't keep your promise to bid that amount, you forfeit the deposit and IRS can even sue you for additional amounts if they were damaged by an amount greater than your deposit by your failure to bid the agreed amount.

What do you get for your deposit and agreement to bid?—the right to bid at an IRS auction. If you are outbid at that auction, you get your deposit back with no interest or profit. I have no idea why anyone would ever put up such a deposit and sign an agreement to bid. To do so requires effort and risk and loss of interest on the deposit. Yet the public at large, not just the one who agreed to bid, gets the benefit of another shot at the property.

However, people **do** sign those agreements to bid. And IRS sales result. Ron Starr lost a bargain foreclosure auction purchase that way. (See below.)

Agreement to not advertise

Beck says investors who sign agreements to bid generally get the revenue officer to verbally promise to not put the particular property in his mailings or on the hotline. That is not illegal *per se* because the law does not **require** mailing advertisements or hot lines. Reg. § 301.6335-1(b)(2) says,

> "The district director may use other methods of giving notice of sale and of advertising seized property... when he believes...wider or more specialized advertising coverage will enhance the possibility of obtaining a higher price for the property."

So you probably can**not** get such a promise **in writing**. Until Congress passes a law which at least pays interest to the person who agrees to bid, the promise to not advertise more than the law requires is necessary to get any body to agree to bid.

IRS can sell its right to redeem or release it for free if it has no value to the U.S. Government. To buy it, contact the IRS district director of the district where the property is located. [Reg. § 301.7425-4(c)(4) and Rev. Proc. 68-10, 1968-1 CB 758]

A crowd in Woodland

Starr bought another property in Woodland, CA in '89 at a foreclosure auction. IRS had recorded a lien which Starr took into account when deciding how much to pay for the equity. IRS exercised their right of redemption and held an auction in Woodland attended by 45 people. Starr lost his bargain purchase and only received the amount he had paid plus the 6% interest provided by law [Regulation § 301.7425(b)] in those types of redemptions. (IRS will also pay for necessary maintenance expenses incurred in excess of rents collected [Reg. § 301.7425-4 (b)(iii)] IRS will **not** reimburse the foreclosure/tax/execution sale buyer for any improvements made or expenses of acquisition like title insurance.)

Financing

IRS can agree to let you pay part of the payment for seized property up to one month after the auction if they want. You can generally expect to pay all cash. If you are the winning bidder and don't have the cash, the IRS will reopen the bidding on the spot.

Starr says the revenue officer typically requires 20% down and the rest in a week or two. He has seen some auctions where it was 20% at the time of the sale and the rest by 4:00 PM the same day. The sale Beck missed out on was an all-cash-right-now sale. The notice of the sale states the "conditions of the sale" which means the amount required at auction and the amount of time available to get the rest of the money.

Title

Uncle Sam is a tough seller. He sells "as is, where is," and "without recourse against the United States." Furthermore, the buyer gets only "the right, title, and interest of the delinquent taxpayer in and to the property…" [Reg § 301.6335-1(c)(4)(iii)] In other words, it's as if you got a quit claim deed from the delinquent taxpayer and there was no purchase agreement with any representations. That is, the delinquent taxpayer may **not own** any interest in the property. And if you buy his interest in such a situation, tough. IRS makes no warranties including even the most basic warranty that the delinquent taxpayer **owned** any part of the property.

Hazard insurance

The "risk of loss and responsibility for preservation of the property" shifts to you the moment the IRS accepts your bid. So you'd better work something out with your hazard and liability insurance agent **before** you go to the auction. The agent can bind coverage a day or so in advance.

One of Beck's students did nothing about fire insurance and the previous owner burned the property down a couple of days before the redemption period expired. The owner admitted he burned it down and was arrested for arson, although that did not help the investor.

Cornucopia

The laws governing IRS liens provide a one-stop-shopping cornucopia of bargain-purchase opportunities. They are analogous to numerous bargain-purchase techniques I've written about—ranging from rights of redemption to pre-foreclosures to OREOs to discount lien releases.

Special expertise required

You need to know the pertinent IRS regulations. I've explained them in this chapter. But to pursue this opportunity, you need to know them cold and keep up to date with any changes. You also need to learn the procedures of the local IRS offices where you plan to buy.

Full-time or part-time possible

You'll recall I said there were five ways to profit from IRS property seizures:

1. buy real estate from an owner who is **about to lose it** to an IRS seized property sale,
2. buy real estate at IRS **seized property sales,**
3. buy real estate **owned by IRS** because no one bid the minimum bid at a previous seized property auction and the IRS elected to become the owner of the property,
4. buy real estate from previous owners or lien holders who have the **right to redeem** properties lost at IRS seized property sales,
5. buy real estate which has gone to a "nonjudicial" sale [trustee sale, delinquent property tax sale, etc. (Reg. §301.7425-2)] but which the **IRS has the right to redeem** because of an IRS lien having been recorded against the previous owner at least thirty days before the nonjudicial sale.

Methods 2, 3, 4, and 5 can probably be done successfully by a part-timer because they all involve dealing with the government. The government is not a fast-moving entity. You may need to take off work during business hours to attend an auction or visit an IRS office. But such absences would probably be limited enough for most employers.

Method 1, however, involves dealing with private parties who are in financial difficulty. These folks are hard to get hold of. They avoid strangers, assuming they are bill collectors. They are also typically the targets of many people hoping to capitalize on their distress—like yourself.

Consequently, to be successful in buying from them, you must be ready to react on a moment's notice. It's like catching a fish. When you feel a nibble, you need to promptly reel them in. That generally takes full-time availability if not effort.

Regional variations

Logic would suggest that there would be regional variations based on the regional **economies**. Ron Starr says it appears more related to **policies** of the IRS personnel involved. That is, some districts have lots of IRS property sales because their directors favor seizing and selling property. Also, all districts have an upsurge in IRS property sales when DC orders a crack down. So there **are** some regional variations, but they are not caused by regional economics. They are caused by district directors. You can only find out where the opportunities are by inquiring at the various IRS district offices. Over time, you'll see the pattern. For example, Starr says he has never seen an IRS sale out of the IRS's San Jose office.

Ethical considerations

With all non-auction bargain purchases, you need to refrain from making misleading statements regarding the value of the property. And in the case of an agreement to bid on property to be redeemed by IRS, you need to be careful you don't violate the law. The only unethical conduct I can conceive of when buying direct from the IRS is bid chilling. That is, agreeing with other potential bidders to bid less than you normally would then paying off those other would-be bidders or being paid off by the winning bidder. That's unethical and illegal.

Screening procedures and sequencing

Use the same screening procedures and sequencing pros use in analogous situations. That is, use pre-foreclosure screening and sequencing for pre-IRS sale deals. Use foreclosure auction screening and sequencing for IRS auction purchases. And so forth.

Environmental liability considerations

Take the normal precautions when you buy pre-IRS sale property. Take more than the normal precautions when you buy from the government. Their "as is, where is, without recourse to the United States" terms are tougher than those of any other seller. You are left holding the bag more when you buy from the government than when you buy from any other seller.

Need for secrecy

IRS sales are in the nobody-knows-it's-for-sale category of bargain purchase. It is in your interest to keep it that way. You cannot control IRS's marketing. But you can refrain from helping them by blabbing all over town about your deals.

17

Bankruptcy

How it works

When a person or company declares bankruptcy, a trustee is appointed to sell their assets and distribute the proceeds according to law. The trustee must obtain an appraisal to guard against the property selling too cheap.

Liens against property are generally not wiped out by bankruptcy. Only unsecured debt is wiped out. So you can only get a bargain when the total liens on the bankrupt's property are less than the market value. Some times you can get a bargain even if the liens equal or exceed the value of the property. That occurs when the creditors who own the liens agree to take less than 100 cents on the dollar to release the entire lien off the property. They do that when they figure they won't get a better offer. Also, the court can sometimes order creditors to take less than face value for secured liens.

If the IRS had previously seized a property which was owned by the bankrupt person, the bankruptcy trustee has the power to force the IRS to return it. (*U.S. v. Whiting Pools, Inc.*, 103 S.Ct. 2309)

The trustee has wide discretion as to how to market the property. In the case histories below, the trustee listed the houses with a real estate agent. Others are sold by auction. The trustee can sell either by public sale or private sale. *Forced Sale Workbook* author John Beck says they often sell by private sale with the court's permission.

The bankruptcy court supervises the sales. In general, you must identify the trustees in your area and learn how they market bankrupt real estate so you can learn about and bid an their properties.

Why it works

When home owners sell their own house, they try hard to maximize the sale price. In bankruptcy, the home owner is not selling. The bankruptcy trustee is. Depending on state law and the amount of equity in the house, the owners may receive nothing at all from the bankruptcy sale. As a result, they have little motivation to cooperate with showings and keep the house in tip-top showing shape.

The agent and bankruptcy trustee want the sale to be as easy for them as possible. So their incentive is to get their respective commissions with the least effort. The incremental commission they get from a better price is insignificant so they have little motivation to push for more money from the buyer.

If the court gives permission for a private sale, the trustee is not required to advertise the property to the general public or to hold an auction. Only creditors of the bankrupt must get notice of the sale. The court sets a minimum price in those cases. That minimum may be too low, in which case the lack of advertising can give rise to a bargain.

According to *How to File for Bankruptcy* by Elias, Renauer, and Leonard, "In a bankruptcy sale, a typical home goes for 10% to 30% less than what it would bring in a normal sale."

How to find them

John Beck says there are no universal publication points in bankruptcies the way there are in foreclosures and tax sales. Bankruptcy trustees have **wide discretion** so you must contact them individually asking to be put on their mailing lists or just repeatedly contact them to see what they have at present.

They are **not** required to advertise in legal newspapers the way other forced-sale instigators are. You simply have to track down the trustees and agents who handle bankruptcies and **persuade** them to tell you about upcoming sales.

Creditors get notified about asset sales. But no law requires **public** notice—although the notices are generally addressed to "the debtor, creditors, and persons interested in the above bankruptcy case."

The "persons interested" phrase suggests the court and trustee must comply with reasonable requests for information. If they refused, questions could be raised as to whether they are discharging faithfully their duties to the creditors and debtor to maximize the sales proceeds. The bankruptcy court proceedings are generally public—as are their files. But neither the bankruptcy court nor the bankruptcy trustee are required to notify bargain-seekers like yourself or any other non-creditors about upcoming sales. You can and should ask the court and/or trustees to notify you about upcoming sales. They may. Then again they may not.

Look for the phrase "subject to court approval" in MLS write ups. One investor reads Chapter 7 bankruptcy court files and calls trustees when he sees real property. You can read the files in the court. Bankrupt persons and entities are required to list their assets, including real estate, when they file bankruptcy. In a Chapter 7 bankruptcy, it's on "Schedule B-1—STATEMENT OF ALL PROPERTY OF DEBTOR—Real Property." Addresses, legal descriptions, nature of interests, and estimated value are supposed to be given in the statement. Schedule B-4—Property Claimed as Exempt, lists the property which the bankrupt person believes is protected from creditors.

Homestead exemption

As far as real estate is concerned, only the homestead (residence of the bankrupt person) is exempt. And then only in some states. Homestead exemption amounts vary by state. Bankruptcy is a federal law, but each state passes its own list of exemptions from bankruptcy. Bankrupt persons can use their state's exemptions or the exemptions contained in the federal Bankruptcy Code. There is no federal homestead exemption. Here is a list of the homestead exemptions from *How To File For Bankruptcy* by Elias, Renauer, and Leonard.

State	Homestead exemption
AL	$5,000. Land under home may not exceed 160 acres. Homestead declaration must be recorded.
AK	$54,000.
AZ	$100,000. Homestead declaration must be recorded.

AR	No dollar limit if 1/4 acre or smaller and in city, town, or village or 80 acres elsewhere. $2,500 if between 1/4 acre and 1 acre in city, town, or village or 80 to 160 acres elsewhere. No exemption for properties larger than one acre in city, town, or village or 160 acres elsewhere.
CA	$50,000 single; $75,000 family; $100,000 65 or older, disabled, single and earn under $15,000, married and earn under $20,000.
CO	$20,000.
CT	None.
DE	None. *
DC	Residential condo deposit. *
FL	No dollar limit if one acre or less in municipality, 160 contiguous acres elsewhere.*
GA	$5,000.
HI	$20,000; head of family or over 65, $30,000. No bigger than one acre. *
ID	$30,000. Homestead declaration must be recorded.
IL	$7,500.
IN	$7,500. *
IA	No dollar limit. No more than one acre in town or city, 40 acres elsewhere.
KS	No dollar limit. No more than one acre in town or city, 160 acres elsewhere.
KY	$5,000.
LA	$15,000. No more than 160 acres on two or more tracts if home on one tract and field, garden, or pasture on others.
ME	$7,500; $60,000 if over age 60 or disabled. Double for joint debtors.
MD	None. *
MA	$100,000; $150,000 if over 65 or disabled. Homestead declaration must be recorded. *
MI	$3,500. No more than one lot in city, town, or village, 40 acres elsewhere. *
MN	No dollar limit. No more than one acre in city, 160 acres elsewhere.
MS	$30,000. No more than 160 acres.
MO	$8,000. *
MT	$40,000. Homestead declaration must be recorded.
NE	$10,000. No more than two lots in city, 160 acres elsewhere.
NV	$90,000. Homestead declaration must be recorded.
NH	$5,000.
NJ	None
NM	$20,000. Double for joint debtors.
NY	$10,000. Double for married couple.
NC	$7,500. *
ND	$80,000.
OH	$5,000. *
OK	No dollar limit if not exceed 1/4 acre. If over 1/4 acre, $5,000 on one acre in city or 160 acres elsewhere
OR	$15,000. $20,000 for joint owners. No more than one block in town or city or 160 acres elsewhere.
PA	None. *
RI	None.
SC	$5,000. Double for joint owners.
SD	No dollar limit. No more than one acre in town, 160 acres elsewhere.
TN	$5,000. $7,500 for joint owners. *
TX	No dollar limit. No more than one acre in town and 100 acres for a single person or 200 acres for a family.
UT	$8,000 single. Add $2,000 for spouse and $500 per dependent. Homestead declaration must be recorded.
VT	$30,000. *
VA	$5,000. $10,000 for married couple. Homestead declaration must be recorded. *

WA $30,000. Homestead declaration must be recorded.
WV $7,500.
WI $40,000.
WY $10,000. *

   * This is a state in which tenancy by the entirety properties are exempt without dollar limit if only one spouse is bankrupt.

   If the equity in a home equals or is less than the state homestead exemption, the bankruptcy trustee generally will **not** sell the home. What would be the point? All the sale proceeds would have to go to the debtor and would be exempt from the creditors. Bankruptcy trustees do not foreclose on behalf of secured creditors. They are expected to look out for themselves by foreclosing if the loan is in default.
   The home may be foreclosed by the lender if the mortgage has not been kept current. To buy those houses, follow the procedures in the pre-foreclosure, foreclosure, and OREO chapters. In *How To File For Bankruptcy*, they say,

   ...losing your home in bankruptcy will often be a better deal than losing it in a foreclosure sale. There are two reasons:
   First, a forced sale of your home in bankruptcy is supervised by the bankruptcy trustee, who will want to sell the house for as much as possible. In a foreclosure sale, the foreclosing creditor will try to get only a high enough price to cover the amount due on the mortgage. If you have a homestead exemption on the house, the more the house is sold for, the more you get on the homestead exemption.
   Second, in some states, a homestead exemption yields you nothing in a foreclosure sale.

   Bargain hunters have the opposite perspective. They prefer to buy at foreclosure auctions because the bargains are generally bigger there.
   Checking the court files is probably the only sure way to make sure you don't miss any sales. It's time-consuming. But that's also precisely what limits the number of competing bidders thereby increasing the chances you'll get a bargain.

Special expertise required
   If you are studying the court files, you'll need to learn the procedures of your local court. You also need to know your state's homestead exemption law, if any, to figure out whether homes listed in the court files will be sold.

Tax Ramifications
   There are no special tax considerations for bankruptcy purchases. The bankrupt person does have many special considerations. For details on them, see my special report on *Distressed Real Estate Times*. But those do not affect you as a bankruptcy buyer. Nor can you benefit from knowing the other guy's perspective because the bankrupt person is not the other guy. You negotiate with the trustee and indirectly, with the creditors.
   There is one exception. If you are **related** to the bankrupt, you cannot buy one or more of his or her debts for a small amount so as to reduce the bankrupt's discharge of indebtedness income.

Full-time or part-time possible
   Part-time investors would probably have some trouble pursuing bankruptcy properties. When the trustee lists them with a real estate agent, you have to work fast to beat the other buyers. When the trustee sells them privately, you need to move fast. An investor with

another job would have trouble dealing with the during-business-hours aspect of court proceedings and access to court files.

Regional variations

Bankruptcies increase when the local economy sags. The incidence of bargains is also a function of how the local bankruptcy judges and trustees conduct the marketing of bankruptcy real estate. Finally, there are differences in state homestead exemption laws. So the availability of bargains and the proper approach to getting them will vary from region to region, state to state, and from judge to judge and from trustee to trustee.

Ethical considerations

Bankruptcy is a scandal-ridden aspect of our justice system. The officials and attorneys charged with disposing the bankrupt's property often loot it. That is, they do sweetheart deals that benefit themselves or their cronies. There have been kickbacks. At least one attorney in the San Francisco area was mysteriously murdered after he began exposing corrupt bankruptcy officials. Northern California bankruptcy trustee Charles Duck pleaded guilty to embezzling $1.89 million from debtor's funds in 1989.

You cannot participate in any of this. You should steer completely clear of it if you get even a hint that your local bankruptcy courts or trustees are crooked. There is nothing wrong with getting a bargain if you do so in an arms-length deal. But if you conspire with crooked officials to screw the bankrupt or his creditors out of some of the money they would get from honest sales of the property, you have committed both civil and criminal offenses as well as ethical breaches.

Environmental liability considerations

You need to perform the same due diligence as with any purchase. Since you are buying from a federal court, your ability to go back against the seller if you later find environmental problems is extremely limited. So you'd better be even more careful than when buying from a private party.

Need for secrecy

No matter how you buy bankruptcy property, you'd better kept it to yourself. In general, the bargains stem from lack of market exposure. The more you say, the more exposure you give it.

$20,000 in a week

The best thing Eileen Thompson got out of attending Robert Allen's $5,000 seminar was meeting a young couple who introduced her to Sandra Yarrow (not her real name). Sandra is a Realtor® who specializes in selling property sold by bankruptcy courts. (Thompson also gave Allen's seminar credit for motivating her. But she said she has not used a single technique he taught.)

The young couple had agreed to buy a bankruptcy condo for $160,000 less a $1,600 credit for carpet and painting. But they were unable to qualify for a mortgage. They assigned their agreement to Thompson for $2,000 on June 18, 1990. Net of the credit, her purchase price was $160,400. Inexplicably, the painting and carpeting had been done at no cost to Thompson before she took possession. Closing costs took the total cost up to $161,253.67.

She estimated the property was worth $200,000. Closing was July 13, 1990.

Thompson began advertising the property for sale the day after she bought the purchase agreement, June 19th. By June 26th, she received an offer for $175,000. She negotiated them up to $190,500. That deal closed August 9th. Net of commission and other closing costs, she received $183,376.46.

The property

The property Thompson bought is a two-bedroom, two-bath condominium. It was vacant when Thompson inspected and bought it.

I am not listing the location of the properties in this case to protect the privacy of the bankrupt persons and to avoid riling other involved parties.

The bankruptcy court was in another, nearby county. *Distress Sales Report* (415-523-6115) editor John Beck once bought land in Florida out of a bankruptcy in San Jose. Bargains are likely to be proportionate to the distance between the bankruptcy court and the property in question.

Commissions

The bankruptcy court pays a 6% commission to Yarrow when she produces accepted offers. Bankruptcy trustees generally have wide discretion as to **whether** to list a property, **how** to list it, and **with whom** to list it.

When she **sold** the property, Thompson paid a 3% commission or $5,715.00.

Inspection

When you buy at property tax, foreclosure, or IRS auctions, you generally do **not** get to inspect the property unless you privately contact the occupant and get their cooperation. But when you buy out of bankruptcy, you **can** make an appointment to inspect just as you would with a house in the multiple-listing book. Agents even hold open houses in bankruptcy properties when they are still occupied by the bankrupt family.

Procedure

With bankruptcy property, you inspect and make an offer just as you would with a regular seller. But the bankruptcy trustee's acceptance is only **tentative**. He or she then sends notices to the creditors and, in some cases, publishes notice of your bid and invites other bidders to overbid you at an auction in the trustee's office twenty days hence. The trustee does **not** have to accept the highest bid if there are other considerations.

The trustee in the county in question requires a $5,000 non-refundable deposit from winning overbidders.

Overbids

Such bidding after an acceptable offer is anathema to real estate agents in all other situations. Real estate agents hate multiple offers which turn into auctions because all but one of the agents stand to lose everything.

My impression is that most real estate companies will **not** submit offers until the seller has accepted or rejected a prior offer—even when the subsequent offer might be **higher**. That's an outrage. But it was generally accepted in the real estate brokerage industry last I heard. Because the agents are more sympathetic to the agent who loses his commission after bringing in an acceptable offer than they are to the seller who could have gotten more for his property.

The way this manifests itself in the multiple listing service where I worked in 1974 as an agent, was that when you called to submit an offer, the agent who answered the phone would say, "There's an offer on the property." No one would mention the price on either offer and the second agent would retreat for a few hours until the first agent got to present his offer with**out** the seller knowing there was a second offer. This is especially true when the first offer is **in-house** (same company as the listing agent) and the subsequent offer is from another company.

In any event, the overbid invitation represents a **threat** if you are the original bidder; an **opportunity** if you are not. No one overbid Thompson in this deal or the other bankruptcy property she bought.

Timing

Thompson's second bankruptcy auction purchase took place in November of 1990. That's four months after she made the offer.

Yarrow says you need more patience with bankruptcies than with normal deals because the debtor or creditors can object to the sale adding months or years to the process.

In the second deal, Thompson offered $275,000 for a property appraised at $340,000. Liens on the property totaled $293,872.75. Normally, the trustee will **not** sell for less than the total liens unless enough creditors agree to release their lien for less than face value. If there is no such agreement, the trustee will **abandon** the property to the secured creditors who must then foreclose in the normal manner. Yarrow thought the offer was probably too low to be accepted because it was less than the total liens. But some creditors agreed to take less so it was accepted.

I said $275,000 was too **high** because it did not produce a 20% margin. What the trustee and creditors will accept is irrelevant when one gets above 80% of value. Bankruptcy buyers must make the offers they **need** to make, first and foremost, and only secondarily worry about making the offer which is likely to be accepted. If **none** of your offers are accepted at 20% below market value, look for another investment niche.

Thompson sold the second property, a four-bedroom, two-bath, detached single-family house on April 24, 1991 for $$290,000 without a real estate agent. She found a buyer by putting out flyers at a meeting of a real estate investors club. Thompson said she only broke even on this deal in spite of not paying a commission, thereby proving my point that the profit margin was inadequate. You must buy for at least 20% below market value.

Financing

Thompson is a flipper (wants to resell immediately) so she paid **all cash**. But with bankruptcy auctions, unlike property tax, foreclosure, and IRS auctions, you don't **need** to pay all cash. The bankruptcy trustee will give you reasonable time to arrange financing in the normal fashion. You may be able to take over existing financing. Yarrow says that's very rare. The bankruptcy authorities can even take back a mortgage or do an exchange.

Other trustees use **auctions**. There, the winning bidder typically must put 10% down in cash on the day of the auction. Terms vary on when you have to pay the rest.

Title insurance

You **can** get title insurance when you buy bankruptcy property. With some other forced-sale auctions, that is sometimes **not** the case. All liens can be wiped out by the bankruptcy if the trustee so chooses.

Ted Thomas dropout

Thompson is a drop out of Ted Thomas's $5,000 pre-foreclosure course (See the pre-foreclosure chapter). She was turned off by the first night's assignment: writing letters to people against whom notices of default have been filed. She was uncomfortable with trying to persuade people in financial distress to sell their homes at a big discount.

Thompson was also uncomfortable with negotiating across the kitchen table with the financially distressed sellers. Foreclosure auction buyer Paul Thompson says he likes foreclosure auctions rather than pre-foreclosures for the same reason. (Paul is no relation to Eileen.)

Eileen Thompson prefers dealing with the bankruptcy trustee and avoiding negotiating with people in distress. She prefers bankruptcy to foreclosure auctions because of the opportunity to inspect the property and to get title insurance.

Resale

Thompson advertised her first purchase for resale as soon as she bought the purchase agreement—**before** she even closed on the property. She ran a for-sale-by-owner ad in the newspaper classified section. And she held an "open house" and put a sign on the sidewalk out front.

Incidence of bankruptcies

According to the *Statistical Abstract of the Untied States*, 642,993 bankruptcies were filed in the U.S. in 1989 (the most recent year in the *Abstract*). That's about one for every 420 people so you can get a rough idea of the number of bankruptcies in your area by dividing your population by 420. Or you can simply call the local bankruptcy court and ask them.

18

Execution sales

How it works

Civil suits that go to trial end in judgments. In many cases, the judgment entitles the winning party to obtain money from the loser. The losing party (judgment debtor) often does not voluntarily turn over the money.

When that happens, the winner (judgment creditor) needs to execute. That is, he or she obtains a court order which seizes property owned by the debtor, sells it, and gives the sale proceeds to the creditor. The creditor is typically entitled to the amount of the judgment plus court costs and interest. If the sale proceeds exceed the amount the creditor is due, the excess is paid to lien holders junior to the judgment creditor, if any. If there are sale proceeds left over after the creditors are paid, they go to the debtor or former owner of the property that was sold.

In many cases, the property that is sold is real estate. The sale of the property pursuant to a court order obtained by a judgment creditor is called an execution sale and is generally carried out by the sheriff. The standard format is an all-cash, open-bid auction.

Why it works

As with other government-run forced sales, execution sale procedure is a textbook example of how **not** to sell real estate. In fact, execution sale procedure is probably the absolute **worst**. As a result, the bargains are often astounding in execution sales. Here are some of the reasons the number of bidders is extremely small:

• all-cash required
• no opportunity to inspect the property
• poorly publicized in legal notices
• so few execution sales that there are generally no private services that track them.

Tax Ramifications

For federal income tax purposes, property bought at an execution sale is the same as property bought in a normal fashion. If you get it at a superbargain price, your depreciation basis is still your cost and that will be quite low. You cannot depreciate based on market value.

Full-time or part-time possible

There are few execution sales and few bidders. That means you can do this part-time. On the other hand, you need to do a title search and attend the auction. Title searches can generally only be performed during business hours. And the auctions are held during business hours. So although the number of hours per week that you need to spend is low, they happen to be during business hours. If you have a job working for someone else during business hours, you'll need to get time off.

It would not be possible to be a full-time execution sale investor unless you covered such a wide geographic area that several sales a week were occurring in that area. If you are a full-time investor, execution sales would have to be one of several strategies that you pursued.

Regional variations

State laws on execution sales vary. You need to know your state's law. State laws which were less anachronistic would produce fewer and/or smaller bargains. There may also be variations in the procedures used by various sheriffs. Logic suggests that there should be more execution sales in hard times. But execution sales seem to be more a function of the tenacity of the creditor rather than the regional economy.

Environmental liability considerations

Execution sales represent a high degree of environmental risk. That's because you cannot inspect the property. (Actually, in California, you can demand that the sheriff escort you and the other bidders to the property for an inspection. But that probably will not afford your environmental inspectors a full opportunity to do their job.) Furthermore, you are buying from the government and they are notorious for taking no responsibility whatsoever for problems. So you'd better be careful. See the chapter on delinquent property tax auctions for a horror story similar to what you could encounter in sheriff's sales.

Need for secrecy

Execution sales offer not just bargains, but superbargains. Consequently, you need to keep them as quiet as possible. Especially when you are poking around the court house or recorders office. The bigger the bargain, the more people will want in on it if they know about it. Sheriff's sales fall into the nobody-knows-about-them category. Do your best to keep it that way.

In theory, one could approach the sheriff's sale at any of three stages:

- pre auction
- auction
- post auction.

But since the owner not knowing or realizing the full implications of the sale was a key in the case histories in this chapter, you should probably **not** stir up the owner **before** the auction. I see nothing wrong with approaching the winning bidder **after** the auction. Often an investor who got a superbargain is willing to sell at a still bargain price for a quick profit.

A $58,000 property bought for $577.77

In one case history in John Beck's *Forced Sale Workbook* (510-523-6115), a man who bought a car repair shop and its miscellaneous assets like uncollected debts, discovered the previous owner had won a $500 small claims case against a woman who did not pay a car repair bill.

He then had the sheriff sell a duplex the debtor owned and since no one bid, the car repair guy became the owner. By then, the judgment had grown to $577.77 from interest and costs. He took no action, however, and the woman who had refused to pay the repair bill behaved as if she still owned the duplex.

Two years later, a title company told him the duplex was being sold and asked him to sign a quit-claim deed. The sale price was $58,000. He refused to sign the deed.

Deadbeat sues

He was promptly sued by the deadbeat. The totally meritless complaint alleged in part that the repair shop owner had purchased a property worth $58,000 for a mere $577.77. That was **true**. It was also perfectly **legal**. The repair shop owner figured such a harsh result might bother the court so he settled out of court for half the $27,937.37 sale proceeds or $13,968.69 ($700 legal fee). Legally, he appears to be entitled to not only the entire property but also to all the **net rental income** since the sheriff's deed was recorded.

Seems to me he might have gotten the suit dismissed quickly on summary judgment. I'd have argued that the deadbeat was a chronic scofflaw who ignored the many ominous notices which have to be sent in order for a judgment to be won, executed, property auctioned, and the redemption period, if any, to expire.

I'd have also asked in court papers, "Where was the plaintiff's attorney when all the notices were being ignored?" If the attorney was aware of the collection efforts before expiration of the redemption period, the deadbeat probably has a great case for recovering the lost equity and rent through a **malpractice suit** against the attorney. The suit against the new owner may be merely an attempt by an incompetent attorney to distract his client from his own malpractice.

Finally, I'd have argued that the procedure under which title passed is well-established. That people who do not like it ought to write to their legislator—not sue good faith execution-sale bidders. And that a judicial requirement that such bargains be undone would reduce interest in government-sponsored auctions in general. Lowered interest in the auctions would mean lower sale prices which would harm all future creditors including local governments seeking back taxes. The debtors themselves would be worse off in many cases because they are entitled to the excess proceeds of such sales, if any.

Case history of an execution sale superbargain

On November 17, 1985, *60 Minutes* aired a segment about a superbargain real estate purchase. It told how two men bought a three-bedroom, 1,190 sq.ft. house worth $110,000 to $115,000 in Milpitas, California (San Jose suburb) for just $25,000 at an execution sale.

I figured that would be a good deal to reinvestigate, only this time from a **real estate investor's** perspective. I thought I'd call one of the guys who did the deal and ask how it turned out. Maybe write up some of his other deals if he does this systematically. So I bought a transcript of the broadcast (212-227-7323) and began calling people.

What I found was far more complicated than I expected. **Amazing** in some respects.

Homeowners association dues chronology

In 1974, Joan Williams (I have changed the names except for the association attorney) first became **delinquent** on her **homeowners association dues**. Here is the chronology:

- 1979 Williams owed $133.50 She said she could not afford to pay.
- Association forgave the debt.
- 1981 delinquent again.
- 12/81 & 2/82 letters to Williams offering a payment schedule. She said she could not afford to pay.
- 4/83 & 12/83 two more letters sent.
- 1/84 association referred to attorney, Charles Morrone. Due: $360.
- 1/27/84 Morrone demanded payment and threatened to foreclose. No response.
- 2/28/84 Lien Claim recorded. Copy sent to Williams by the Recorder's Office. No response.
- 3/19/84 the association foreclosed.
- 3/25/84 Williams served a copy of the foreclosure suit.
- 3/28/84 Williams called Morrone and said she could not pay.
- 4/9/84 Williams paid $100 but said she could not afford to pay more.
- 5/22/84 Morrone offered Williams a monthly payment schedule. Williams said she could not pay more.
- 6/13/84 Morrone told Williams bill now $615. No response.
- 8/9/84 Court awarded default judgment for $1,010 and directed home be sold.
- 8/10/84 Morrone sent Williams a copy of the judgment and requested payment in seven days or else auction. No response.
- 8/20/84 Morrone sent appropriate papers to sheriff.
- 9/18/84 Williams called Morrone and said she was getting legal counsel. Morrone also learned Williams had made $105 in payments to association bank unbeknownst to anyone. She refused to pay court costs or collection fees.
- 10/11/84 Sheriff auctioned house.
- 11/5/84 Morrone received letter from Williams' attorney, Samuel Johnson. I read the letter. It borders on incoherent.

Auction

There was an existing $15,000, 7 1/2% mortgage on Williams' house. The **minimum** bid for the equity was $1,010, the amount owed. The **winning** bid was $10,000.

That meant the winning bidders, attorney George Smith and his apparently silent partner, Rajiv Yastha, put $10,000 down and bought subject to the $15,000 mortgage for a total price of $25,000. Mrs. Williams got $10,000 - $1,010 = $8,990.

Redemption period

At that time, there was a **120-day redemption period** on sheriff's sales in California. Although Mrs. Williams had an attorney, she did **not** redeem the property during the redemption period so the sheriff's sale became final. (The redemption period has since been replaced in California by a longer **pre**-sale notice period.)

60 Minutes version

The broadcast gives the impression Mrs. Williams was a simple, religious grandmother who didn't understand enough legal mumbo jumbo to realize what was happening, and whose attorney was no help. Her children would have paid the bill "the next day," said her son-in-law, if only they had known.

Eviction

The case came to the **public's** attention when the buyers evicted Mrs. Williams on February 14, 1985. They had filed an unlawful detainer (eviction) suit on January 25th and won a **default** judgment. They waited until the 120-day redemption period had expired before contacting her. On April 26, 1985, Mrs. Williams asked the judge to set aside the default judgment in the eviction suit. He agreed to a delay so she could seek relief in superior court but she did **nothing** so her motion was denied.

The eviction apparently involved **pushing and shoving** with the old and new owners of the house each alleging the other started the violence and that they only acted in self defense.

The *San Jose Mercury News* carried a **front-page** story about the eviction and Williams made the local TV news. *60 Minutes* heard about it and came to film the story in June. Local 7/11s collected money to help. Mr. Smith was quoted in the paper saying Mrs. Williams was a "shrewd, rich woman who had hoodwinked the media and the public into thinking she is a poor little old lady who lost her house through no fault of her own."

Civil suit

Mrs. Williams got a new attorney and sued every person, association, or government agency involved on March 26, 1985. The defendants, in turn, generally **sued each other**. Williams and her husband alleged **wrongful foreclosure, slander, libel, assault and battery** (during the eviction), **destruction and theft of her personal property, intentional and negligent infliction of emotional distress, improper notice, malpractice**, and **constructive trust** (claiming that attorney/buyer Smith had a fiduciary relationship with her and was her trustee). She sought actual and punitive damages in the hundreds of thousands of dollars. In the cross complaints, the various defendants sought indemnification from each other for Williams' suit.

Yastha's attorney tried to get him tried separately on the grounds that the **pretrial publicity** involving others would inflame the jury unfairly against him. In that motion, Yastha's attorney cited the *60 Minutes* broadcast and other coverage.

All the cases except Mrs. Williams case against her original attorney, Samuel Johnson, were settled. The *Mercury News* reported that "a source close to the case" said Mrs. Williams got a total of $40,000 from the various non-Johnson defendants including $25,000 from Smith and Yastha. Johnson failed to appear at his malpractice trial and Mrs. Williams won a default judgment against him for $94,000. I don't know whether she has collected on that judgment. Johnson died in 1990.

Mrs. Williams never got her house back. Yastha resold it for $120,000 on December 5, 1986. Smith sold out his share to Yastha on August 1, 1986.

Can such bargains be overturned?

If the forced sale is conducted properly, the fact that the property sold real cheap **cannot** in and of itself cause the sale to be overturned. However, in *Bank of Seoul & Trust Co. v. Marcione*, (198 Cal. App. 3d 113), the California Supreme Court said,

> *While mere inadequacy of price, standing alone, will not justify setting aside a trustee's sale, gross inadequacy of price coupled with even slight unfairness or irregularity is a sufficient basis for setting the sale aside.*

It seems to me that forced-sale auction buyers ought to **videotape** the auctions they go to. I'm told this is only rarely done. But I'm also told numerous stories of **collusion** between the auctioneer and the winning bidder, auctioneers who unexpectedly announce the sale is **over** and refuse to reopen bidding in spite of protests from stunned would-be bidders, auctioneers who hold auctions on the **back** or **side** steps of the courthouse instead of the front steps, etc.

Financial matters of great importance are decided at these forced-sale auctions. Yet there is **no** paper or other **record** of what happens at them—other than the auctioneer's signed statement of the end result.

The process is anachronistic, inadequate in protecting the interests of the property owner and junior lien holders, and an open invitation for abuse. I'd be tempted to videotape every one I attended to protect **me** from allegations of impropriety and to either discourage auctioneers from misbehaving or to create the evidence to go after them if they **do** misbehave.

Be more careful than in foreclosures

Unlike trustee sales and foreclosures, you can**not** rely partly on the due diligence of the lender who is foreclosing. Because there is no lender in many cases. So you have to check title more carefully. Specifically, you must check for name liens which were recorded between the grant deed or senior trust deed and the recording of the lien being executed. A name lien is a judgment against the individual who owns the house. You cannot be sure you are getting them all. No services report on sheriff's execution sales so far fewer bidders show up.

No evidence of bid chilling

Although there was extensive local and national media attention and litigation in this case, I found no evidence that any media or legal people investigated the possibility of **bid chilling**. Bid chilling is the first thing that comes to the mind of an experienced **trustee-sale** (foreclosure) buyer when they hear about the deal. Bid chilling is an agreement between prospective bidders to refrain from bidding at a prearranged, artificially low level. At § 4:14 of *California Real Estate Law 2d*, Miller and Starr say,

> *It is unlawful to offer or accept consideration not to bid at a foreclosure sale or to fix or restrain bidding in any manner at a sale of real property conducted under a power of sale and a deed of trust. California Civil Code § 2924h(g)*

Bid chilling is a misdemeanor punishable by a fine of up to $10,000 or up to one year in the county jail or both. There is a one-year statute of limitations. (PC §802)

In the typical scenario, the conspirators repair to a nearby coffee shop immediately after the **public** auction and hold a second, **private** auction. The high bidder at that private auction gets the **property;** the other bidders split the difference between the two auction prices equally among themselves in **cash.**

When a three-bedroom, detached single-family house in a decent neighborhood sells at a **foreclosure** auction, it generally sells for a discount of 15% to 30%, unless only one bidder shows up. *60 Minutes* said that there was more than one bidder at the Williams auction.

If foreclosure property sells for a discount **greater than** 30%, one should suspect bid chilling. The greater the discount, the greater the probability that bid chilling occurred. The discount in this case was **78%**.

Execution sales different

But *Distress Sales Report* editor John Beck says execution sales are **quite different** from foreclosure sales when it comes to the discounts obtainable. The discounts at execution sales can be **much larger** than 30% with**out** bid chilling according to Beck.

Incidence of this opportunity

The reason is that there are **far fewer** execution sales. In fact, they are so rare that it does not pay any private publishers to report on them as they do on foreclosures and probates. Real estate educator Ron Starr says there are probably fewer than a dozen execution sales in the nine-county San Francisco Bay Area per year. So the investor wishing to pursue execution sales has to be **his own** reporting service.

How to find them

Notice of execution sales must be published in **newspapers of general circulation**. So you have to check the appropriate paper for each sheriff's jurisdiction. Or you could monitor notices of attachment filed in the county recorder's office.

Start your own executions

One way to get around both the rarity of execution sales and the minimal advertising, might be to **buy judgments** at a discount, then execute them yourself. You're sure to know about **those** sales.

You need to learn your **state law** on execution sales. For example, you cannot, as a practical matter, execute involuntary liens on a debtor's **homestead** in California because the law requires that homesteads sell for at least 90% of market value.

With no opportunity to inspect, finance, or get title insurance, virtually no one will pay that much. (Mrs. Williams' house was not protected by this law because the homeowners association dues are a **voluntary** lien like a mortgage.) Debtors are generally permitted to **stay** in the house until the redemption period, if any, expires.

To instigate your own execution sales, you would have to become a judgment investor like Lloyd Walters in the judgment investing chapter of this book. But with a twist. Whenever you bought a judgment in which the debtor owned **non-homestead** real estate—and in which the ratio of your lien plus senior liens to the value of the property was **50% or less**—you would execute the lien.

Many, if not most, debtors will **pay off** the debt rather than let the property be sold. Which is fine because you bought it for 8¢ on the dollar (at least that was Walters' experience). And if the execution sale actually takes place—and you are the winning bidder—you make **even more** than a 92% markup.

Where are they now?

Is George Smith the kind of man who would commit misdemeanor bid-chilling? I wanted to ask him. But when I called the number listed for his law office in the San Jose phone book, it was **disconnected**.

I tried to call John Brown, the attorney who represented Smith in the civil litigation. But the only listing was for "Jon" Brown, which turned out to be a different attorney. He suggested I track the various attorneys down by calling the State Bar of California because all attorneys have to register annually with them.

"George Smith resigned from the bar with charges pending," the State Bar told me. Oh, really? How about Mrs. Williams first attorney, Samuel Johnson? "He was suspended for nonpayment of registration fees in September 1986." Hmmm.

I **was** able to find the attorney for the homeowners' association, Charles Morrone (his real name). He told me Smith was recently convicted of **embezzlement** in an unrelated matter.

I went to San Jose and read the court files in both the civil and criminal courts and the news stories in the *San Jose Mercury News*. I also drove by the property in Milpitas. It is your basic one-story, two-car garage, working-class house in a working-class neighborhood.

The saga of George Smith

George Smith was not just the shrewd real estate investor I expected.

In the early seventies, he had put a loaded pistol in his mouth and pulled the trigger. The suicide attempt failed but left him with one eye, fewer teeth, and a scar on his face where doctors operated on the damage done by the bullet.

In October of 1987, he had been designated a trustee in a divorce case. In conjunction with that case, he was supposed to put $56,423 in proceeds from the sale of the divorcing couple's house into a trust account. Instead, the bachelor attorney put the money in his **own** account, used it to buy travelers checks, and, on November 7, 1987, disappeared.

While Smith was missing, his physician brother offered a $2,000 reward and was quoted in the *Mercury News* as saying he was convinced his brother did nothing wrong. "He is compulsively honest."

An attorney friend described Smith as a "loner" but also strongly doubted he had done anything illegal. Smith had previously disappeared briefly on what turned out to be an apparently innocent but unannounced vacation to Florida. After that vacation, which resulted in a visit to his apartment by police responding to a missing-person report, Smith installed a booby trap, i.e., a live electric cord attached to the doorknob and lock. A warrant was issued for the police to disarm that booby trap.

Arrested

Smith was arrested in a transient hotel in Springfield, MO in the fall of 1988 and extradited to San Jose. Psychiatric reports in his criminal file reveal that he went to Hong Kong twice immediately after disappearing. Smith said he believed he was entitled to the $56,000, although I found no indication of **why** he thought that. His defense was that no court ever ordered him to return the money. Say what? He told one psychiatrist that he was "Pleasantly surprised to find [jail] pleasant and nicer than freedom."

Smith was indicted for **felony grand theft embezzlement** (California Penal Code §§ 487, 506). He pleaded insanity, which was disputed by two court-appointed psychiatrists. He was defended by the Public Defender's office, which only works for indigent defendants. Smith insisted on acting as his own attorney (co-counsel). The Public Defender was later quoted in a *Mercury News* story as saying Smith did not cooperate with him.

The jury said Smith was both sane and guilty on March 22, 1990. He got the max: four years in state prison. By the time the trial ended, Smith had already spent 622 days in the county jail and had received credit for an additional 311 "local conduct" days (time off for good behavior). He was also sentenced to pay full restitution to the victim plus pay her a $2,500 "restitution fine."

Meaning for investors

Bargains which are extraordinary even by the standards of forced sales may result in new dimensions being added to the deal. In this case they were:

- possibility of bid chilling
- widespread media attention
- civil litigation.

Bid chilling did not come up in this case. But it might in similar cases. I presume that you will be innocent of bid chilling. But **proving** your innocence could become an issue where there are multiple bidders and you buy the property for more than 30% below market value.

Extreme bargains may "offend the conscience" of the community to use a phrase often used by judges. Even though the law clearly entitles the bargain purchaser to his bargain (in the absence of bid chilling or other unfairness), the person who lost a large equity can effectively appeal to the emotions of both the public and the courts. Furthermore, as the *Bank of Seoul* decision shows, the courts will look for **any excuse** to overturn a sale when a huge bargain is obtained. Your state law may be different.

Media coverage

The *Mercury News* stories were deliberately designed to appeal to the **emotions** and were **stereotypical** in their depiction of the parties. Mrs. Williams was "elderly…gray-haired …living on a fixed income…tall, elegant looking woman…tired yet determined." The *Mercury News* implied that "her dog, Skipper" died as a result of the eviction—a connection which was not even alleged in Mrs. Williams' you-name-it-we-claim-it lawsuit. One *Mercury News* story erroneously claimed that "Penalties quickly increased her debt to more than $10,000…" It was neither quick nor $10,000.

All stories about Smith's disappearance and embezzlement contained a paragraph which described him as, "an attorney who once forced an impoverished couple from their home…and sold the house at a profit."

What the heck does all that have to do with anything? The lady lost her house because she ignored multiple demands and notices to pay her dues and collection costs.

60 Minutes came closer to the truth in their account of the warnings leading up to the eviction. And Morley Safer's indignation over the $90,000 loss Williams ultimately suffered for her failure to pay a $1,010 debt is warranted. But I disagree with Safer's statement that, "She has every right to be a confused woman." The notices and warnings she received may not have been models of readability. But I doubt that any sane adult would miss their point.

Bad publicity can be very costly and/or painful to some people, like children or other relatives of the publicity targets or those who sell products or services to the public, politicians, or people who are active in community affairs. Others couldn't care less about bad publicity.

Title trickier

Title searches are trickier with execution sales than with foreclosure auctions. With a foreclosure, you can generally assume that an institutional mortgage lender got a title search making sure they were first in priority when they made the loan. And if you buy at auction, you know that all **junior** liens are wiped out.

But execution liens are generally **involuntary** liens from court judgments. So there was **no title search** made in connection with their creation. Consequently, you have to search from the last likely clean title report to the recording date of the lien being executed.

You must look for both mortgage liens and involuntary property and **name** liens. The more common the name of the debtor, the harder to tell whether the judgments you find apply to the property in question. You also cannot get **payoff statements** from the lien holders the way you could in a normal purchase. So you have to **guess** at what their current balance is from their original amounts and such information as recording dates and statutory interest rates.

All of this is complicated by the fact that you generally cannot afford to spend much time on a property until the **day before** the auction. That's because the vast majority of scheduled auctions are canceled or postponed. You have to call the **day before** to see if the auction is still on. **Then**, you do your title search.

Deal killers

Another problem bargain purchasers have to deal with more than those who pay market value is people trying to kill their deal. The greater the bargain, the harder people try to kill the deal. In the Williams case—where the bargain represented $90,000 lost—Mrs. Williams understandably fought **fiercely** to kill Smith's deal.

Smith got to keep the property. And he probably could have come out better in the litigation if he had been more careful about the **eviction** and his public comments about Mrs. Williams. Handle hostile evictions with great care. Better yet, get **someone else** to handle them. If you must be present, take a witness and **videotape** and audiotape everything that happens with the knowledge and consent of the parties. (If you can't get their consent, leave and come back with additional witnesses and/or the police as appropriate.) Don't say anything about former tenants or employees.

If you can't stand the heat of bad publicity, stay out of the super-bargain kitchen. If you **chase superbargains**, expect bad publicity and litigation trying to overturn the deal. Make sure your profit margin is big enough to cover the litigation costs. Not all super bargains involve these kinds of troubles. In fact, most don't. But it is a hazard of superbargain purchases for which veterans of market-value purchases may be unprepared.

Apartment complex for a security deposit

I read back in the seventies about a tenant who moved out of a Sacramento area apartment complex. As is too often the case, the complex neither sent him his security deposit nor told him why not. That's against the law. You have to do one or the other within 30 days in most states—two weeks in California.

It happened that the tenant was a law student. He sued. There was no response from the complex so he won a default judgment. He then obtained a writ of execution and the complex was auctioned off to pay his judgment.

No bidders appeared. So he became the owner of the apartment complex for the amount of his security deposit plus the statutory damages and costs he was owed. Last I heard, he had finally gotten the complex's attention and the complex owners were trying to extricate themselves from the situation. I suspect the law student received tens of thousands of dollars if he did not get to keep the building. Par for the course in these things seems to be about half the equity. That's because both sides are terrified the other may win in court.

$40,000 for $7,000

Bill Stubbs attended a sheriff's execution sale in 1988 in Northern California. A contractor had occupied and simultaneously renovated three stores. His $7,000 bill was not paid. He sued the owner and won. Then he had the sheriff execute by auctioning off the building which was worth at least $40,000 and had no other liens on it.

Stubbs planned to bid but the contractor verbally promised to sell him the property for $10,000, so Stubbs remained silent during the auction. Afterward, the contractor refused to sell him the property. Stubbs now believes the contractor made the $10,000 promise solely to convince Stubbs not to bid. Lesson learned, bid. Don't fall for verbal promises in any real estate deal. If it's not in writing, it's not enforceable. Also, such an arrangement probably violates laws against bid chilling.

19

Condemned property

In January of 1990, a working woman in her sixties was released from a hospital on The Peninsula, a generally affluent area directly south of San Francisco. As was standard in such cases, a visiting nurse was assigned to check on how she was doing.

"Unfit"

When she arrived at the woman's house, the visiting nurse was appalled at its condition. The roof had holes in it big enough to allow not only rain but also leaves to come in. More than 20 cats lived in the attic producing the sort of stench you'd expect. As required by law, the nurse reported the condition of the house to the city. A city inspector visited the property and promptly posted a sign reading:

"Unfit for human occupancy."

The city ordered the gas-and-electric company to turn off those utilities and forced the couple to move out **immediately**.

How he found it

Bob Bruss, an investor and nationally-syndicated real estate columnist, had been watching the house for some time. In addition to the bad roof, its grass was never mowed and two vehicles sat unmoved and covered by tarps in the driveway for years. Like many investors, Bruss tries to contact the owners of such neglected properties on the theory that they are often willing to sell at bargain prices. In this case, he had left two or three notes for the owners over the years. But he got no response.

Fortunately, he also made it known to all the real estate agents in the area that he bought fixer uppers. One such agent learned of the condemnation of the house and tracked down its owners, who had moved to a boarding house in San Jose.

The owners refused to sign a listing or even state an asking price. Nevertheless, the agent decided to call Bruss in the hope that a specific offer might get the sellers to act.

Offer

Bruss said he was interested, inspected the property, and offered $212,000 including a 6% commission for the agent. Had it been maintained in a normal fashion, the two-bedroom, one-bath house would have been worth about $320,000 in that neighborhood, according to Bruss.

The owners neither rejected nor countered the offer. After waiting two weeks, Bruss called the agent and said if he didn't get an answer in the next four days, the offer would be withdrawn. When presented with that ultimatum, the owners countered at $216,000. Bruss agreed and the papers were signed.

Bruss then introduced himself to the neighbors, told them of his rehabilitation plans. He gave them his card and invited them to call him if they saw any suspicious characters around the property. Shortly thereafter, a neighbor called and said she had seen a man on the property and asked what he was doing. He said he was about to buy the property. She took his name then called Bruss to tell him.

Interloper

Bruss recognized the name as that of an aggressive local real estate investor. Upon investigation, he learned that the investor had agreed to buy the property for the same price as Bruss—only there would be no commission. So the sellers would net 6% x $216,000 = $12,960 more than selling to Bruss through the agent. Of course, that would require them to breach their agreement with Bruss.

Bruss, who is a lawyer, called the investor and told him that he would enforce his purchase agreement against the seller by filing a specific performance suit and would file a *lis pendens* (lawsuit regarding ownership pending) against the property if the owners did not perform at closing a few days later. The investor knew such a suit would probably prevail and immediately abandoned his plans to buy the building.

Gut rehab

The owners **did** sell to Bruss. They owned the house free and clear and had even paid the 1990 property taxes in advance. The closing went smoothly.

The house required a gut rehab. It's the worst house Bruss ever bought in his many years as a fixer upper. The tax assessor split Bruss's $216,000 purchase price into $215,000 for the land and **$1,000 for the improvements**.

The hardwood floors were destroyed by the rain but the underlayment was OK. The floors were removed and replaced by carpet. All non-carpeted floors got new vinyl. Because of mildew, all the walls and ceilings were replaced. The appliances and plumbing fixtures were also unsalvable and were replaced. The fireplace, on the other hand, was in great shape because it had never been used in the property's 40- to 50-year history.

The house has a 6' x 15' front porch which was under the main roof and was surrounded on three sides by the house. Bruss enclosed that porch and thereby added a third bedroom and expanded the living room. He also turned part of the living room into a second bathroom.

Bruss's fixed-price contract with the general contractor was for $62,000 and took four months to complete. Change orders typically added a bit more. When complete, he figures the expanded house will be worth $350,000. Bruss had a lessee optionee to take the house before closing.

Financing

Bruss financed the purchase and renovation as follows:

- Construction loan of $170,000 at prime plus two percent
- Secured line of credit drawn down $50,000 at same rate
- Unsecured line of credit drawn down $60,000 at same rate.

He says all three loans came from the same local bank. He recommends against banking with more than one bank or with large banks. Rather he says you should cultivate a relationship with a **small bank** in your community—a bank which only has one or two branches and which is **not** a subsidiary of a large bank—where your business will be more appreciated. Of course, in this age of big banks buying up little ones, one can never be certain that a community bank won't become part of BigCitiMegaBanc next year.

Hedge floating-rate loans

Bruss's loans were all floating rate. I believe it's financial Russian Roulette to finance real estate with floating-rate loans. Rather, the investor should use either **fixed-rate** loans or **hedge** using interest-rate futures contracts or, in this case with its six-month holding period, the simpler interest-rate futures options. Although the use of interest-rate futures hedging is inexplicably rare among real estate investors, it is common among builders. In this deal, Bruss is operating more like a builder.

Ethics

There is no ethical issue for Bruss in this deal. A buyer has the right to make any cash offer he wants and owes no one an apology if the seller agrees to sell cheap or to forego the possible profits which might be obtained from renovations.

An **agent** representing a seller has a duty to make a full and complete disclosure of all material facts which might influence the seller. According to *Fisher v. Losey*, 78 C.A. 2d 121, that includes "the price that can be obtained, the possibility of a sale at a higher price, dealing with the property in another fashion..." Bruss says the agent did his duty in this case and that the seller got top dollar for the property considering its condition. Bruss's profit stemmed from his general contracting of the renovation rather than his getting a bargain purchase.

Tax ramifications

Bruss kept this property and lease optioned it as he often does. He could begin depreciating it when the house was ready to be rented. Bruss's **basis** is the sum of:

- $216,000 purchase price
- $4,000 (approx.) in closing costs
- $62,000 (approx.) in fix up costs
- construction period interest.

The fix-up costs were 100% depreciable because they are 100% attributable to the improvements. The other basis items must be allocated to land and depreciable improvements.

Replacement cost

To do that, Bruss will ask his insurance agent for the **replacement cost** of the improvements. That's one of the main methods I advocate in my book, *Aggressive Tax Avoidance for Real Estate Investors*. Furthermore, Bruss says he was audited by IRS a couple years ago and the auditor **liked** the insurance-agent-replacement-cost-estimate approach.

Many investors would use the tax assessor's breakdown. In this case, that would give the absurd result of saying that Bruss got a three-bedroom, two-bath house built for $62,000—on a lot worth $215,000.

The ultimate depreciation schedule ought to have a **personal property** component for the appliances, drapes, and carpet; a **land** component; a **land improvements** component; and a **structure** component. The personal property basis would be simply the cost of the appliances. The closing costs, fix up costs, purchase price, and construction period interest would be allocated into the land, land improvement, and structure categories.

Lessons learned

Bruss regrets that he did not follow the "unfit-for-human-occupancy" notices filed in building inspectors' offices in the cities near where he lives. Had he known that the owners of this property had a new and compelling reason to sell then he probably would have tracked them down on his own. Presumably, he could have split the $12,960 commission savings with the sellers.

He does **not** regret telling that agent and others of his interest in such properties. Doing so enabled him to be the first buyer to make an offer on this property and that was crucial to making the $68,000 or so profit.

How it works

Local boards of health have the power to declare buildings unfit for human occupancy. That is an emergency power which can be employed without hearings or other delaying procedures. Occupants of the building must leave immediately regardless of almost any other circumstances.

Although they do not need to hold preliminary hearings, the health officers must give public notice of what they have done. That's done on the property in question and in the public records of the government entity the health officer works for.

Why it works

Condemnation puts almost instantaneous pressure on the property owner to sell. That's because carrying costs like mortgage payments and property taxes continue after the occupants are forced out of the building, but all benefit of owning the building like using it or collecting rent abruptly stops. Condemned buildings also constitute a public nuisance. So the government will not only tell you to abandon the building, they will insist that you repair or demolish it.

Relatively few people are competent to accurately estimate the cost of repairing the extreme conditions found in condemned buildings. As a result, most people tend to overestimate. That creates an opportunity for an investor who **can** accurately estimate the cost.

The combination of extreme pressure from the government to stop using and abate the nuisance the building represents and the overreaction of the market to the imagined repair cost often allow the investor to buy the property cheap enough to make an adequate profit after repairs.

Incidence of this opportunity

I am not aware of any statistics on condemned properties. An average of 362,907 housing units were demolished per year in the seventies. Those do not all represent opportunities to make a profit by repairing the house. Many were condemned to make way for roads and such. Those need to be moved rather than repaired.

Condemned properties are sometimes created en masse by natural or manmade disasters like hurricanes, earthquakes, riots, and floods. You need to be careful about trying to make a buck of disasters, though. There is tremendously increased media attention and there is a bias against "profiteers" and such. Ethically, there is nothing wrong with offering to buy a condemned property for cash. But many regard it as unseemly especially in the aftermath of a disaster.

Because condemned properties are relatively rare, you probably cannot make a living just doing condemned properties. You'd have to cover a wide geographic area to get more than a few properties per year this way. Rather this would be one of several approaches you follow.

How to find them

Call your local or county government and find out who does the condemning of properties. Then call that agency and ask what public notice they give of their condemnations. You then need to check those public notices at appropriate intervals. How often will depend on how convenient it is for you to check and how many condemned properties there are per year in your area. It's possible the convenience can be greatly increased by just telephoning the agency periodically.

Kill ratio

I don't know of anyone who does enough of these to have discerned a kill rate. But I can say that persistence and contacting as many possible sellers as possible appear to be necessary for success.

Special expertise required

Repairing condemned properties requires general contracting skills. That is, you need to know how to get repairs done on time and on budget.

Full-time or part-time possible

You almost have no choice. This is a part-time opportunity in the sense that there are not that many condemned properties. On the other hand, as Bob Bruss's deal illustrates, you need to move quickly when you get a bite or you'll lose the deal. That implies you need to be able to respond on a full-time basis. So the answer to the full- or part-time question is yes and no. Actually doing the deals will only consume part of your time. But you'd better be available full time to pounce on them. I am an example of a person who could do this. I work at home as a self-employed writer. I could switch focus to the condemned properties when needed and go back to writing when there were no condemned properties to work on.

Regional variations

Aside from whether a disaster has hit, the only regional variations would stem from variations in the diligence and standards of the various health inspectors. Some are strict and/or work hard. Others are lenient and/or lazy. In lenient/lazy jurisdictions, there will be fewer condemned properties.

Environmental liability considerations

There are two environmental issues with condemned properties:

• Do you have enough time to make an adequate inspection?
• Asbestos-containing building materials affect demolition and renovation.

As Bruss's deal shows, you often have to act quickly to avoid losing the deal to someone else. But haste can make waste in the sense of overlooking environmental problems. Try to sew up the deal quickly, but put a contingency clause in the agreement allowing you to have the property inspected for environmental hazards. If the seller won't agree to such a clause, think twice about proceeding with the deal. The seller may have environmental problems that he or she is deliberately trying to foist off on you.

Demolition and renovation have predictable costs. But those costs are now dramatically higher when the property contains asbestos-containing building materials. Asbestos is indestructible. It generally cannot be disturbed without extraordinary precautions and care. And as you would expect, those precautions and care increase the cost.

Even rubble can contain asbestos. When it does, it must be disposed of in a special, high-cost manner. Furthermore, you never stop owning asbestos. It continues to be your property in the dump. And if, for some reason, it has to be relocated in the future, you're liable.

Make sure you inspect for the presence of asbestos-containing building materials before you buy a condemned property. If asbestos is present, make sure you accurately estimate the cost of disturbing and disposing of it.

Need for secrecy

Every technique in this book tells you about a very good deal. The world is full of people who want very good deals. Some of the techniques do not require much secrecy because the expertise required to use that particular technique is extremely rare. That is **not** the case with condemned properties. **Many** people can accurately estimate the cost of renovating a condemned property. So you have to act quickly and keep the deal as secret as you can. Bruss almost lost his deal when another investor found out about it.

Tornado-damaged apartment house

In 1974, a tornado hit a wealthy area of Louisville. One severely damaged property was a six-unit apartment building. It had lost its roof—and, as a result, its tenants.

Probate property

The property was also part of an estate at the time. Probates, like severe damage, often create bargain opportunities. In this case, Louisville, KY investor George Davidson (502-896-9068) found two bargain causers in one deal.

High class building

Each apartment in the damaged building had 2,000 square feet, two bathrooms, plaster walls, fireplace, and hardwood floors. The previous owner had put in new kitchens not long before the tornado. Under the building was an enclosed garage for six cars.

Partly finished roof

The estate had replaced the flat roof frame and deck. But they had not completed the job with built-up tar and gravel to make it waterproof.

The building still contained the furniture of the tenants who lived there when the tornado hit. Because of water damage, the furniture was reduced to trash which had to be removed. The walls and floors were severely water damaged by the rains which fell after the roof was destroyed. A general contractor bid over $100,000 to do the rest of the repairs for the estate.

Davidson was able to buy the property from the estate, as is, for $15,000 in 1975. That's $15,000 **total—not** $15,000 per unit.

Refinanced $35,000 out

He then installed new windows and some sheet rock, refinished all the floors, and painted. The repairs cost about $20,000 giving Davidson a total cost of about $35,000.

When he was done nine months later, he figured the building was worth about $125,000. He refinanced by getting a new $35,000 first mortgage, thereby extracting all the money he had put into the property.

He eventually sold the property for $183,000 after commission in 1980. Actually, he delayed exchanged out of it.

From 1975 to 1980, this six-unit, tornado-damaged building was his main source of cash flow and equity for other projects.

Fire and tornado damage

While driving through the neighborhood where he lived in 1975, Davidson spotted a burned-out, boarded-up, five-unit apartment building. This was not a look-for-property drive around—just his normal coming and going.

The property had a **furnace fire** which damaged several apartments. The property also had some tornado damage which was unrelated to the fire. The worst damage came from just sitting unoccupied for a year with no heat or water. No pipes had burst. But apartment interiors are not designed to be exposed to the extreme temperatures of the Louisville climate.

$2,000 a unit

Davidson tracked down the owner and agreed to buy the property for $10,000. That also is the **total—not** $10,000 per unit. The financing was $2,000 down and an $8,000 first mortgage taken back by the seller.

More than tripled his money

Davidson spent $5,000 total fixing the property up. He acted as his own general contractor. When he was done about nine months later, he figured the property was worth about $50,000.

He got a new first mortgage of $25,000 which enabled him to pay off the $8,000 seller first mortgage and put $17,000 cash in his pocket.

In November of this year, Davidson had paid off the mortgage on that property entirely. He now owns it free and clear.

Six-plex from same owner

The same owner also owned a boarded-up six-plex. There had not been a fire or anything. It just was not up to the housing code and had been declared uninhabitable by the local board of health.

The owner was too busy in his other business to fix it. Davidson bought it for $20,000; $2,000 down. The seller took back $18,000. Davidson spent about $9,000 fixing it up. He sold it for $40,000 less than a year after he bought it.

Another fire-damaged building

In 1978, Davidson bought yet another fire-damaged building. This property happened to be a duplex on the street behind the probate/tornado-damaged building. Davidson noticed it while working on the tornado building.

It had been boarded up for two years because of an appliance fire. Davidson looked up the owner in the tax assessor records. Turned out the owner lived just three doors from the building in question. He was not ready to sell at first but Davidson kept in touch over a year and finally got it for $15,000.

This property was a gut rehab and then some. Davidson held it boarded up himself for about two years then spent $20,000 repairing it. He figured it was worth about $65,000 when he finished it. He sold it in 1984 for $75,000.

20

Delinquent tax auction

How it works

About 5% of the properties offered at delinquent property tax auctions sell for 50% of market value or less.

When you don't pay your property taxes, the government auctions off your property in many states. That's a forced-sale auction. As with all other forced-sale auctions, you and the public receive notice of the auction in advance. You are given a certain time period in which to bring your account current. If you don't, they auction off your property.

As a general rule, the only properties that get auctioned off for non-payment of property taxes are those which have **no mortgage** on them. That's because any lender on the property will usually pay the property taxes when they receive notice of the delinquency to protect their interest.

As with other forced-sale auctions, you can buy the property from the owner before the sale, or at the auction, or after the auction from the winning bidder.

Regional variations

In many states, they do not auction properties off for non-payment of property taxes. Some states auction **tax certificates**—a sort of interest-bearing account receivable secured by the property. Other states auction off tenant-in-common interests to the bidder who is willing to pay the back taxes for the lowest percentage of ownership. That's an intriguing way to buy partial interests, the subject of another chapter in this book.

Actual case histories

Talking to real estate author and investor Ron Starr one day, I asked him, "What was your greatest hit as an investor?"

2021 Sonoma Way

2021 Sonoma Way, Oakland, California was a 4-bedroom-and-den house which Starr bought for $275 in 1981. Starr figured the fair market value was $20,000 to $25,000 at the time.

Starr learned about the property from notices of pending delinquent tax sales. Call the tax assessor in your area to find out how to get the list of properties to be auctioned. The auctions are held annually or semi-annually in most areas. Starr contacted the owner who turned out to be what the seminar gurus used to call a "don't wanter."

The owner had bought it as a fixer upper. But it was in a very bad neighborhood. He tried to fix it up. One improvement he made was installing new aluminum windows. They were all stolen within 24 hours. While he worked in the house, passers by would throw large bags of trash into his pick up. He was disgusted with the property and had stopped paying the property taxes.

Tough negotiation

The owner said, yes, he'd be willing to sell it and asked Starr and his partner to make him an offer. Starr thought $800 would be good. The partner said, "Why not $200?" Starr couldn't think of a reason why not so they offered $200. The seller countered at $300.

They compromised by splitting the difference and settled on $250. But, they did not put it in writing.

One of the common occurrences in bargain purchases is third parties find out about your deal before it's consummated and try to either steal it or kill it. In this case, the seller mentioned it to a friend who said, "Hey, I'll give you $275." The seller agreed. But the buyer backed out after he saw the property.

Unfortunately, the seller was now attached to the $275 figure. Starr and his partner said OK to $275 and the deal was done at that price.

Let it go to tax sale

Starr and his partner planned all along to let the property go to tax sale. They were not trying to save it from tax sale or do anything with it. They just wanted to be the owners when it went to tax sale figuring it would sell for more than the taxes owed and they would receive the excess proceeds as the new owners.

The tax sale was held but nobody bid on 2021 Sonoma Way. That meant Starr and his partner still owned it.

HUD-style boarding up

They decided to board the house up rather than renovate it. Starr had seen some HUD houses and was impressed with the way they boarded them up.

The plywood is cut to fit the window frames. It is attached to the house by carriage bolts which go through the plywood and through a sturdy post on the inside of the window frame. The nut is on the inside. On the outside, only the round, unslotted head of the carriage bolt shows. Starr and his partner did a HUD-style boarding-up job, painted an outbuilding on the property, and replaced one siding board.

Marketing

They then advertised the property for sale in the paper. A buyer was found at a price of $14,500. But the deal fell through. No other buyers came forth.

Starr then tried to list the property for sale with an Oakland broker who specialized in selling junky properties. But the broker didn't want a listing **that** junky.

'Tax Collector Realty, Inc.'

So they ended up "listing" the property with another big seller of junk: the county tax collector. The county tax collector does not take listings *per se*. But he does sell your property for you if you don't pay the property taxes for an extended period of time. Starr and partner never paid.

After four more years, the tax collector finally sold it.

Bought by City of Oakland

State law in California gives any taxing entity the right to buy delinquent-tax properties for the minimum bid **before** the public auction. That's a blatant screwing of the property owner to the tune of the difference between the minimum bid and what a higher bidder would have bid at the public auction. Government has its privileges.

The tax assessor set the market value at $25,000. At that time, California law said the minimum bid had to be 50% of the market value or, in this case, 50% x $25,000 = $12,500. And that's what the City of Oakland paid for it.

Why did they buy it? Starr does not know. All he **does** know is that they tore down the buildings that were on the parcel and did nothing further with it. Your tax dollars at work.

Excess proceeds

At that time, the delinquent property taxes had accrued to $3,069.27. Oakland's $12,500 paid that $3,069.27 and the remaining $12,500 - $3,069.27 = $9,430.73 went to Starr and his partner as excess proceeds.

1% of market value

If the assessor was correct and the property had a fair market value of $25,000, Starr and his partner got it for $275 ÷ $25,000 = 1.1% of market value. If you figure that the $9,430.73 excess proceeds was the market value, they got it for $275 ÷ $9,403.73 = 2.92% of market value.

Spectacular as it is, that one deal would be hard to live on. So pursue pre-tax auction properties as part of other investment efforts.

Returned to sender

A significant percentage of the tax bills which have not been paid are returned to the tax collector by the post office. To find those owners, you may have to resort to the techniques in the "Owner unknown" chapter. Then on the other hand, the U.S. Postal Service has been known to return as undeliverable mail which is correctly addressed to a person who has not moved.

Rights of redemption

If the state in question gives the delinquent owner and/or others with interests in the property a **post**-auction **redemption period**, then you can buy the property from them **after** the auction as well—at least until the redemption period expires.

Mostly vacant land

Starr has been to dozens of tax auctions and says fewer than 10% of the properties offered have buildings on them. And those are frequently ramshackle.

Mortgages and most other liens are **junior** to property tax liens and are therefore wiped out by property tax auctions. (If the buyer at auction is the delinquent taxpayer himself—or his agent—the junior liens are reinstated in California and most other states.) Some liens like government agency liens may **not** be wiped out by property tax sales. You need to learn the rules in your area. IRS liens are wiped out if the IRS does not redeem the property within 120 days. If IRS **does** redeem the property, you as the investor who bought at the tax auction only get what you paid plus 6% annual interest.

Few people who own a house with, say, $100,000 equity are going to lose that equity for the want of several thousand dollars in property taxes. Although I must add that virtually everything can and does happen at forced sales. There have been people who lost valuable homes at tax auctions.

Junk land at that

Not only is much of the property offered at tax sales land, it is **junk** land—about a third of the time in Starr's experience. That is, it is **useless**. You can't build on it because it's too small, too steep, too wet, too rocky, too inaccessible, or too something. Delinquent tax auctions are real estate's equivalent of an unclaimed property sale. People usually let properties go to tax sale because they don't want them or forgot they owned them—not the sort of behavior one associates with prime, or even ordinary, land.

Deceased/moved owners

A third of the properties are owned by heirs who either don't know about the property or don't care about it. Another final third are owned by people who have moved and did not get the bill. Not getting the bills does not relieve you of paying them. You're supposed to know when taxes are due and make inquiry if you don't get a bill.

Size of the bargains

The best California property tax-**auction** bargain I've heard of was 21% of market value. (Starr's 1.1% deal was bought **before** the auction.) Better bargains have been obtained in other states. Twenty-five to fifty percent is par for selective professional tax auction buyers in California. When you are dealing with bargain purchases, 80% of market or less is generally adequate. But because of the illiquid nature of **land**, the difficulty of appraising it, and the many uncertainties associated with it, professional tax auction buyers generally insist on paying no more than about 50% market value.

Prices

As you would expect, "unclaimed," free-and-clear properties generally are not high in value. Opening bids typically range from $50 to $50,000 with sale prices most commonly under $10,000. So this is a game you can play with relatively little cash compared to most other real estate deals. Unfortunately, real estate available at less than $1,000 attracts dozens of incompetent bidders. As a result, you generally cannot buy any bargains below about $3,000 at auction.

Plus there is a certain amount of due diligence you must do before you buy any real estate. And you cannot **afford** to do much due diligence—even on a property you're getting for 25¢ on the dollar—if its market value is less than $4,000.

Minimum bids

Your state or local law may require certain **minimum** bids. In California, the state law says the minimum bid should be at least 25% of fair market value as determined by the assessor. Some counties, like Alameda, set their minimum bids at **50%** of the assessor's opinion of market value. In other states, there may be no minimum bid or the minimum bid may be the amount of taxes owed.

Assessors vary greatly in their competence, conscientiousness, and time available. So their opinion of value may be quite accurate or wildly **in**accurate—in either direction. The fact that many properties do not sell at auction prices which are supposedly one half or one fourth of market value proves that the assessor's opinion of value is often much too high. In California, the winning bidder also has to pay **transfer tax**. There may be such a tax or other additional costs in other jurisdictions.

Price layers

It appears to me that there are three layers of tax sale prices. At each layer, you get different bidder behavior as follows:

- $10 to $3,000 — Attack of the bargain-killer bees, worthless properties bid up to several thousand dollars over assessor's opinion of market value
- $3K to $10K — Too much for bargain-killers, some bargains available
- Over $10,000 — Hardly any bidders, but often overpriced

So the tax sale action is primarily in the $3,000 to $10,000 range. There are exceptions to that rule. One exception is that you can often buy the $10 to $3,000 parcels from their owners **before** the tax sale for $500 or less. Then you just let them go to tax sale and file a claim for excess proceeds if they sell for more than the taxes owed and other liens.

Rural and inner-city

As is often the case with bargain-purchase techniques, the incidence of bargains in tax auctions seems to be inversely proportional to the distance from the suburbs of a major metropolitan area. I attended the May 29, 1991 Alameda County, CA (Oakland) delinquent tax auction with *Distress Sales Report* editor John Beck and twelve of his mini-"boot camp" attendees. He schedules his boot camps so they can prepare for and attend an actual auction. By the time this one took place, he and his well-trained "boots" wanted nothing to do with **any** of the properties being auctioned. All the decent ones they were interested in were redeemed (the delinquent taxes paid off) before the auction. So they just came to observe.

By reading court records of a lawsuit involving one property, they learned it was contaminated with toxics. Having read the Kenneth Groves story (the guy who bought a chromium-contaminated street car barn) as part of their course, they were quite interested to see if anyone would buy the contaminated property. No one did.

In contrast, Starr bid on three properties at a Yuba County, CA tax auction and got two bargains. Yuba County has a population of about 55,000 and is north of Sacramento.

In spite of its seeming simplicity, land is a much trickier real estate investment than improved property. That's true in urban areas and it's especially true in rural areas. I strongly recommend that you read Les Scher's *Finding and Buying Your Place in the Country* (Collier Books) for background on the nuances of rural land.

Ambience

I am sometimes too clinical and abstract in describing real estate techniques. There is an ambience to each technique. And, when you're actually pursuing the deal, the ambience pervades your life. There's more to life to profit. You need to take note of the world around you as you go. In the delinquent tax auction business, your life consists of:

- reading legal newspapers or property lists from the tax collector
- eleventh-hour title, zoning, contamination and other searches in government offices
- motel stays
- 4-wheel-drive exploration of remote areas accessible only by dirt roads as you try to figure out the location of parcels without street addresses on maps which often show nonexistent streets (watch out for armed and dangerous marijuana farmers)
- rural detective work trying to track down owners
- negotiations with owners you find
- a tension-filled hour or two in an auction room where all your preparation suddenly produces either a seemingly bargain purchase (Hooray!) or the disappointment of hearing the bidding exceed your limit (Bummer).

The sale itself

I'm a forced-sale auction "veteran." (One anyway. Paul Thompson took me to a foreclosure auction.) So I did not find much new to observe at the Alameda County tax auction. There were more people—probably over a hundred. That's because some properties were offered for as little as $50. At the **foreclosure** auction, only those with at least $100,000 or so in cashier's checks in their pocket could bid. That tends to keep out the riff raff.

The 1990 foreclosure auction was attended entirely by what appeared to be business people. I said they looked like off-duty Rotarians. In contrast, the Alameda tax auction seemed to be attended by a mostly working-class crowd. There were also some who looked like working class would be a step **up**. Several mothers brought young children who had trouble keeping quiet. Some observers and participants were shabbily dressed and unshaven. There was an armed, uniformed sheriff's deputy with a two-way radio present the whole time.

Procedures differ from county to county and state to state. So you need to check with the tax collector where you are bidding. In Alameda County, you had to qualify to bid by putting up a cash or cashier's check deposit of $500 with the tax collector's office and filling out a form by noon of the auction day. Apparently, about 40 of the more than 100 present had done that. Qualified bidders were given 8 1/2 x 11 cards with a number printed on them for bidding.

The tax collector was the auctioneer. He started by reading an official description of the auction. Then he read disclaimers including ominously intoning the words, "Buyer beware!"

Finally, he announced the properties one by one. He stated the parcel number, address, and minimum bid, then asked for bids. Bidders raised their numbered card. The collector had stated a minimum bid increment of $100 and he simply added that amount to the last bid whenever someone raised a card—unless the bidder verbally gave a higher number. At times, several bidders simply put their cards up and held them there as the bidding spiraled up. The auctioneer would then arbitrarily assign the various bids sequentially to those who had their cards up. As in, "$4,600 from number 28. Number six bids $4,700." One man became confused and bid twice in succession. The tax collector corrected him saying, "You don't want to bid against yourself."

What do they know that I don't?

I have to warn you about one phenomenon which is spooky in its ability to mess up your mind. The other bidders look very wise as they thoughtfully ponder whether to go higher. They have seemingly intelligent whispered conversations with colleagues before they bid.

What does it mean? What do they know that I don't? I don't know if Shakespeare ever went to a tax auction. But his words describing "a poor player" in Macbeth fit most of the bidders and their cogitations and consultations to a T.

> ...a poor player
> *That struts and frets his hour upon the stage*
> *And then is heard no more: it is a tale*
> *Told by an idiot, full of sound and fury,*
> *Signifying nothing.*

As I listened to the bidding and watched, I reminded myself that they were bidding on properties which Beck and his boots had summarily rejected as having little or no equity. Because many of the bidders looked like they knew what they were doing, I turned to Beck, who was sitting next to me for reconfirmation, "These bidders are idiots, right?" He said, "Yes," and assured me that the properties they were bidding on were either bad deals or were too likely to be bad deals for anyone to spend the time it would take to find out otherwise.

Discipline

The actions and words of the other bidders in an auction are a bit of a siren song. Calculating as I believe I am, I still found myself needing reaffirmation because of the sight and sound of the other bidders. I had not come to this auction prepared to bid and never even gave it a thought while I was there. Had I come to bid I would have followed the standard advice to **write down my maximum in advance** and **drop out when the bidding exceeded it**. Seems to me that you simply join in the bidding for any property which has not yet exceeded your maximum and you drop out when the max is exceeded. Period. There is nothing to discuss or cogitate about.

I **did** attend and bid at another "auction" of sorts. It was the annual draft for my son's Little League. My co-coach and I rated all the available players at the tryout, put the ratings into the computer, sorted them by their overall score, and took the rankings to the draft. You may think that's pretty sophisticated for 9- and 10-year old Little League. I thought it was, too—until I got to the draft and saw that every other team had their computer rankings on **14-inch-wide** computer paper. Mine was just 8 1/2 x 11.

Anyway, we just picked the highest ranking boy who was not yet taken. The other teams would consult and discuss for minutes when it was their turn. We simply called off a player name as soon as our team name was called. If all the other teams had done likewise, the draft would have lasted less than a half hour instead of several hours. In subsequent competition against those teams we have won eight games, lost four, and tied three, so it would appear there was no benefit to agonizing over your selection.

Have a plan and stick to it like a robot. Bid on any property with equity which is available below your maximum. When the bidding exceeds your maximum, drop out and forget about it. The auction is the **last** place you want to start reconsidering your preset maximum bid.

Post-mortem interviews

I did not conduct any post-mortem interviews with the "successful" bidders. One reason was I do not suffer fools gladly. Another was that Starr and Beck have interviewed them at many auctions and gotten the same mindless responses. In general, the "successful" bidders believe you can't go wrong with real estate, that the amount they've invested is so small they won't mind losing it, property in that area sells for $X, that they're going to build on it, etc.

Typically, they have done little or no research on the property. They often consult assessor's maps for the first time **after** the sale to see what they bought. They haven't a clue as to zoning and so forth. They don't know values of similar properties, rather they are vaguely familiar with the single-family house values in the area in question. They are typically unaware that there **is** such a thing as useless, worthless real estate—much less that they just became the owner of some of it.

Beck and Starr tell of one guy they run into at lots of tax sales. He specializes in small parcels. Indeed, he bought a 1/6 interest in a 20 foot by 20 foot parcel for $275. That's $275 ÷ (20x20) = $275 ÷ 400 = $.688/sq. ft. or 43,264 sq. ft. per acre x $.688/sq. ft = $29,765.63 per acre. The guy is reasonably well dressed and well-spoken. He does not seem to need incarceration in a mental institution. Nevertheless, this sort of "investment" is certifiable. When asked why he buys such property he said, "It is like going to an orchard that you own and sometimes ripe fruit just falls into your hand."

Uh huh. I'd be tempted to add, "Yes, and if you gather enough of these fruits you can bake them into a cake that you won't be able to eat because of laws against cannibalism."

Incidence of tax auction properties

An average of 2,730 properties per year were offered at tax auctions in California in the late '80s according to Starr. That is similar to the number of foreclosures which are bought by **investors** in California. (Lenders buy far more foreclosures because no one else bids on them.) Since California's population is about 30,000,000, the ratio of tax sale properties to population sounds like about 2,730 ÷ 30,000,000 = 1/10,000. Although California has a higher percentage of government-owned land than most other states, so other investors may find more properties available through tax auctions than one for every 10,000 people.

And remember that fewer than 10% of the tax auction properties offered are worthwhile deals.

Financing

Tax collectors' policies range from cash or cashier's check on the barrelhead to "personal checks OK" to 10% down and up to 90 days to pay the rest in California. Check your local authorities for the requirements in your area. In general, the tax auction business is a cash business. Although Oregon even takes back long-term land contracts.

Title insurance

Check with your local title insurance companies to see what, if anything, they are willing to do on tax auction properties. In California, they generally will not insure title until at least one year after you record the deed. The California statute of limitations on the previous owner filing suit to overturn the sale is one year. Other states may have longer statutes of limitations. If you cannot wait until the end of the statute of limitations, you can try to render the title insurable sooner by filing a **quiet title** lawsuit.

Another case history

At the 1987 Yuba County, CA tax sale, Starr bought a multifamily lot in Linda, CA for $8,050. The flat lot was 60' x 212', on a cul de sac, and had all utilities in the street. The lot next door contained a "decent-looking fourplex" and a veterinary clinic was being built on a nearby parcel. There was a junior college one block away and the entrance Beale Air Force Base was two miles away. The minimum bid was set at $4,500 indicating the tax assessor thought the market value of the parcel was 4 x $4,500 = $18,000. Starr's research found the property had been sold six years before for $26,000. Within a year, Starr traded that lot and another he had bought at a different tax sale for $2,150, for four houses worth about $160,000 ($30,000 equity above the $130,000 in mortgages). Two months later, he sold two of those houses for $10,200 cash. That leaves him with nothing in the deal and still owning the other two houses that had about $15,000 equity. He still owns them.

At that Yuba County auction he also bought 20 rolling acres for the minimum bid of $10,000. That indicated the assessor thought it was worth $10,000 x 4 = $40,000.

Counting transfer taxes, Starr paid a total of $18,070.35 for properties which he figured had fair market value of $60,000 to $80,000. His total time invested was four days so he made at least $10,000 per day.

For more information:
John Beck's Forced Sale Workbook
2200 Central Avenue
Alameda, CA 94501
510-523-6115

Buying Real Estate Superbargains at California Tax Sales by Ronald Starr
Unlimited Golden Opportunities Press
P.O. Box 27218
Oakland, CA 94602
510-534-6472

In January of 1990, Starr passed up the chance to bet on one real estate horse. A lot and ramshackle house in a poor part of Sacramento were going to tax auction. The owner agreed to sell both to Starr for $500. He passed, figuring the chances of excess proceeds were slim.

One of the two properties did indeed sell for **less** than the taxes owed. So that property would have been a total loss. But the other sold for about $5,000 **more** than the taxes owed. That $5,000 in excess proceeds would have gone to Starr had he bought the two properties for $500. If the auction had taken place in a state where there was a right of redemption (there's not in California), he could have tried to buy the properties **after** the auction **knowing** whether the redemption price was below market.

Ethical considerations when buying

At the auction, there should be no ethical questions. Just refrain from bid chilling. **Before** the auction, you need to refrain from misleading the seller as to the value of their property. You must also refrain from misleading them about the fact that they could get excess sales proceeds if the property is allowed to go to sale.

Sequence

Auctions are frequently postponed or cancelled. So you cannot afford to spend any time checking out the property until the last minute.

Need for secrecy

When you're buying **pre**-auction, you need to keep your deal secret and tie it up in writing as soon as possible. Starr almost lost one deal because he didn't. Auctions are public so you can't control secrecy there.

Unique risks

Some liens stay on the property when it's sold at tax auction. You need to learn the law of IRS liens and your state law on other liens.

You cannot inspect the property without the owner's permission. He or she may give it. But they are not required to. Inspecting without permission is criminal trespassing. You can do a **windshield** appraisal. But that's hardly the kind of due diligence that is required to avoid environmental problems.

Auctions are seductive. You need to be impervious to the behavior of the other bidders in the room. If you get caught up in auction fever, you'd better stay away.

Ponderosa syndrome

In an episode of *Bonanza*, Hoss was escorting a man to the Ponderosa on horseback. The man asked, "How long till we get to the Ponderosa, Hoss?" "We've been on it for the last two days," said Hoss.

Many people are enamored of such empires and have a compulsion to own land—even if it's just a **little** land.

Slivers, vertical land, etc.

John Beck often writes about buyers who buy useless parcels of land at tax sales. For example, he tells of a parcel that sold for $4,000 at a tax sale. According to the assessor's records, the parcel's "use code" was 003 which means "*vacant residential lot---totally unusable (incurable)*."

In March of 1989, Ron Starr and a partner (who spotted the deal) bought a 25-foot-wide useless parcel on a steep hill in Alameda County, California (Oakland area). They paid $500 the day before it was scheduled to be sold by the county for nonpayment of taxes. They let it be sold at the tax auction and it went for **$4,600**. After the back taxes and costs were deducted, they got $2,139.89.

At that same auction, Starr saw two other lots sell for $20,000 each. Those lots were useless because their soil was unstable. A house on one had previously been demolished by a slide.

This does not always work, however. Starr bought two to-be-auctioned lots in El Dorado County, CA (South Lake Tahoe area) for a total of $880. They ended up selling for less than the taxes owed so Starr got nothing for his $880. (Western Land Bank, which is discussed below, bought one and resold it, price unknown.)

10' x 150' lot

Several years ago, an acquaintance of Starr's bought a 10 foot by 150 foot sliver (It was created by a surveyor's error.) in Mill Valley, CA, an expensive suburb of San Francisco. He paid about $800 then resold it for about $3,000 all cash through a classified ad.

In another deal Starr witnessed, a man bought two Oakland lots on an earthquake fault for $1,000. He did not pay the property taxes thereby deliberately letting them go to sale at the tax auction. He received excess auction proceeds of about $21,000 seventeen months later.

These parcels are unsuitable to build on. But the compulsion to own land—and the notion that "you can't go wrong with real estate"—cause some to buy anyway.

Real estate can be useless because it's too small or the terrain is unbuildable or it's in a floodplain or odd shaped or lacks access, etc. Since it's useless, you'd think it's worthless—or at least that's the **logical** conclusion.

Too-small or odd-shaped parcels generally came about in the days before zoning (which arrived in the 1920's) or through surveyor error or as a result of the building of roads or other eminent domain proceedings. You can spot them on tax maps.

Cost, $500; resale price, $2,000

It appears that metropolitan-area, non-slum real estate doesn't sell, when advertised to the public, for less than about $2,000—**no matter how useless it is**. So if you can buy it before the public knows about it for, say, $500, you can probably sell it at a profit.

You can often buy useless property for $200 to $500. The typical seller is someone who finally realizes the property is useless and that its usefulness isn't going to improve. You are alerted to this fact when the property is listed as being in arrears on its property taxes.

The market for these properties is extremely thin. That's why you get a bargain. Two hundred dollars seems to be the minimum amount that's large enough to get the owner to go to the trouble of deeding it to you before the auction.

Now how do you resell it for $2,000 or more? A **classified ad** has worked for some. If you had a bunch of these properties, you might prepare a **catalog** with a title like "Own a lot in the Bay Area for less than $5,000." Offer the catalog in ads.

Western Land Bank

Peter Bogart and his wife Punty are apparently doing quite well with a variation of this approach. Roughly speaking, it appears they gross about $2,000,000 a year on the sale of about 650 properties. The minimum bids printed in their catalog appear to be more than they paid for the property.

According to Beck, the Bogarts frequently buy property at tax auctions, then hire an auctioneer and hold their own well-advertised, resale auctions in Los Angeles area hotels. The ads carry the name Western Land Bank. Beck says Punty Bogart bid on virtually every property at the August 31, 1989 Sonoma County, California tax auction, buying ten properties out of the 25 offered. Although their ad in the 4/10/89 *Daily Commerce* said "liquidation at 50%-60%-70% even 90% below market," she paid 128% to 322% of the assessor's fair market value estimate on nine properties and got one for 85% of assessor's appraisal. Beck says the Bogarts "can afford to pay 'crazy' prices because they can resell the same properties at even 'crazier' prices."

If you buy these properties from the owner **before** the auction, you should kiss the Bogarts for bidding up the sale prices and thereby, the excess proceeds you'll receive. However, if you buy **from** the Bogarts or bid **against** them at auction, kissing may not be what comes to mind.

"Natural growth abounds"

A reliable source says Western Land Bank described one of their properties with the phrase, "natural growth abounds." He visited the property in question and says that while "natural growth abounds" was certainly an accurate description, most people would simply call the property a marsh—or to use one of the most terrifyng words a real estate investor can hear these days—a wetland.

The Western Land Bank offers 6% seller financing and fills its ads with bargain-connoting words like "foreclosures, tax deeds, R.E.O.s, probates, estates, bankruptcies, liquidation, depression priced." I surmise they feel it's appropriate to use those words on the grounds that that's where **they** got the properties. However, some buyers may be confused into thinking the Western Land Bank auction is an event where you can buy R.E.O.s **direct** from the lender or probates **direct** from the estate, etc.

Let it go to tax auction

You might "market" the property through the county tax sale auction if the pertinent state law requires that excess proceeds be paid to the owner. Unlike private auctioneers, the county often charges little or nothing for this service. In California, the charge is $186.50. This let-it-go-to-tax-auction sale method is also the only one I know of where you don't have to sign a contract, get title searched, prepare a deed, etc. Check local law and observe several tax auctions before you assume you can profitably do this in your area.

According to Beck, every one of the twenty-five properties sold at the 8/31/89 Sonoma County auction produced excess proceeds. The excess proceeds ranged from $441.88 to $40,754.04. The average excess proceeds was $8,182.24. Had you bought **all** the properties **before** the auction for an average purchase price of, say, $1,000, you'd have made $8,182.24 - $1,000 = $7,182.24 x 25 = $179,556.

Environmental audit

You should not buy real estate without making sure it's not contaminated. Such audits cost from $500 to $30,000. In general, you cannot afford such audits on useless properties. But you'd better at least do a self-help, on-site inspection.

Another advantage of selling through the tax auction is that you don't have to make any of the usual disclosures, warranties, etc. However, local, state, or federal laws may require that you notify the government if you are aware of contamination. Such a sale would not absolve you of all liability. But it would at least immunize you against any **misrepresentation** charges.

Ethics when selling

There is nothing wrong with selling a property for more than its market value as long as you do **not represent or imply** that the sale price is **at or below** market. You should limit the information you provide to "just the facs, ma'am," things like the legal description, the dimensions, the assessed value. You can say, "I'll let you have the property for $10,000." But do **not** say things like, "It's worth every penny of the price I'm asking."

Don't even imply that it **can** be used. For example, describing a lot as having a **view** implies that one could put a building on it. If building is not feasible, the word "view" could be attacked as deceitful.

In my opinion, you must also give the buyer of a useless lot **fee simple** title. No oddball lesser rights like a lease-option unless the buyer is financially sophisticated.

I also would not use, in an advertisement or elsewhere, any name, word, phrase, or emblem that might cause people to think I was anything other than an individual, private seller. I would **not** use words like "R.E.O., tax deed, bankruptcy, etc." unless I made it clear that the seller was **neither** a lender or government or court or whatever—nor **representing** a lender or government or court or whatever.

Is it right to sell a product which is useless or largely useless? A vast number of common products are.

A guy made a million selling pet rocks. Surely, you are permitted to make yours selling pet lots.

And who is to decide the usefulness of the things people buy? Shall we deny the "bow wow" her bottle of Obsession? The wimp his pack of Marlboros?

The world is full of nobodies yearning to be somebodies. Owning real estate, even useless real estate, makes some people feel better about themselves—gives them a chance to drop lines like, "I own some property up in Sonoma County" into conversations. Attention must be paid to these real estate Willy Lomans as they strut and fret their hour upon the stage. Let he who is without foible cast the first stone at them and the people who sell them their props.

21

Judgment investing

How it works

Lloyd Walters bought judgments. In the typical case, A sued B in small claims court and won. Then A found out how hard it is to **collect** such a judgment and forgot about it. Walters sent A a letter offering to buy the judgment for 10¢ on the dollar. If there are any unusual problems with the judgment, he offered less.

Walters offered 10% of the **judgment amount** only. The amount that can actually be collected is **greater** than the judgment amount because of the right to get court costs and interest from the debtor.

Sometimes, A counteroffered and Walters went as high as 15¢. His cost ran from 2¢ to 15¢ on the dollar, averaging 8¢ or so. For example, he paid $50 for a $2,000 judgment in one deal.

Why it works

Obtaining judgments is easier than collecting on them. Few people have the expertise to efficiently employ collection tactics. As the years pass, they write off the debt in their minds. As a result, your offer to purchase the judgment sounds like found money when it comes.

You, on the other hand, can acquire the expertise, volume, and tools to efficiently collect 100% of the judgments you buy.

Incidence of this opportunity

The only statistics I could find on small claims courts were for California in fiscal year 1991-92. According to the Judicial Council of California of Annual Data Reference, during a twelve-month period spanning those two years, 532,644 small claims court cases were filed. 158,788 were uncontested meaning the plaintiffs won default judgments. An additional 153,691 were contested. Presumably many, if not most, of those resulted in judgments for the plaintiff as well. The statistics do not break it down. I'd guess that about 250,000 judgments came out of the California small claims courts that year. The population of California in 1991 was about 30,000,000. That suggests there is about 250,000 ÷ 30,000,000 = one small claims court judgment per year for every hundred people.

But at that time, the California limit on small claims court judgments was $2,000. It was raised to $5,000 effective January 1, 1991. Raising the limit surely increases the number of cases filed and the number that are filed in the small claims courts. So figure on a one per hundred of population ratio where the limit is around $2,500—more where it's higher.

Financing ramifications

At 8¢ on the dollar and the dollar value being in the $1,000 to $5,000 range, I assume you can pay the $80 to $400 cash required. You can also raise cash by aggressively taking action to force the debtor to pay rather than just waiting until he needs to sell or refinance.

Tax Ramifications

This would probably be an ordinary income activity under section 61(a) of the Internal Revenue Code. That very general section just says that taxable income includes,

"all income from whatever source derived including (but not limited to)...
(2) Gross income derived from business;..."

An argument could be made that pay off of the judgment is a purchase of the judgment which could make it eligible for long-term capital gains treatment. But accountant Bob Baldassari (703-698-6260) says he thinks you're unlikely to persuade IRS or the courts of that.

Kill ratio

Lloyd Walters worked Alameda County, California only. The population of Alameda County then was about 2,000,000. That would suggest an annual judgment rate in that county of .01 x 2,000,000 = 20,000. Walters said he could buy about one a day. There are about 250 business days per year. If he was contacting every single one—which is not likely—his kill ratio was 250 ÷ 20,000 = 1.25/100. I can't find him to confirm. But it would appear that his kill ratio was **better** than 1/100. That is, he had to contact fewer than 100 judgment owners for every one he bought.

Full-time or part-time possible

This can clearly be pursued on a part-time basis. As far as I know, Lloyd Walters was the only one doing it. And he stopped. He mentioned no instances of needing to hurry or losing deals because of third parties. It would be harder to do full-time unless you worked more than one heavily populated county.

Regional variations

The local limit on the amount you can seek in small claims court determines the average value of the judgments you can buy in that jurisdiction. There are also additional relevant laws regarding:

- debt collection behavior
- execution sales of assets owned by the debtor
- levying against bank accounts
- garnishing wages
- seizing business receipts
- and so forth.

These, in turn, affect how you approach a judgment investing program and its potential. In general, this will work best in high limit, relatively pro-creditor states. But it should work in all states. You simply have to use different criteria and screening procedures in low-limit or pro-debtor states. You would need to be more selective about which judgments you bought in low-limit or pro-debtor states.

Ethical considerations

As with virtually all the techniques in this book, you must refrain from misleading the judgment owner about the fair market value of his judgment or the likelihood that he or she will collect it.

Telling a judgment owner that a senior mortgage lien is being foreclosed and may wipe out his judgment lien is a tricky area. For one thing, the foreclosure only wipes out the judgment lien on that property, not the judgment itself or judgment liens on any other property owned by that debtor. For another, if the sale proceeds of the foreclosure exceed the amount sought by the foreclosing lien holder, junior lien holders are paid off in order of priority. So the 'you'll be wiped out' phrase is a half truth at best and could be fraudulent if it is not worded with the utmost care. If I were going to approach the owner of a recorded judgment that was junior to a foreclosing lender, I'd say something like the following:

> *I am willing to pay $X for the judgment you own. You may be interested to know that I found out about it by reading that a mortgage senior to your lien is being foreclosed next Tuesday.*

Actually, I would write out what I was going to say and have it approved by an attorney. Then I would read the words from that approved script like a police officer giving a suspect a Miranda warning.

It is also unethical and generally illegal to mislead the debtor as to the consequences of not paying the judgment off. Phrases like, "Your credit will be ruined," are generally exaggerations and therefore misleading and possibly a violation of both common law and state and federal statutes.

Environmental liability considerations

This is a great technique for this era of environmental liability. You get to acquire a valuable interest in real estate. But you need not worry about environmental liability because you never become the **owner** of the property.

It's possible that your interest could be wiped out by environmental problems lowering the value of the property. But they can't cost you more than the 8¢ on the dollar you paid for the judgment plus the interest that accrues since you bought it. In regular ownership, you could lose your entire net worth because one small property you bought had an environmental problem.

Need for secrecy

In general, there appears to be no need for secrecy in this technique. You might want to keep the big picture secret. But I doubt a friend of a judgment owner is going to say, "Hey, I'll buy it for 10¢ on the dollar!" when they hear of the pending sale.

Check out the debtor

If the owner of the judgment verbally agrees on the price, Walters checks out the debtor to make sure he owns real estate or other assets that can be levied against. If so, Walters completes the deal.

After Walters buys the judgment, he reports it to the TRW and CBI credit bureaus and records it against real estate owned by B, if it's not already recorded. Then he sends B a letter asking that it be paid off.

Death and bankruptcy

In the $50 example above, done when Walters first started buying judgments, he made a beginner's mistake. The debtor had **died** and the probate period of the estate had **expired**. Fortunately, however, the transfer of the real estate had not yet closed. The title company found the judgment Walters had just recorded and sent him $2,000 out of escrow within six months of his purchase.

Dead debtors and those who go **bankrupt** are the big bugaboos in this business. Walters now checks the vital statistics in the county recorder's office for death certificates before he buys the judgment. If the debtor is dead, he checks to see if the probate of the estate has been completed. If the debtor is dead and probate and disposition of the estate have been completed, Walters does **not** buy the judgment. (If the dead debtor had his assets in a **living trust** to avoid probate, you may be able to collect from the trust. The county recorder's vital statistics only cover people who died in the county.)

Walters says that bankruptcy judges generally give short shrift to such "involuntary" liens as judgments. "Voluntary" liens like trust deeds receive more money in a bankruptcy in his experience. Walters says there is little you can do to protect yourself from bankruptcy of the debtor.

Walters tries to avoid the problem by buying only judgments small enough ($10,000 or less) that they are **nuisances** to the debtor; not a debt big enough to throw the debtor into bankruptcy.

Offer to debtor

Walters makes the following offer to the debtor:

If you give me a trust deed (mortgage in eastern states) on your real estate, and agree to pay it off according to a schedule, I will cancel the judgment (by recording a satisfaction of lien) which is currently recorded against you and clear the judgment off your record at the credit bureaus.

He asks for a one-year payoff, but will take what he can get. He adds 10% per year since the judgment was entered by the court to the amount owed. That's the statutory rate at which interest accrues on judgments in California. And his installment notes call for 10% interest as well so that Walters is no worse off interest-wise than he was just holding a judgment lien.

If the debtor agrees, Walters has traded an "involuntary" lien for a "voluntary" one. Then, if the debtor goes bankrupt, Walters believes he'll probably get some of any equity the debtor has in his real estate. In addition, it is far easier to foreclose on a trust deed or mortgage than it is to force the sale of a property to satisfy a judgment lien.

Walters has never had to foreclose on a judgment or a trust deed which the debtor agreed to substitute for the judgment lien.

Unfortunately, the debtor accepts this offer only in a minority of cases.

Wait

If the debtor turns down such an offer, you could just wait. Eventually, the debtor will want to sell, refinance, or just clear their credit rating, and the new buyer or lender will almost certainly insist that the judgment be paid off.

If you could match Walters' experience of buying a judgment a day averaging $1,100 at a cost of 8¢ on the dollar, you'd buy interests in real estate worth $110,000 every 100 working days—at a cost of 8% x $110,000 = $8,800.

You'd have no management, no tenants, and no personal injury or environmental liability. You'd never have to deal with real estate agents, loan officers, or prospective purchasers. The value of your interests in real estate would **"appreciate"** at precisely **10%** per year **by law** (in CA—other states may have different interest rates. A decline in the value of the property could make it impossible to get the 10%.)

Initial cash flow

In several years, the buy-judgments-record-them-and-wait approach should produce $100,000+ in annual cash flow. But initially, cash will flow more slowly. To produce more cash flow in the early years, you could pursue the debtors more diligently.

Depending on state law and the facts of each case, you can garnish wages, force sale of property, seize rental security deposits (in the case of tenant debtors), have the sheriff confiscate their car or other personal property, seize the receipts of the debtor's business, force the debtor's own debtors to pay you money they owe him, or levy against the debtor's bank accounts.

Special expertise required

Essentially, producing initial cash flow in judgment investing is a **collection agency-**like operation. Special state and federal laws apply to debt collection. Learn them before you act.

Faster payoff

Walters experimented with buying judgment liens on properties on which a **notice of mortgage default** has been filed. He figured the judgment lien holder will be eager due to the threat of being wiped out. And if the property sells for a high enough price, Walters will be paid off quickly with no collection effort on his part.

Foreclosure is rare. Only 3% of the default notices actually lead to auction. And completed foreclosure only wipes the lien **off that property**—and then only when the high bid is inadequate to cover the judgment.

Foreclosure does **not** wipe out the judgment entirely. The debtor is **personally liable** for the judgment. It is **not** like a nonrecourse trust deed—even in California where virtually all trust deeds are the sole security for the debt.

You can leave the abstract of judgment in the county records thereby attaching a lien to any other property the debtor owns or buys in the future. You can record it in as many counties as you wish as long as you pay the recording fees. And you can still use such collection methods as levying against bank accounts or garnishing wages.

How he finds them

Walters worked with small claims and municipal court records. He did not buy judgments held by landlords against tenants (because evicted tenants rarely have assets). Most of the judgments he bought involved bad debts between friends, car accidents, and contractor or repair work that was done unsatisfactorily.

There are no data bases or printed summaries of the cases where Walters operated (Alameda County, CA). He or his assistants had to look at the case files. (There are, however, statewide data bases which can be used for **tracking down** the debtor.)

Walters conducted his business with both the owner of the judgment and the debtor almost entirely **by mail**. In spite of that, he said the one-a-day pace he achieved was very hard work.

In California, judgments are good for ten years. And they can be "revived" routinely for additional ten-year periods.

Walters never tried it, but I am intrigued by the possibility of buying judgments against former **college student** tenants. Let's say four guys rent a house. They don't pay the last several months rent and do some damage. The landlord sues and wins. But the students are judgment proof or go off to grad school or the army or whatever.

Years later, they come back as lawyers, doctors, businessmen, etc. I presume you can buy such forgotten judgments real cheap. And that the former students will have had both an attitude adjustment and a loss of their judgment-proof status.

Gotcha!

Higher court limits

Walters bought judgments with an average value of just $1,100. But that was because California small claims courts then had relatively low $1,500, then $2,000 limits. The limit in California has since been raised to $5,000. That should gradually raise the size of the judgment which Walters' program buys by 2.5 times to $2,750—with little or no increase in **effort** required. Other states have even higher limits. Some Tennessee counties have a $15,000 limit.

"Big-time" real estate investors used to making multimillion dollar investments may scoff at such piddling amounts. But people have gotten quite rich from even smaller deals. Names like Wrigley and Gillette come to mind. Make it up in volume.

Small amounts per deal have a distinct advantage in one sense. They enable you to achieve far more **diversification** of risk than the typical real estate portfolio. Only a person who makes many small investments can legitimately claim to be a calculated risk taker.

Other courts

Why not buy judgments from courts other than small claims—courts with no upper limit? Walters said the **bigger** the judgment, the more **sophisticated** its owner and the harder it is to buy for a big enough discount. Also, the bigger the judgment, the harder the debtor fights to avoid paying it.

Small claims court, on the other hand, yields judgments which are typically owned by **unsophisticated** private citizens and are small enough that they represent a **nuisance** rather than a threat to the debtor. Walters also said small claims courts judgments are all **money** judgments. That is, the defendant is ordered to pay money to the plaintiff. In higher courts, the decision often produces injunctions, recisions, or "other equitable relief." Sorting through the **non**-money judgments wastes research time, and, in Walters' opinion, made those court decisions unacceptably "low-grade ore."

Recession plants seeds

You might think hard economic times would cause an increase in the number of judgments available. They do. But that does not mean an immediate increase in the number of judgments you can profitably buy.

For one thing, the judgments need to **age**. The people who own them are not inclined to sell them at a huge discount until several years have passed and they've given up hope of collecting.

For another, the business cycle applies to the individual debtors as well as to the economy as a whole. That is, the debtor typically does not have **assets** to collect from at the time he loses the lawsuit. But several years later, his financial situation may have improved. So you need a **whole** business cycle, not just the down half of it, to generate judgment investing opportunities. The best judgment investing opportunities today would generally involve judgments generated during the late eighties boom years or the early eighties recession.

Out of county

Plaintiffs who live out of the county are good targets. Out of state are even better. Because it's more time consuming and expensive for them to try to collect on the judgment. The **opposite** is true of out-of-area **defendants**. You should avoid them because they are more time consuming and expensive for **you** to collect from.

How to find them

Walters found the judgments he bought by laboriously digging through small claims court records and dictating pertinent information into a tape recorder. That works. But so do two less labor-intensive methods: advertising and foreclosure notices.

Advertising

Walters found classified ads under the "Miscellaneous" or "Personals" headings worked best. He ran them in an all-ads paper that circulated county-wide. Headlines that worked included "Cash for judgments" and "Can't collect your judgment?"

Foreclosure notices

Foreclosure notices are "high-grade ore" because they name people who:

A. Have **not paid** one of their most important bills thereby indicating they probably have not paid other, less important ones, and
B. Own **real estate**.

Walters looked up the names of the foreclosees in the county recorders office to see if any judgments have been recorded against them. If so, he contacted the judgment owner and told him that the property which secures his judgment was in the process of being foreclosed which could wipe out his lien. The letter also offered to buy the judgment.

Small businesses

Small businesses often have a drawer full of uncollected judgments. Unfortunately, small business owners are also often sophisticated enough to want more than pennies on the dollar for them. But some either are not that sophisticated or they just don't want to be bothered.

One of the best deals I've ever heard about involved a "drawer judgment." That was not a case of judgment investing *per se*—because the buyer bought a business not just its judgments—and because the original owner of the account receivable had not yet obtained a judgment when he sold it. But you can see the potential in unpaid bills. I told you about that deal in the execution sale chapter.

To buy judgments from small businesses, contact them by **direct mail** or by **advertising** in appropriate periodicals.

Microfiche in your office

When a judgment owner you located, other than through foreclosure notices, bites on your inquiry, promise to get back to them within 24 hours. Then check to see if the debtor in question owns any real estate. You do that by looking them up in the **assessor's records**. Nowadays, you can do that most efficiently by leasing **your own** copy of the assessor's records. They can generally be obtained on microfiche from Real Estate Data, Inc. (800-327-1085). Walters said that you can buy a used microfiche reader for $30 to $50.

Don't call him, he'll call you

Walters said **don't call** judgment owners to see if they want to sell. Just write to them and wait for them to contact you. Calling them cold is too time consuming and not cost effective.

Assign with warranty

Walters' purchase documents included an assignment with warranty in which the judgment seller represents that the judgment has **not been paid** or otherwise **rendered valueless** and that the seller will return Walters' money if it has. Walters never had to enforce that warranty.

Confiscate the bail money

I was surprised to learn that creditors can seize **rent security deposits** of judgment debtors. In other words, if one of your tenants owes a judgment, the judgment holder can get a court to order you to turn the money over to the creditor. You then have to collect **another** security deposit from the tenant.

Another surprising "asset" which can be confiscated is **bail money**. When you hold a judgment against someone, you can obtain an Order of Examination—every 120 days in California. An Order of Examination orders the debtor to appear in court to answer, under oath, your questions about his assets. He also has to bring financial documents which you request.

As you might expect, debtors are not fond of this procedure and often do not show up. You can then have them **arrested**. To get out of jail, they must post bail money. If you so request, the court will give **you** the bail money as partial or complete satisfaction of your judgment: You'd get $150 or $500 in Walters' area.

Skim the cream

Walters said his deal-a-day pace was very strenuous and difficult to maintain. I suspect that pace is beyond the point of diminishing returns. Real estate investors could adopt a much less strenuous goal like a judgment purchase a week or two a month.

If you could make, say, $1,500 profit per judgment, a deal a week would produce profits of 52 x $1,500 = $78,000 a year. That pace may let you skim the cream—perhaps skipping the court records altogether and just relying on classified ads or foreclosure notices.

Judgment investing would be a good **supplement** to some other investment program. It's not wise to rely on one formula. Judgment investing can provide a relatively steady income which is high in relation to the hours and investment required—while other investment programs wax and wane.

I like the judgment investment strategy from a lifestyle standpoint, too. You would typically never lay eyes on a debtor. You would spend your time at your home office and in the recorders office.

You have no tenants. Your name appears on no deeds, thereby insulating you from property-related lawsuit liability.

186

22

Regulatory loopholes

How it works

Government regulations depress property values in many cases. Most of those regulations contain **exemptions**. In some cases, you can buy a property at its depressed value because of the regulation, then raise the value up closer to normal by revealing the property to be completely or partially exempt from the regulation.

Why it works

Most people tend to focus on the main thrust of a law. They do not read the literal words of the law with an eye toward obtaining an exemption. Furthermore, few people are willing to fight city hall the way you sometimes need to do to obtain the exemption. The few who are can, in effect, buy property for much less than its market value will be after its exemption from the value-depressing law is revealed.

Actual case history

This specific case history involves escaping Berkeley, California's rent-control law by converting apartment buildings to owner-occupied tenancies in common.

Berkeley

I have contributed to overreactions to rent control in general and Berkeley rent control in particular. But perhaps I can be forgiven when one considers such incidents as landlord Jon Vicars claiming in a lawsuit against Berkeley that he was being forced into **slavery** by its rent control law. Then there was the president of the Berkeley Rent Stabilization Board who, during her tenure as president, was arrested while she was spray painting "Amazons Unite!" on someone's wall at two o'clock in the morning.

Kim Marienthal

Kim Marienthal is a Berkeley real estate agent and investor (Coldwell Banker, 510-486-1495). He began buying Berkeley apartment buildings because they were the only non-slum apartments in the San Francisco Area with **positive cash flow**.

He has converted two buildings to tenants in common. And he brokered six other similar deals.

You convert by selling the buildings to a group of tenants in common. The number of tenants in common in the group equals the number of units in the building and each tenant in common occupies one of the units.

Apartments sell cheap

You can buy some Berkeley apartment buildings for **eight** times gross. Decent-neighborhood apartment buildings sell for ten to twelve times gross in non-rent-controlled San Francisco-area communities.

Building size

Under Berkeley's rent-control law at the time, only owners who owned 50% or more of the building could evict a tenant in order for the owner to move in. As a result **duplexes** sold for twice as much per unit as larger buildings. Triplexes also sold for more per unit because they are close enough to two units to make 50%-owner evictions feasible.

With five to ten units, you can create a tenants-in-common-occupied apartment building by simply getting each buyer to sign a statement to the Real Estate Commissioner saying (a) he is fully informed about the undivided interest he is acquiring and its risks, (b) he is buying for himself and has no present intention to resell, and (c) he expressly waives the protection of the Subdivided Lands Act. If the assessed value of the **land** is less than the assessed value of the **structure**, you don't even need the statement. [CA B&PC § 11000.1(b)]

Adler v. Elphick

In 1986, the First District Court of Appeal in California decided *Adler v. Elphick* (184 CA 3d 642). Triplex tenant Sheila Elphick argued that landlord Albert Adler could not evict her because he had created a "community apartment project" which must be approved in advance under the California Subdivision Map Act (Govt. Code §66410).

In addition, "community apartment projects" were prohibited by the Berkeley Tenants Rights Amendments Act of 1982 (Berkeley Municipal Code §13.76.010) unless the vacancy rate in Berkeley was 5% or more. (BMC §21.52.070) Landlords wonder if the number of units voluntarily taken off the market isn't **already** over 10%. If so, the law arguably should have ended.

The court said tenant-in-common conversions were **not** "community apartment projects" as long as the right to occupancy of a particular unit was not specified in the **deed**. (CC § 1352)

While they were at it, the court said Elphick, who had refused to move, would have to pay damages for "unlawfully withholding property" and that the amount of rent allowed by Berkeley's Rent Stabilization Law on her unit was **irrelevant** in determining the damage amount. All right!

The *Bakanauskas* decision

In 1988, the court of appeals again shot down a tenant who tried to fight eviction by a 50% owner from a tenant-in-common conversion of a Berkeley triplex. Both the tenant's arguments and the court's reasoning were about the same as in *Adler*. (*Ruth Bakanauskas v. Nancy Urdan*, 206 CA 3d 621)

In both the *Adler* and *Bakanauskas* cases, the court knew there was a recorded, tenant-in-common agreement which gave the owner the exclusive right to occupy the unit in question.

The strategy

Marienthal and his partners paid $210,000 for one six-unit building which would sell for only about $125,000 if there were no tenant-in-common possibility.

But he could only get a $100,000 mortgage because the lenders base their loans on the **registered** rents, which in this case were about $200 per unit per month. So they financed the deal by buying **subject to** the existing (pre-rent control) $100,000 first, the seller taking back a $50,000 second, and Marienthal's group putting down $60,000.

Then, you either **evict** by invoking the 50%-owner prerogative or you **pay** the remaining tenants to move (about $4,000 to $20,000 depending upon how low the rent is).

There are lots of **vacant** units in Berkeley now. Because, when tenants move out, landlords would rather hold them off the market than let another tenant in. Holding units off the market is typically **illegal** in rent-controlled cities. But California has the Ellis Act (Govt. Code §7060) which says landlords may go out of the rental business.

In this case, Marienthal's six-unit building came with five apartments already vacant. And the lone remaining tenant paid to join Marienthal's investor/conversion group.

Improvements = increases

Marienthal studied the rent-control law and found that you could get rent increases if you **improved** the property. He **did** improve it—then asked the Rent Stabilization Board to increase the allowed rents from $200 to $600 per unit based on those improvements. The Board **approved** the increases, mainly because no tenants opposed them.

Refinancing

By tripling the registered rents, he tripled the mortgage amount the property qualified for and obtained a new $300,000 mortgage. That cashed him out.

He then **sold** the tenant-in-common units for about $100,000 each (taking back an average second mortgage of $25,000) by selling the entire building to six tenants in common for around $600,000. The tenants in common will, in turn, make additional big profits if condo conversion is ever allowed.

Conversion to condo

Conversion to condominium is still prohibited in Berkeley. But it appears that the combination of the rent-control law, the *Adler* and *Bakanauskas* decisions, and the Ellis Act, are turning Berkeley tenants into an endangered "species." The great irony—and poetic justice—is that the tenants themselves put this in motion by voting in such a vicious rent-control law.

As the number of tenants declines, the percentage of homeowners increases. That means increasingly more votes **against** rent control and **for** allowing condo conversion. A measure to eliminate rent control from two thirds of Berkeley's units lost in a 1990 election—but only by about 800 votes.

The increasing number of tenants in common in Berkeley (about 1,500 units in 1991) have a powerful incentive to vote for condo conversion: condos sell for about **30% to 50% more** than tenant-in-common units.

Rent to the government

There are other ways to escape rent control. For example, federal and state governments generally have the right to preempt local rent controls. (e.g., 24 CFR §246.21, *Ocean House Corp. v. Permanent Rent Control Board*, 147 CA 3d 395). In one case, Marienthal was able to raise the rents in some units from the $300 per month required by Berkeley rent control to $500 by putting in Section 8 tenants.

Santa Monica attorney Tom Nitti, (213-829-2287) believes landlords can escape municipal rent-control by leasing units to federal or state entities, like military bases or universities (U.C. Berkeley won such a case). See Chapter 13 "Escaping Rent Control" of my book, *How to Increase the Value of Real Estate,* for more ways.)

No day at the beach

Don't get the wrong idea. Berkeley and other rent-controlled cities are extremely hostile environments for landlords. In one of Marienthal's units, the tenant left town and illegally subleased the property. The subtenant skipped. Marienthal changed the locks. The original tenant broke in **under supervision of the Berkeley Police Department**.

Later, when the tenant's electricity went off through no fault of Marienthal's, he found a message on his answering machine saying, "Our power is out. If it's not back on in twenty minutes, we will have you arrested." And in Berkeley, where just being a landlord is *prima facie* evidence of criminal intent, they weren't kidding.

Another stunt they pull is reporting building code violations in order to get protection from **anti-retaliation** laws (e.g., CA CC § 1942.5)—then charge retaliation when they receive a 50%-owner-move-in eviction notice.

Opportunity short lived

Loophole-type opportunities are generally short-lived. That's because legislators and the rest of the market find out about them.

For example, two San Francisco Supervisors introduced a bill in that rent-controlled city to raise the minimum ownership share needed to evict a tenant for owner occupancy. The minimum in early 1991 was 10% which meant tenant-in-common deals requiring eviction could be done there in buildings with about **ten** or fewer units. The proposed minimum of 25% would mean you could only do tenant-in-common deals requiring evictions in buildings with **four** or fewer units. (Of course, both minimums are far lower than Berkeley's 50%.)

But those buildings already benefit from a San Francisco law which says there is **no** rent control on buildings with four or fewer units if one of the units is owner-occupied.

That means the prices of duplexes, triplexes, and fourplexes in San Francisco are only **slightly** depressed by the rent-control law. San Francisco attorney, John O'Reilly (415-392-2860) says they even do tenant-in-common deals in **two- to four-family** buildings in San Francisco and in similar buildings in **non-rent**-controlled Bay Area cities. The profit margins are apparently too thin for **pros** in such properties. In one San Francisco district, the average duplex sold for $233,540 per unit during the first eight months of 1990. But the average **six**-unit building in that same district sold for $118,000 per unit during the same period.

By April of 1991, Berkeley passed an ordinance banning tenant-in-common conversions of apartment buildings. In March 1990, Santa Monica passed an as yet untested law prohibiting tenant-in-common conversions.

Tenant-in-common conversions are now so widely known that many ads using the abbreviation "TIC" appear in Berkeley and San Francisco newspapers. That's another reason why loophole opportunities are often short-lived. The sellers demand ever increasing percentages of the converters' profits.

End of rent control?

The Ellis Act and court decisions have knocked holes in the bottom of the rent-control "barrel." Every day, more tenants "drain" out of California's rent-controlled cities. Eventually, landlords should achieve the critical political mass needed to emancipate their buildings. If they do, formerly controlled apartment buildings will leap in value. But landlords are generally pessimistic because of bad news like the vacancy controls that were added to San Francisco's rent control law after many years of interim decontrol.

Santa Maria deal

A group of buyers in Santa Maria bought a rent-controlled apartment building. They withdrew it from the rental business in accordance with California's Ellis Act (GC § 7060). That let them evict the tenants. The partners then moved into the building and shared the operating and finance expenses of the building.

Santa Maria sued saying the partners had, by occupying the property as residence, gone back into the rental business and therefore had to offer the apartmments to the old tenants at the old rents. The Rent Control Board lost. (*Santa Maria Rent Control Board v. Bluvshtein* (5/23/91, 230 CA 3d 308)

Greenmail For Real Estate Investors?

Settlement offers and agreements are usually confidential. But I heard a rumor that a city with rent control laws offered to settle an anti-rent control suit out of court for big bucks. Other cities rewrote their rent-control ordinances so that they no longer applied to the landlord who sued.

Fontana, CA and El Monte, CA went the exempt-the-plaintiff route. (Such exemptions seem to violate the equal protection clause of the Constitution. Fontana is now being sued by another landlord who alleges unconstitutional taking.)

California's Center For Property Rights (415-845-8944) says in its 11/88 newsletter that Berkeley has made "...*offers of economically viable settlements in order to evade adverse judgments when judicial success by an owner appears imminent.*"

Rent control is a fundamental part of the political base of most politicians in rent controlled towns. And rent control is increasingly coming under more effective legal attack (outside of New York).

Scared politicians would rather pay a sort of **greenmail** to the few landlords who sue than risk losing their jobs if the rent control bandwagon were judicially junked. In **corporate** greenmail, executives fearful of losing their jobs pay **shareholder**'s money to get the attackers to go away. In **rent-control** greenmail, it's **taxpayer's** money.

Rent-control greenmail delays the judicial day of reckoning for rent-control laws. That hurts landlords as a group. But you can't blame the individual landlord who takes the greenmail and runs. It's a sure thing compared to a "maybe" in court.

Rent-control greenmailing leads to 2 conclusions:

1. If you are a rent-control victim, you ought to consider suing to collect **your** greenmail.
2. The industry as a whole should fund suits so the landlord whose case is being used has no incentive to bail out before a decision. Class action suits seem appropriate as well.

The more people who follow advice number one above, the quicker the politicians will run out of taxpayers' money for greenmail purposes.

I've heard of one settlement offer in the million-dollar range. So greenmailing may be a viable business strategy all by itself—just as it is on Wall Street. (Note: I believe the **payment** of corporate or municipal greenmail is an outrage which is arguably an illegal breach of fiduciary duty. And if it isn't, it **ought** to be. But I find no fault with **recipients** of greenmail who honestly admit what they're doing.)

Wetlands

In the last five or six years, those who hate the rich have found a bunch of powerful ways to torment and transfer wealth from real estate investors. One of the most vexing to owners of raw land is the way Section 404 of the Clean Water Act of 1972 has been used to regulate so-called wetlands.

Oddly, the word "wetlands" does not appear in that law and arguably such lands are not covered by it.

Draining the swamp

Harried managers of the '70s often displayed a gag sign which said,

When you're up to your a__ in alligators, it's hard to remember that your original objective was to drain the swamp.

Now, if you succeed in draining the swamp in spite of being up to your a__ in alligators, you will soon be up to your a__ in Army Corps of Engineers litigation. Draining swamps is now a **crime**. And alligators are an endangered species.

What's worse, swamps and other wetlands are described by a definition so broad and vague only an environmentalist, or sadist, could love it.

One such environmentalist is an official charged with promulgating rules regarding wetlands, EPA Administrator William Reilly. He has said that private property rights are no more than "a quaint anachronism" according to *Land Rights Letter* (301-797-7455).

Corps of Engineers

If you want to drain a swamp or fill a wetland or build on a wetland, you have to get a permit from the Corps of Engineers. And the Environmental Protection Agency has veto power over the issuance of the permit.

What is a wetland?

People who own raw land which is **not** a swamp may think upon first hearing the term wetland that it does not apply to them. Not so fast. According to attorneys William Kelly and Sheldon Fisher (Latham & Watkins, Washington, DC) in the October 1991 issue of *Urban Land*, "critics charge [the definition of wetlands] includes prairie potholes and other areas that are dry most of the year."

The Manual definition

The official definition was in a book called "The Federal Manual for Identifying and Delineating Jurisdictional Wetlands" which was promulgated by four federal agencies in 1989. That book says your property is a wetland if it is "covered or saturated with water for seven consecutive days each growing season," and "...contains certain soils and vegetation..." says *Urban Land*.

The manual says your land is wetland if, in addition to the required moisture, 50% or more of the plants are the type usually found in wetlands. They say the type usually found in wetlands includes "facultative" plants, that is, plants which grow in **both** wet and dry conditions.

On August 17, 1991, Bush signed the Energy and Water Developments Appropriations Act which gives land owners the right to have already **pending** permit requests decided according to the more favorable wetlands definition contained in a 1987 Corps of Engineers manual.

How much wetlands?

A 1985 inventory by the U.S. Fish and Wildlife Service found there were 105 million acres of wetlands. But Rhode Island Senator Chaffee says about 200 million acres should be considered wetlands. The total land area of the U.S. is 2,271,343,000 acres, so about 4 to 9% is wetlands.

George Bush

During the 1988 presidential campaign, George Bush tried to kiss up to environmentalists by promising "no net loss of wetlands." On August 14, 1991, Bush reneged on that promise by proposing that the definition of a wetland be change to land

"...covered with water for 15 consecutive days or saturated with water for 21 consecutive days each year."

Bush's proposal would also have substituted a complex weighted average scoring system regarding the nature and extent of wetlands vegetation.

The Bush proposal would have freed 10 to 25% of the current wetlands from that classification. Bush would also have said that if the Corps of Engineers did not approve or disapprove your request for a permit within six months, the permit would automatically be granted.

I can picture developers and land owners giving each other high fives on the 21st day when dry weather desaturates their land while devastated environmentalists scurry around frantically digging holes to find moisture.

$29,000 building lot worthless

In 1970, Dick Bryant and his wife bought a building lot on the Outer Banks in North Carolina. All the lots around his have homes on them. But when he sold it in 1988 for $29,000, the Corps of Engineers killed the sale on the grounds that the lot was a wetland. Bryant, now 80 years old, had planned to live off the income from the lot sale. The Private Property Rights Act would require that the Bryant's be compensated for the taking of the land by the government. The Constitution arguably already requires such compensation. But the above-mentioned William Reilly said in a land use report he once wrote that "...mere loss in land value will never be justification for invalidating the regulation of land use."

Changed grading on neighbor's property makes hers wetlands

A case reported in the 8/5/91 Realtor® News suggests wetlands don't have to be natural to be protected. Eloise Seamon, an Alexandria, VA real estate agent and developer, says five acres she owns in Ocean City, MD became wetland because the Corps of Engineers changed the grade of a nearby parcel causing storm water from that parcel to run onto Seamon's parcel. When she dug a drainage ditch at the edge of her property to stop that, the state fined her for unlawfully disturbing a wetland.

Hungarian refugee jailed for cleaning up dump

John Pozsgai, a self-employed truck mechanic from Morrisville, PA was sentenced to three years is prison, five years probation, and fined $202,000 for placing clean fill and topsoil on a property he owned. The property had been a dump and he had to remove 7,000 old tires first. Pozsgai was also ordered to "restore" his property to its wetland condition by the Corps of Engineers. Pozsgai, ironically, fled Hungary in 1956 as a result of the uprising against that country's communist government.

Two jailed for cleaning 300-foot ditch

Ocie Mills and his son were fined $5,000 each, denied eligibility for parole, and locked up for 21 months for cleaning out a football-field-length drainage ditch and putting 19 loads of clean fill in it on a half acre lot he owned in Florida. They were also ordered to restore the ditch within 90 days of getting out of prison.

Land owners win millions in court awards for wetlands 'takings'

The Corps of Engineers denied Loveladies Harbor, Inc., a developer, a permit to develop 12.5 acres. The developer sued and a judge pronounced the denial a "taking."

According to the last twelve words of the Fifth Amendment to the Constitution, takings must result in "just compensation." The judge ordered the federal government to pay Loveladies Harbor, Inc. $2.5 million for the land and take title to it.

In another case, the U.S. Court of Claims ordered the Corps of Engineers to pay a New Jersey developer $2.7 million plus court costs for refusing to permit development of 11 acres of wetlands.

$40,000 building lot worthless

A buyer paid $40,000 for a 28,000-square-foot building lot in South Nags Head, NC contingent upon a detailed site evaluation. The lot was surrounded by similar lots which already contained homes.

The local health department required the lot be cleared of its overgrown vegetation in order to do its septic system evaluation. This was done. Then the local health engineer decided there was a wetlands problem and called the Corps of Engineers. They declared the lot a wetland and threatened to sue to force restoration of the overgrown vegetation.

The local health department required fill be added to the land to support a septic system. But the Corps of Engineers refuses to allow any filling. The sale fell through and the lot is now worthless.

$2.5 million parcel bought for $125,000

Bellingham, WA investor David Syre specializes in buying property nobody else wants—property with seemingly intractable development obstacles like massive title problems.

He recently bought an apparent bargain in the Northwest. The property was on the market for months at $2.5 million. But there were no takers or even lookers because it was a wetland. The sellers got fed up. Syre got it for just $125,000. He expects to sell it for a profit after obtaining permits for all or part of the property.

Your money

You can get your financial clock cleaned if land you own is declared a wetland. Because if it's a wetland it's of value only to the mosquitoes and other creatures whose rights to the property take precedence over yours.

On the other hand, some people have escaped from this environmental Devil's Island. Some have escaped by getting the courts to order compensation. Others have no doubt obtained permits which were originally **expected** to be denied or which **were** denied.

Mitigation

In some cases, permits are issued if the landowner mitigates the damage, for example, by creating a new wetland at another location to compensate the mosquitoes for the one that was lost. As far as I know, the mosquitoes moving expenses are not required to be paid—yet.

The Council on Environmental Quality lists the following ways to mitigate destruction of wetlands:

• " limiting the degree or magnitude of an action"
• "compensating for an impact by replacing or providing substitute resources or environments."

That's a bunch of vague, environmentalist gobbledygook. But the basic idea is that there are times when the environmentalists and their political and bureaucratic dependents **will** let you develop a wetland. If you can make the appropriate sacrifice to the environmental gods cheaply enough, a wetlands deal can be profitable. Heck, maybe you can even build your project on pilings. If it's retail, you can set up nature observation points to illustrate the role of wetlands in nature. And maybe establish a little a mosquito petting zoo.

Incidence of this opportunity

The number of property-related regulations is large and growing. Examples include zoning, wetlands, rent control, etc. The loopholes are most prevalent at the **beginning** of the life of the law. As investors take advantage of the loopholes, the legislature or city council modifies the law to stop the loophole users.

How to find them

Just look for properties that have obviously depressed values. Ask why. And if the answer is regulation, get a copy of the regulation and read it with a magnifying glass. There is no standard way of approaching these properties because by their very nature, the loopholes are more or less unknown. You simply have to be one of those pioneers who often end up with arrows in their back.

Tax Ramifications

You probably have to capitalize (depreciate or amortize) the cost of your efforts to obtain the regulatory exemption. That's the way property tax appeal costs must be handled and that is a close cousin of loophole escaping.

Kill ratio

Because this is a sort of guerrilla, political warfare type of activity, there is no basis for calculating a normal kill ratio. Some loophole strategies are quite successful for a time, Others are moderately successful, others are failures. You have to do your own handicapping.

Special expertise required

Government expertise would be very helpful. I suspect the best person to do this would be a former employee of the agency in charge of granting exemptions to the regulation. You'll need to know the law or regulation in question.

Full-time or part-time possible

This can probably be done part-time although I suspect full-time would have a greater chance of success. Government tends to operate on public hearings that are held after business hours. That lets a part-timer in. But on the other hand, periods of intense activity are often required when fighting city hall at crucial times in the battle.

Regional variations

You bet there are regional variations. Municipalities and metropolitan areas vary enormously in the regulatory area. Rent control is always municipal. Anti-growth is generally a regional phenomenon. Urban areas create regulations designed to force the use of union labor. And so forth.

Ethical considerations

When you deal with politicians, there's a good chance you are the only honest man or woman in the room. Take care to keep it that way. You may be asked for bribes. You cannot pay. Bribes are illegal, immoral, and if that's not enough, they may be setting you up in a sting operation complete with hidden cameras and microphones.

You need to resist the temptation to mislead sellers as to the possibility of obtaining an exemption. It's best to not say anything about exemptions. Just buy the property or option it.

If tenants are involved and you want to move them out or convert them to owners, you also need to be scrupulously careful that you do not succumb to the temptation to mislead.

Finally, you need to be very careful to not mislead the regulators. Not only is it immoral. It's generally illegal and the regulators have the power to hurt you severely if you make them angry.

Need for secrecy

Secrecy is important but difficult given the public nature of most regulations and procedures for seeking exemptions. Just avoid unnecessary disclosures to people who don't have a need to know. As I said above, escaping loopholes generally anger the regulators.

Unique risks

The unique risk in trying to pull a property through a loophole is that you cannot generally know in advance if you will succeed. By their very nature, these are ephemeral, pioneering strategies. The more you do them, the more you know about your chances of success—except that the more you do them, the more the regulators or legislators are likely to find out and change the rules.

Criteria

The regulation in question must depress the property value by at least 20% or double the cost of obtaining the exemption, whichever is greater. Obtaining exemptions is analogous to renovation. In his book, *How I Turned $1,000 into $5,000,000 in Real Estate in my Spare Time*, he says to always increase the building value by at least $2 for every $1 spent on the renovations. In regulatory matters, you are likely to spend a lot of your own time. The value of that time should be included as part of the cost of obtaining the exemption.

Study the law

Land use regulations, like rent control or zoning or wetlands, are frequently so onerous that they drive away virtually the entire market. In many cases, that is an **overreaction**. Overreactions breed profit opportunities like wetlands breed mosquitoes.

The regulation is bad, but not quite as bad as the emotional response of the market would suggest. The key is to become expert in the regulation in question and learn when and where property can be exempted from it.

Other laws, too

Rent control and wetlands regulations are not the only laws that scare off real estate investors. Nor are they the only such laws with loopholes. Other laws which artificially depress values include zoning, the Tax Reform Act of 1986, California's Coastal Commission, and so forth.

Whenever you find real estate values **artificially depressed by a law** or regulation, examine the law with a magnifying glass to see if it contains a loophole through which you can profitably pull a property.

196

23

Owner unknown

In 1991, I got a book from my friend, Jane Bryant Quinn, the financial columnist. It had been sent to her in the hopes that she would review it. She thought I'd be interested. The book was published by the Genealogical Publishing Company.

The Genealogical Publishing Company?

How, you may wonder, would a genealogical book interest hard-nosed investors?

According to author Jay Segel, it would take three lifetimes to research the "owner unknown" real estate parcels just in his state of Massachusetts. And he says similar parcels exist in many states. And that the profit potential on larger parcels runs "...into the millions."

My county assessor's office says there are 99 unknown-owner parcels in Contra Costa County, California—out of a total of 289,604. Segel says he found 174 in Los Angeles County and about 75 in San Diego County. One Texas county assessor sent Segel 17 pages of owner unknowns from their computer. Making random calls to county assessors in preparation for TV appearances, he quickly found over 10,000 acres worth of owner-unknown land in 45 different states.

"Eastern seaboard"

Segel says, "You will not find owner-unknown land in every town. In fact, certain states and regions have a higher propensity than others—owing to disparate statutes, historical circumstances, and attitudes of civil servants—the Eastern seaboard seems to be the most fertile territory for real estate treasure hunting."

Turning genealogical research into money

The trick is you find the owners—typically heirs who lost touch with or did not know the last known owner of the property. You offer to buy their interest in the property. But you don't tell them where the property is. Then, if they try to cut you out, they have to redo most of the research you've done—in reverse. That's a daunting task—especially for those who are not skilled in genealogy.

The sample deal in Segel's book has him buying a parcel of land worth $50,000 to $80,000 for about $4,000 including all out-of-pocket expenses. The book, *Owner Unknown—Your Guide to Real Estate Treasure Hunting*, tells how to play this game ($25, 1001 N. Calvert Street, Baltimore, MD 21202, 800-727-6687).

Owner unknown

I didn't know there **was** such a thing as owner-unknown real estate. Unknown owners obviously don't pay their property taxes. I thought the tax assessor assessed everybody in the county, sent a bill to everyone, then auctioned off the properties on which the owners failed to pay their taxes—regardless of the **reason** they didn't pay.

Apparently, not always. Remember, we're talking about the **government** here. Segel says, "Whatever the specific circumstances…you can bet that the municipality is always at least partly responsible…an owner-unknown label is an official admission of carelessness, mismanagement, lack of effective oversight, or outright ineptitude by local authorities."

States typically have special laws to protect unknown heirs. The local government may have to try to find the heirs before they can sell the property. They often don't want to be bothered. That's where you come in.

Starting point

Start with the assessor's records. Segel recommends focusing on **rural** areas—a recommendation often encountered in other bargain-purchase techniques. He also finds **resort areas** good hunting because lots bought with the intent of some day building a second home are more likely to be overlooked by executors and heirs.

Prime land is "low-grade ore" when it comes to owner unknowns. That's because some developer has probably tried to buy any owner-unknown **prime** property. He may not have been a genealogist, but he likely consulted with attorneys who knew something of how to clear title to and buy the property. Generally the only prime properties still available are the ones not likely to produce an adequate return on your time.

Size is a factor. The effort to find the owner is considerable. That eliminates very low-value properties. How big you go depends on what you can afford. The opportunities come in all sizes according to Segel.

Typically, you will find a number of owner-unknown properties. If you don't find **any**, pick another county.

The law of descent

Every state has laws regarding who inherits property when someone dies. The laws cover both those who left a will and those who did not. Generally, the laws say that when someone dies, the property they own goes to the following people in the following order:

Spouse, or if none,
Descendants, or if none,
Parents, or if none,
Siblings, or if none,
Nieces and nephews, and so on.

The entire property goes to the next level only and is divided equally among those at that level or their heirs if they are no longer living.

Remember, this is the **general** rule. You have to check your state for the specific law there. The laws of descent may rule even if a will calls for another way of splitting the property. For example, some states prohibit disinheriting wives or children.

Your investigation

When you find an owner-unknown property, you first figure out who the last known owner was. You do that by performing a title search on an **abutting** property that was likely once combined with the property in question. Once you find the name of the last owner, you are usually in the heir-tracing business to find the current owner(s).

Segel gives dozens of tips on how to do that in his book. Heir tracing sounds like a combination of Indiana Jones, Perry Mason, and Woodward and Bernstein. It can lead you to other states or even other countries. In one of Segel's cases, he traced the ownership to a 70-year old man who married a woman in her forties. He found the **man's** probate; but not the **wife's**. Finally, it occurred to him that since the marriage only lasted a few years before the husband's death, she may have returned to her home state. The marriage certificate gave that state and Segel found her probate there.

(You don't necessarily have to go there **in person**. You can investigate a lot of things by phone and mail. I got a lot of documents on *Nothing Down* author Robert Allen from the Utah County Court House in Provo, Utah by phone and mail for an article I did on his financial difficulties in September of 1987.)

Secrecy

If you are buying a $60,000 lot for $4,000, you'd better not let it get around.

Segel told me he tells the various clerks and others he encounters exactly what he's doing and isn't concerned about them stealing his deal. He's found few have the diligence and skill to pull it off. He sounded a bit like a football coach who told me he used to diagram all of his plays on the blackboard in the **visitors** locker room before games and write, "Here they are. Try to stop them."

Sequence

In owner-unknowns, Segel says the most efficient sequence goes like this: First you find a parcel whose ownership is unknown—a sort of **un**title search.

Then you inspect the property. If there is a **building** or signs of **recent occupation** of the property, Segel says to **forget it**. He opposes using his techniques to throw someone out of their home. Even if it's not a home, signs that the property is being used probably mean that the user became the owner it by virtue of **adverse possession**. So you're looking for **unoccupied raw land**.

Then you look for the last recorded owner in the recorder's office. You copy his deed and related information and begin your search for those to whom he sold, gave, or left it.

Tricks of the trade

Segel's book is full of nuts-and-bolts tricks of the real estate genealogy trade. He tells you to buy a magnifying glass to read old documents, special references like the *County Courthouse Book* and the *International Vital Records Handbook*, and a software program called *Family Roots®* to prepare "pedigree" charts.

He tells you how to organize the voluminous files this technique generates. He provides insider tips like look for various spellings of the names in question because misspellings are common.

Tenants in common

Tenancies in common are usually the way in which the current owners of owner-unknown land hold land. That is, when you finally figure out who the current, living owners are, there are a **bunch** of them—each owning a fractional interest according to where they are in the family tree.

We're talkin' old

Owner unknown searches can lead you not only to other countries, they can also lead you to other **centuries**. Title searches in market value purchases typically only go back to the last sale or refinancing—on the theory that the title was searched adequately before then in order to permit that sale or refinancing. You can apply the same principle to owner unknowns. However, the last known sale or refinancing was a **long** time ago. Segel says the typical owner-unknown parcel has been so listed in the assessor's records for 60 to 100 years! He has had to go back to the year 1637 on at least one search. So you will be researching documents from the nineteenth century through the depression at the start of your tracing investigation.

Resources

You may be tempted to conclude that such records would be next to impossible to come by. Certainly the average person's house and other day-to-day experience does not bring him or her into contact with such old records. But the most fascinating aspect of Segel's book is his revelation of the vast researching resources which are little known beyond the esoteric world of historians and genealogists. And by Mr. Segel's account, those resources and the expertise to use them efficiently are generally accessible to ordinary people.

The resources include places your are aware of but whose genealogical aspects you may not have known the extent of like local libraries, the Library of Congress, courthouses, cemeteries, the U.S. Bureau of Prisons, and newspaper morgues. He also tells of less well-known resources like the registry of probate, bureaus of vital statistics, the Bureau of Land Management, the Bureau of Indian Affairs (Indians used to own it all, you know), U.S. Immigration and Naturalization Service. And he tells of such little-known resources as local historical societies, the genealogical files of the Mormon church, the Federal Archives and Record Center, and U.S. Census records (they become public after 72 years).

Gaps

In a typical case, there will be many living owners—but you will not be able to find them **all**. In the sample case history in Segel's book, he finds the widower of a descendant. That widower owns 2/3 of the property and agrees to sell it to Segel. The other third is owned by a daughter who got pregnant before she was married and ran away from home never to be heard from again.

What to do?

File a lawsuit for **partition**. You buy the interest of the heir or heirs you located. Then you ask the court to sell the **whole** property. You need to prove that a diligent search for the missing heir has been made. You do that with your records on this property. The court then orders a sale and public notice is published in legal newspapers and on courthouse walls and such. You or someone else buys the property at the auction.

If it's you, you can file a suit for **quiet title** to convert the title you get from the court to a marketable (insurable) title. The classic quiet title suit I recall reading about involved Alaskan "gold country" land. I was one of those who lost his interest in the property in question. You may have been, too.

In the fifties, when I was a kid, a breakfast cereal promoted itself by putting a deed to one square inch of "Yukon Gold Country" in the cereal boxes. I remember comparing "holdings" with my friends. I think my share got up to six square inches or so.

Years later, they discovered oil on the land. Talk about a title problem. I read somewhere that it was solved by a quiet title suit involving published notices and all that.

Legal work

It may sound like a prohibitive amount of legal work is required to play this game. Segel says it's not. The $4,000 total out-of-pocket cost in the sample deal described above

includes legal expenses. He says you can generally get the legal work done for a small retainer and a piece of the action. To the extent that you can do repeated deals in one state, I suspect you could learn to do most of the legal work yourself.

Meeting the heirs

Segel says his heart is on the verge of pounding a hole in his chest when it comes time to contact the heirs for the first time. For days or weeks or months, he has been on their trail, tracing their family history through the words on headstones; yellowed birth, marriage, and death certificates; and so forth. Now a real human being is to be substituted for the abstract names he has been dealing with—and the work he's done will produce a return or he'll end up with nothing for his efforts.

He tells them they may own a fractional interest in a property and that he has spent a great deal of time trying to clear its title. He gives them a copy of their family tree and "other interesting artifacts" and asks them to sign a deed quitclaiming their interest to him in return for some cash.

He says the heirs are usually more interested in the family history information he provides than in the money he offers. He typically pays between one dollar and six hundred dollars for their interest in the property. The price is low for the same reasons I've cited in other bargain purchases: there is no market for partial interests and the owners of these interests are subject to the easy-come-easy-go syndrome. In addition, their alternative is nothing at worst and a bewildering search for an unknown property at best.

If they need time to consider the matter, he leaves them only the genealogy chart. He waits ten days before calling "...so as not to appear pushy."

Finder's fees

Segel says the payment of finder's fees to those who track down heirs "...is usually accepted and regulated by state statute." I checked California's statute (Probate Code §11604). It provides much protection to heirs and cold comfort to heir hunters. It gives the court the right to investigate any transfer, assignment, etc. from the beneficiary of an estate to another person. And it gives the court the right to refuse to "distribute" the property in question or to

> *order distribution on any terms that the court deems just and equitable, if the court finds either of the following:*
> *(1) The fees, charges, or consideration paid or agreed to be paid by a beneficiary are grossly unreasonable.*
> *(2) The transfer agreement, request, or instructions were obtained by duress, fraud, or undue influence.*

Turning that upside down yields the strange principle that heir hunters are entitled to **unreasonable** compensation, as long as it's not **grossly** unreasonable.

I suspect most judges would regard Mr. Segel's buying $50,000 to $80,000 of real estate for $1 to $600 as "grossly unreasonable." Check your state statute before you start.

Fun

The various techniques for buying real estate for at least 20% below market generally involve work or even downright drudgery like repairing bad foundations, finding owners of remainder estates, sending letters to people who are being foreclosed, and so forth.

Genealogy, on the other hand, is a **hobby** to many. From Segel's account, it sounds like fun or an adventure—playing private investigator and getting paid handsomely for it.

I once researched Robert Allen's legendary *Los Angeles Times*, nothing-down deals. Those were the ones he did when the *Times* took him up on his ad claim that he could go to any city with just $100 and within 72 hours buy an excellent piece of property for nothing down. When the document I had been looking for popped up on the microfiche screen, I had the sense of excitement and tension one might experience as a Watergate burglar—in spite of the fact that researching public records is perfectly legal.

Leigh Robinson, author of the book *Landlording*, told me he had a similar experience when, as a graduate student, he traced the movements of a prominent nineteenth century Californian who shot his wife's lover north of San Francisco. Robinson had to read old newspaper after old newspaper looking for the name of the man in question on passenger lists of ships heading out of San Francisco. Suddenly, there it was.

The novelty can wear off, though. Bill "Tycoon" Greene was a well-known real estate guru in the late seventies—before he was convicted of income tax evasion—and escaped from prison while on emergency leave. Before he became a real estate guru, he was a worldwide heir hunter seeking heirs who were entitled to cash. He said it was profitable and exciting, but that after a while, it got old.

Escaped land

There is a subcategory of owner unknown land which is even more obscure. That's **escaped** land. Escaped land is land the tax assessor lost track of altogether. He not only doesn't know who owns it, he doesn't know the parcel **exists**. How could such a thing happen? Well, in my county they have 289,604 parcels of real estate. Did you ever try to keep track of 289,604 of something—with a staff of government bureaucrats—and a budget set by politicians? It may be that my county has 289,628 parcels having lost track of 24 of them.

How do you find escaped land? Look for blank areas in the assessor's maps. Or compare the assessor's maps to aerial photos or other maps of the same area. If the assessor's map stops where the aerial photographs or other maps show additional land, you may have found some escaped land.

I asked Jay Segel if he could send me an example of escaped land. He sent the map shown on this page. It's from somewhere in Maryland. The odd-shaped parcel just north of P.637 has no parcel number indicating it is not on the assessor's books.

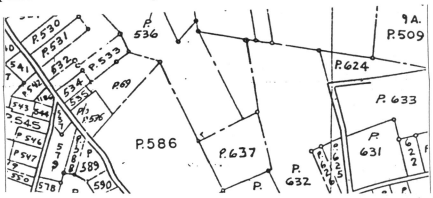

Just keep in mind that the assessor's list of owner unknown properties is probably not a complete list.

Adverse possession

Every state has an adverse possession statute. That's the one that says if you possess real estate "openly, notoriously, and continuously for a statutory period of time," you become the owner. Most people only encounter this concept when they study for a real estate license. A few have occasion to deal with it when a neighbor claims adverse possession of part of adjacent property because his fence or driveway or whatever has encroached for the requisite number of years. Some real estate seminar gurus have taught adverse possession as a technique. It certainly has the necessary something-for-nothing aspect.

Adverse possession is easier taught at seminars than done. For one thing, states also have **criminal** laws against **trespassing**. It's hard to possess someone else's land without trespassing on it. So the trick is to trespass and get away with it for the statutory period of time (for example, five years in California). If you get caught and run off sooner, you could be in a bit of trouble. Use of property also causes a **damage** in the sense that fair market **rent** should have been paid by you to the owner.

In many cases, to become owner by adverse possession, you may have to pay the real estate taxes on the property in question—either because it's an **explicit** requirement of adverse possession in your state or to prevent the property from being sold by the tax collector before you have completed your statutory possession period.

In some states, you can only succeed as an adverse possessor if you do so **in good faith**. That is, you must have truly believed that you had some right to the property. An **opportunist** investor wandering around playing finders-keepers-losers-weepers with abandoned land would win no adverse possession suits in those states.

Adverse incarceration

In his November/December 1988 *Distress Sales Report* (510-523-6115), John Beck told of a student of his who got into big trouble trying to play adverse possession. The guy took "adverse possession" of 21 empty, mortgage-encumbered houses and rented them out in Riverside County, California. He was arrested, indicted, and convicted of trespassing upon lands (CPC 602) and grand theft (CPC 487). He literally was sentenced to jail. Had he done it **after** January 1, 1987, he most likely would also have been indicted and convicted for violating California's **rent-skimming** statute (CC §890). If the mortgages on those properties were **federally** related, his attempt at adverse possession and subleasing the properties might have violated the **federal** rent-skimming law (12 USC 1709-2).

Al Lowry reportedly recommended taking possession of and changing the locks on abandoned houses in his book, *Foreclosure Hidden Treasures*. This and other actions, he said, could lead you to adverse possession of the properties in question. He also said that if you got caught, you'd be reimbursed by the owner for the money you spent on taxes and improvements. That's only the case if you can prove you were a **good-faith** improver, that is, that you believed you were the owner of the property when you made the improvements. (CCP § 871.1).

Buy from the good faith possessor

So adverse possession is not a very good way to invest in real estate in states requiring good faith possession, right? Not so fast. If you pursue owner unknown property, you will most likely come across adverse possessors. They may have occupied the land in good faith. But if they try to **sell** it, the title report will reveal that they have never been the legal title holders. That, in turn, will scare off virtually all prospective buyers, thereby enabling **you** to acquire their interest **cheaply** if they are inclined to sell. You could then file a quiet title suit to convert your quitclaim deed from the adverse possessor into a marketable (insurable) title. The beauty of adverse possession and quiet title actions against unknown owners is that there is virtually zero chance that they will contest.

Case history

How could the adverse possessor be there in good faith? Beck tells of an actual case history where preforeclosure investor Ted Thomas was one of the people scared off. We'll never know what would have happened because Thomas let someone else buy the property at the foreclosure auction. But here was the adverse possession situation.

A house at 2122 Funston Avenue in Stockton, CA was worth about $50,000 to $60,000. It had just a $5,300 private mortgage on it which was $1,200 in arrears. The "owner" was actually the ex-husband of the title owner. He had quitclaimed his interest in the house to her as part of the divorce settlement. She had died twelve years before the house was on the way to foreclosure. He apparently moved back into the house after her death and had paid the taxes since.

$43,500 lost

He was willing to sell the house to Thomas for nothing ($1 to make it legal)—he just wanted out. Had he bought it and converted the title to a marketable one, Thomas's profit would have been about $50,000 - $6,500 = $43,500 before legal expenses. The possibility that the "owner" might indeed be the lawful owner as a result of adverse possession never occurred to Thomas. The house sold at the foreclosure auction for $20,200 after Thomas dropped out of the bidding at $20,100.

Although the ex-husband occupied the house more than the five years required by California law, it's **not** clear that he would be entitled to ownership by adverse possession. If the deceased wife left the property to others either by will or by the laws of descent of California, **they** would be the title owners. Courts generally do **not** like to grant adverse possession to one family member against his close relatives like his spouse, parent(s), or child(ren).

Forget it?

Segel's book can work as a way to find real estate bargains because he has identified a situation where virtually all potential bidders say, "Forget it," namely, property whose ownership is unknown. That is one of the basic principles of bargain real estate purchases. Look for situations where the rest of the market runs away—like bad foundations, remainder estates, toxic contamination, etc.—then carefully and expertly estimate the cost of correcting the problem which is causing the rest of the market to shun the property.

But having discovered the principle so well as to owner unknowns, Segel promptly goes the other direction when it comes to owner-unknown property **other than** unoccupied raw land. "Forget it," he says if the property has buildings or is occupied and being used in some other way.

I prefer to apply the principle of, "Never say never." If the property is occupied, see if there might still be a legitimate, ethical bargain-purchase opportunity like the deceased-wife/ex-husband situation described above. That ex-husband would have been better off if he had sold the house to a Jay Segel or Ted Thomas than he was to let it go to foreclosure.

Check your state law

If you want to play the adverse possession game, you need to become familiar with your pertinent state laws. The time period varies from five to twenty years. Many states have different time periods for different situations. Some require payment of property taxes; others have a shorter possession period requirement if you pay the taxes, and so forth. Because of the possibility of criminal trespass violations, you'd better work with an attorney.

Pre-tax sale applications

In forced sales like foreclosures and delinquent property tax sales, there are generally three phases at which you may be able to make a bargain purchase: **before** the forced sale from the delinquent owner, **at** the forced sale, and from the winning bidder **after** the forced sale.

You can**not** have an owner-unknown situation when a property is going to a foreclosure or trustee sale because, by definition, such sales are instigated by lenders with a security interest in the property. That interest makes them "owners" in a sufficient sense to take the property **out** of the owner unknown category. The same is true of execution sales for nonpayment of an involuntary lien.

But owner-unknown property can be and is sold at delinquent property tax sales. Your competitors at such sales often try to contact the owner of the property **before** the sale to buy it on a bargain basis from him. If the property is owner unknown, they can't contact the owner because they don't know who or where he is. But **you** can, if you can learn and efficiently apply the real estate title and genealogical research skills Segel talks about in his book.

How long does this take?

On May 3rd, 1991 Segel researched three parcels in Massachusetts from start to finish in one day. And he had to go back to 1840 on one.

Other variations

Segel says a lot of owner unknown parcels are not listed as such in the assessor's records. Rather they are listed as owned by the **municipality**. But if you check the grantee indexes, you will find no document deeding the property to the town. They just put their name on it—an unconstitutional and eminently overturnable action. That is, when you find the heirs and buy from them, you can tell the town to bug off.

Segel also notes that the owner unknown technique works on mineral rights, in Canada, and that it sometimes applies to properties with dwelling units like empty mobilehomes.

Financing ramifications

The bad news on financing owner unknowns is that it's next to impossible to get institutional financing on raw land especially before your quiet title lawsuit succeeds. And it's impossible by definition to get seller financing on owner unknown property.

The good news is owner unknown properties don't cost very much so you can probably afford to pay cash. Once you've obtained clear title to the entire property, you'll have no more difficulty than any other owner of raw land—although that's a lot. So owner unknown is almost entirely a self-financed, all-cash approach to investing.

Tax Ramifications

As with any bargain purchase, your basis will be your cost and that will be quite low. If there were buildings on the property, that would reduce your depreciation deductions. But since the owner unknown technique applies almost entirely to raw land, depreciation is not an issue. Your low basis will mean a large capital gain tax when you sell. And if you hold the property primarily for resale, you'll be a dealer and have to pay tax on the profits at ordinary income tax rates.

Full-time or part-time possible

Because hardly anyone is doing this, there is no rush. So part-time is possible. However, if you have a 9 to 5 job, you may have trouble getting to the government records offices that are only open during those hours.

Ethical considerations

There is a temptation to try to get the heir to sign a quitclaim deed by saying or implying that their signature is just one of those technicality loose ends that come up in title matters. Be careful. Do not understate the probability that the person is an heir. In other words, if you are 98% certain they own a 1/21 interest, it would be deceitful to say something like, "Because of the sloppy way this was handled sixty years ago, your signature is needed to remove a cloud on the title."

A better, more ethical solution might be to say, "The owner sixty years ago appears to have died without a will and the people who handled the probate appear to have overlooked the fact that the deceased owned this parcel of land. I think you now own a small portion of it by virtue of the state's laws of descent. It would take a law suit to be sure. If you are the owner, you may owe back real estate taxes on the property. I specialize in buying interests like the one I think you own." Then you offer whatever you normally offer and go from there.

Environmental liability considerations

Raw land is generally the least likely property to have environmental problems. On the other hand, unauthorized dumping is more likely to take place on owner unknown land. So you need to inspect. Although it is technically trespassing to set foot on land which does not belong to you, by definition, there is no owner to complain about your inspecting owner-unknown land. So you can probably inspect to your heart's content—and you should.

Kill ratio

Jay Segel says his kill ratio is about 10% to 20%. That is, he buys about 10% to 20% of the properties he researches. Most of the others turn out not to be owner unknown. That is, the **assessor** listed them as owner unknown. But the **owner** knew he owned the property. The others are simply owners who refused to sell. When he encounters such a person, Segel simply tells the tax assessor and the recalcitrant owner gets a big bill for back taxes. In Segel's state of Massachussetts, the new owner of such a property gets it free of the back taxes.

24

Discount lien release

Value, $330,000; liens, $405,000

Ted Thomas found a man whose California house was being foreclosed. The house was worth about $330,000. I drove by it and confirmed that value with a local Realtor®. John Beck examined the documents relating to the deal at the county courthouse and in Thomas's files. The first mortgage lender was foreclosing on their loan which had a current balance including costs and arrearages of $178,000. The owners said they'd sell to Ted for $52,500 cash above the $178,000. Heck of a deal: a $330,000 property for just $178,000 plus $52,500 = $230,500.

The bad news was that there were really **more** than $178,000 in liens against the property. $405,000 in fact.

The extra $227,000 in liens were **judgment** liens owned by recreational-vehicle finance companies. They had sued the home owner and won judgments in those amounts.

How did Thomas make money on such a deal? He persuaded the two creditors to **release** the property from their liens for $5,000 each or a total of $10,000. That made his total cost $178,000 + $52,500 + $10,000 = $240,500 which is still a good price for a property worth $330,000.

Lien release is not judgment release

If it seems unlikely to you that creditors would do such a thing, you may be confusing **lien** release with **judgment** release. Neither creditor forgave the **entire** debt. Rather they executed a "Lien Release and Partial Satisfaction of Judgment." That means the debtor still has to pay the rest of the judgment.

The value of a lien

A lien is worth the discounted present value of the amount the lien holder is **likely** to receive multiplied by the probability that he will receive that amount. When the lien is about to be wiped out by a foreclosure or other forced sale, there is no need to discount to present value.

In Thomas's deal, the senior judgment holder was owed about $132,000 and the junior judgment holder, about $95,000. The title report showed an additional $22,000 attachment lien. But it had expired. Since properties rarely sell for more than about 80% of market value at forced sale auctions, the **junior** judgment holder would probably not get anything at all from the auction.

A fool and his lien are soon parted

I once tried to write an article on the subject of deliberately buying **mortgages** which were already in default at bigger-than-normal discounts so you could foreclose and either get a high yield if a third party bought the property at auction—or buy the property yourself for a credit bid which was well below market value. But my research indicated that plan was **not** viable—because the owners of mortgages are generally **too sophisticated** to sell the mortgage for a big enough discount.

But I **did** write an article entitled "A corporation and its real estate are soon parted" in the April 1988 issue of my newsletter. The point of that article, which **was** supported by my research, was that non-real estate corporations usually lack both real-estate expertise and the motivation to obtain it. As a result, they sometimes stupidly **overpay** for real estate or sell real estate which they consider "surplus" **too cheap**.

Let's marry those two ideas. Non-real estate corporations not only sell **real estate** too cheap sometimes, they agree to **release liens** too cheap, too. And as I said in the April 1988 article, therein lies an opportunity.

Assumption is the mother of all screw ups

In the Thomas deal , the two judgment creditors were **not** real estate investors. The senior judgment creditor was in **Indiana**. **Sophisticated** real estate or mortgage investors would **not** agree to a lien release for $5,000 until they ascertained the current market value of the property.

In his letter to the judgment creditors, Thomas said the total liens on the property exceeded his purchase price by far more than $100,000. He also told them a senior mortgage was in the process of foreclosing. He told them he had arranged to buy the property but was on the verge of backing out of the deal because of the unexpected liens. He said he would go ahead with the purchase only if the liens could be released at less than face value. He did **not** tell them his purchase price, the amount of the mortgage, or the fair market value.

The judgment creditor apparently **assumed** Thomas was paying approximately fair market value and that their lien was mostly or completely **unsecured**. Releasing an unsecured lien is the equivalent of selling someone the sleeves off your vest.

Worth far more

The **second** judgment holder was **smart** to sell a lien release for $5,000.

But the **first** judgment holder should have held out for a higher price to release the lien—or bid at auction. Since they were a creditor on the property, they could have bid as high as $310,000. The amount above $178,000 would be excess proceeds and would be returned to that first judgment creditor. Such a bid would release the debtor from as much of the judgment as the excess proceeds (above the foreclosing $178,000 mortgage) covered—and it would make the judgment holder owners of a property with $330,000 - $178,000 = $152,000 of equity—which is **more** than the amount of their judgment.

If they then resell the property for $330,000, they are entitled by well-established precedent to keep the **entire** $152,000 even though they were originally only owed $132,000. By selling to Thomas for $5,000, they blew about $152,000 - $5,000 = $147,000.

Uncertainty for judgment holder, certainty for Thomas

The judgment holder's motivation to deal with Thomas at all is the certainty of his offer versus the **un**certainty of what the property will sell for at auction.

From Thomas's perspective, however, there is **no** uncertainty at all. His deal with the debtor is he'll buy the property for $230,500 **only if** there are no liens above $178,000 on the property. So if he cannot get the judgment creditors to agree to big enough discounts, he just walks away—perhaps bidding on the property at the foreclosure auction itself.

"Assumable" liens

Suppose I offered you a loan on the following terms:

- 10% interest
- no monthly payments
- fully assumable with no credit check
- nonrecourse
- If I forget about it for more than ten years, you don't have to pay it back **at all**.

That's a deal and a half, isn't it? Yet real estate investors **walk away** from such deals every day. How so? They agree to buy a property. The title report comes back with one or more judgment liens as **"exceptions"** to the title report. The investor and or his attorney automatically tells the seller, "That lien has to be paid off at closing." Your basic knee-jerk reaction.

Why would you want to do a stupid thing like pay off that lien? Leave the darned thing on the property! Just pay the seller that much less for his equity and buy the property **subject to** the lien.

State law

In California, a judgment accrues interest at 10% per year. Other states would probably have similar interest rates. Also in California, the lien must be renewed in ten years or it expires. Other states probably have expiration dates. Do corporations forget to renew such liens? Corporations do. Windfall City!

New financing behind judgment liens

Many title companies will even help you get a **new mortgage** with**out** paying off such a lien. They just make you put up 150% (typically) of the lien amount as a sort of security deposit or bond with the title company. They'll then remove the title exception for that lien which makes the new mortgage a first, in effect.

As long as the lien exists, the title company is protected by your deposit. And if the lien **expires** without being renewed, you get your money back. This is analogous to defeasance which I discuss starting on page 165 of my book, *How to Use Leverage to Maximize your Real Estate Investment Return*.

Wipe-out auctions

Junior lien holders are most likely to agree to release liens at a discount when their lien is on the verge of being wiped out by a **foreclosure** of a senior lien or an auction initiated by a **government** tax or other agency which is owed money by the property owner. You find those situations by following notices of the various kinds of forced sales.

No competition

Competitors are the bane of any business person including those who buy properties which are going to foreclosure, tax, or other forced-sale auctions. But those competitors are typically **only** interested in properties which have **equity**—at least 20% equity for most professional investors. That is, they **reject** properties which have liens totaling more than 80% of market value.

That dramatically **reduces** the competition for those properties—which, in turn, dramatically **increases** the bargains which the remaining buyers can get.

Big discounts from mortgage lenders are rare

In general, you can**not** obtain big discounts from mortgage lenders. Although you can sometimes buy the note from them at a discount. For example, Ernie Kessler, owner of Foreclosure Research of America (301-294-2274), routinely tries to buy notes on properties he owns or is about to own. He approaches the owner of the note through a separate corporation he owns. The corporation does not give any indication it is related to anyone who owns or is buying the property in question. In other words, it's a straw man.

In one deal, Kessler bought a house which was in the process of foreclosure and simultaneously bought the second mortgage on the same house at a discount. The $50,000 **first** mortgage was foreclosing. The owner of the $10,200 second agreed to sell the note for $8,000. Kessler bought the house and the second mortgage then resold the house all on the same day. Had he not bought the second at a discount, his profit on the deal would have been $4,000. By buying the second at a $2,200 discount, he increased his profit from $4,000 to $6,200.

Author George Coats (*Smart Trust Deed Investing in California* 818-339-0270) says he tried to buy second trust deeds at a discount four or five times with no success.

George **did** succeed in getting a discount on a first trust deed on an avocado grove. The property value appeared to be greater than the trust deed, which was in default. But the note holder did not want to foreclose. So George bought the trust deed for a 35% discount off its face value of $80,000. Although the deal turned out to be more difficult than George expected, he made a $20,000 profit.

If there **is** already a default, they may be willing to sell at a discount, even a big discount, if they fear their lien will be wiped out. But mortgage lenders and note buyers will generally do a **competent** job of estimating the equity in the property available to pay off their lien at the auction. Consequently, they will generally **not** release or sell their lien for enough to make it a good deal. But what about lien holders who are **not** competent.

Incompetent lien holders

Are there incompetent lien holders? You bet. Not all lien holders are mortgage lenders or note buyers. Many obtained their lien as a result of a successful **lawsuit**. They are called **judgment** lien holders. It was an out-of-state judgment lien holder who stupidly agreed to release a $132,000 lien for just $5,000 in Ted Thomas's case.

Are there a lot of judgment lien holders? You bet. Note buyer Lloyd Walters estimates about 20% of those who default on their mortgages **also** have outstanding judgments.

"We wrote it off"

It is a basic principle of bill collecting that the longer a bill is outstanding, the lower the probability it will be collected. Consequently, accountants, bookkeepers, and business-people are in the habit of "writing off" long-overdue debts. That is, they reduce the value of the debt to zero in their books.

People who have no accounting books *per se* also tend to write off long-overdue debts **psychologically** as well.

Lien is additional security for a judgment

In the case of a mortgage, the lien on the property is of **primary** importance. Owners of mortgages hardly ever agree to release a property from the mortgage lien unless they are paid off **in full**.

But **judgments** are generally the result of an **un**secured extension of credit (many are the result of **torts** like auto accidents). From the perspective of the judgment lien holder, the lien itself, as opposed to the judgment, is a sort of unexpected bonus. It is viewed as extra or additional security for the original unsecured loan.

I have often noted that many real estate bargain-purchase opportunities arise out of the easy-come-easy-go syndrome. The fact that the original extension of credit was **un**secured, and that the lien arose **unexpectedly** out of legal procedure, gives the lien an easy-come cast in the lien holder's mind. That, in turn, often leads to an easy-go laziness when you offer to buy a lien release.

Found money

Your offer to pay for a lien release some years after the original judgment was entered seems like found money to a judgment lien holder.

The reaction may well be, "You mean the guy's willing to **pay** us for just a lien release on that judgment we wrote off three years ago?! And we can still go after the rest of the money?! Take it!"

Wipe-out auctions

When there is a wipe-out auction impending, junior lien holders have a powerful impetus to seriously consider any offers for their lien. The following are examples of wipe-out auctions:

- foreclosure of a mortgage
- trustee sale (in states which use trust deeds)
- sales for nonpayment of taxes including:
  - local property taxes
  - state income or other taxes
  - federal income or other taxes
- sheriff's sale (demanded by an impatient judgment holder)
- all sorts of other situations like resale of property seized because it was being used by drug dealers

An impending wipe-out auction is **good** news to a junior lien holder if his lien will be covered by the likely auction sale price. But the junior-lien holder can only recognize that fact if he or she is knowledgeable about the current market value of the property and the bidding patterns of local auction buyers on such properties.

Professional auction buyers and pre-auction buyers **do** possess that knowledge. But the lawyers and business executives who decide whether to accept your discount lien release offer generally do **not** possess that knowledge or even know where to get it. That is especially true when they are non-real estate people and when they are not located in the same area as the property in question.

On the other hand, virtually everyone knows that forced sales wipe out liens junior to the lien which triggered the forced sale.

Two case histories

Chicago-area investor Esther Joyal has obtained discount-lien releases twice. She buys foreclosures at or before the auction. If there are liens in excess of 80% of value on the property, she contacts the lien holder, tells him of the impending auction, and asks, "Do you intend to bid?" If they say, "Yes," or "Why do you ask?" she explains that she is interested in buying the property but only if the lien in question can be released at a discount. She then asks if they would like to get "something" for their lien, leaving them to mull over the implicit thought that they may get **nothing** if they **don't** come to agreement with her.

In one deal in 1988, she got a $13,000 judgment lien released for just $1,000. In another, she got the lien holder to agree to release the lien for less than half its face amount. She notes that institutions like retail chains and credit-card companies will often agree to release the lien for 50% of its face value.

Types of lawsuit lien

There are three types of lawsuit liens in California. Other states probably have similar liens. They are:

- attachment lien
- judgment lien
- execution lien.

Each of these has an expiration date. That is, on the anniversary prescribed by law, the lien expires, if it is not renewed. In California, judgment liens expire on the 10th anniversary of their being recorded, attachment liens, the 3rd; and execution, the 2nd.

Attachment liens are a sort of advance lien which is granted **before** trial if there is a high probability the creditor will win and a danger that the debtor might dispose of assets before the judgment is entered.

Homestead and other laws

Many states have homestead laws which make it hard or impossible for creditors to execute liens on the debtor's residence. To execute a lien means to get the sheriff to auction off the property to pay the debt. For example, in Texas, which has the homestead exemption most favorable to debtors, a person can declare bankruptcy and exempt from the bankruptcy up to one acre in a "city, town, or village," or up to 200 acres elsewhere. There is no dollar limit on the **value** of the property in question (Texas Property Code Annotated §41.001). That is, the Texan who lives on and owns a free-and-clear 200-acre ranch worth $10,000,000 can emerge from bankruptcy with the entire $10,000,000 ranch even though his creditors had to settle for pennies on the dollar.

By making it harder or impossible to get paid off out of the home owner's equity without his cooperation, these laws increase the probability that you can get a lien released at a discount. So if you want to play the lien-release game, you should become informed on the creditor/debtor laws in your state.

How to find them

In general, this formula involves finding greater-than-80%-lien-to-value-ratio lawsuit-based liens on properties which are about to be sold to pay off a senior lien which is in default. You find them the same way you find all other forced-sale bargains: by following legal notices of defaults and auctions. The fact that a property is over encumbered will come out in your conversation with the seller or in the title search.

Approach

Since the owners of such liens are generally unsophisticated in the ways of real estate, you should educate them **selectively**. That is, you inform them as to the **dis**advantages of their position. For example, that the sale will extinguish their lien, that you won't buy unless they release their lien at a discount.

But do **not** inform them of the **advantages**, like the fact that they might get some excess proceeds from the auction. As always, do **not** do this with widows and orphans. It's OK to take advantage of sophisticated business people who simply disdain real estate expertise. But **not** people who lack any business sophistication at all but who have somehow come into ownership of a lawsuit lien.

When you seek to buy a lien at a discount—as opposed to merely seeking its release from one property—you are well advised to keep the connection between the current or future owner of the property and the would-be lien buyer secret. Do this by **silence**, **not** by false statements.

Efficient screening of pre-forced-sale opportunities generally requires you to wait until about a week before the auction to contact owners. But don't wait that long with **over encumbered** properties. You need extra time to contact and negotiate with the lien holder(s).

Tax Ramifications

As a buyer you're only tax ramification is that your basis is your cost and that includes only the discounted price you pay for the lien release, not the face value of the lien.

Full-time or part-time possible

You could probably do this part-time because the rest of the market assumes the deal in not worth pursuing. That takes the pressure off and lets you pursue the lien holder at a more leisurely pace.

Ethical considerations

You need to be careful to not mislead the lien holder explicitly or implicitly. There is a temptation to lead him to believe that the forced sale will wipe out their lien and that they will get nothing as a result. Since you will only be buying release of the lien at a discount in situations where that would **not** be the case, you can't say or imply that. Just state the facts and offer to buy.

Need for secrecy

You need to keep your negotiations to get a discount lien release secret from the other parties and the other interested buyers. If they find out, they will likely overbid you. The owner who's losing his property to the forced sale is probably not a threat to overbid. He doesn't have cash or he wouldn't be in this fix. And the lien holder is less likely to agree to a discount when dealing directly with the dead beat. But you still need to keep the negotiations secret from the property owner because he may blab about it to people who do have the wherewithal to overbid you.

25

Condo reconversion

As you probably know, many condo developments flop. When that happens, they usually become rental apartments. But the condominium deeds have still been recorded separately, albeit all in the same owner's name. The fact that the condo deeds are already recorded saves anyone who reconverts the project to condos a lot of time, hassle, and expense.

In recent years, many of those flopped condos flopped **again** as apartments and end up owned by banks or federal-deposit insurance agencies. From there, they are sold—often real cheap. Enter Jim Tucker (803-252-4849) and his Bonaventures partners. Bonaventures buys rental condos from lenders and federal agencies and markets them again as condos.

Idlewood Condominiums

Idlewood Condominiums is a 65-unit (22 two-bedrooms and 43 threes) townhouse development in Tucker, GA. Tucker, GA, which is no relation to Jim Tucker, is a northeastern suburb of Atlanta.

Idlewood had been built as a condo in the early seventies. But it bombed and was turned into an apartment complex. A syndicator bought it. The syndicator went bust after the Tax Reform Act of 1986. First Chicago Bank foreclosed and became the owner.

Persistence

First Chicago spent $400,000 on fix-up. Then they made half-hearted efforts to market it at prices that were too high. An agent with whom the property was listed brought it to Bonaventure's attention in 1988.

Bonaventure tried to buy it from First Chicago repeatedly for three years. Tucker does not know, but suspects that First Chicago did not want to take the hit of selling it for market value during '88 or '89, but was finally willing to do so in 1990. He speculates that they had more losses than they were comfortable with in '88 and '89 but that they had some profits which could absorb the loss in 1990. It's also possible that regulators leaned on them to get rid of the property in 1990.

Whatever the reason, they did not want to cut the price to what Tucker needed in 1988 or 1989, but they suddenly were willing to do so in 1990.

Many are called but few are closed

This need for persistence when pursuing OREOs ("Other Real Estate Owned" by lending institutions as a result of foreclosures) came up in the OREO chapter earlier in the book. That told how Ernie Kessler pursues OREOs by calling the bank officer in charge of the property every Monday until they either sell it to someone else and close it or sell to him. He gets about one out of every 25 he pursues and he generally does not get a 'yes' until the 3.7th call.

Tucker calls on about 100 properties a month. He also has a huge loose leaf binder containing every property he's heard about. He leafs through it every three months or so and follows up on properties that might have become available on the terms Tucker wants. One of the main differences between investors like Bonaventures and Kessler, who succeed at OREO buying, and those who don't, is **persistence**.

Call us, we won't call you

Tucker also says, "The lenders will never call you. You always have to call them." I suspect this is a habit they got from their days as loan officers. They are used to, nay **addicted** to, borrowers coming to them hat in hand.

That's **not** how you market property. But bankers self image is that they are **Bankers**. They just don't **do** things like solicit offers on the properties they want to sell. OK. So play their silly game. That lack of willingness to actively seek buyers is one of the reasons you get OREOs cheap.

Protect commissions

Most of the properties he hears about are brought to him by agents. Bonaventures encourages that by always protecting the commission of the agents who bring them deals. When an agent tells them about a property, they often send the agent a letter saying you are the first to tell us about such-and-such property and we will not buy it in the next two years unless you get a commission on the deal.

I paid similar attention to winning over agents when I was in an acquisition mode. You not only need to convince them that you will protect their right to a commission, you also need to convince them that you have the wherewithal to do deals and that you will not take an inordinate amount of their time in the process.

The first buyer agents call is the one who seems **easiest** to please and **quickest** to act. To get the best deals, you need to be the first buyer every agent calls.

Rent more than carrying costs

Bonaventure's formula is to sell condos cheap enough that owning one of their units costs less than renting a comparable unit. That is, the total of the mortgage payment, home owners association dues (which includes fire insurance), insurance, and taxes is less than the rent would be. That's **before** the value of home owner tax benefits.

Idlewood had large 1,456-square foot, two-bedroom, two-and-a-half bath apartments and 1,625-square foot three-bedroom, two-and-a-half bath units. The twos rented for $550 to $600 and the threes, $620 to $670. Tucker's condo resale prices were $39,900 for the two-bedroom unit. The monthly payment was $475.80 including principal, interest, homeowner's association dues, property taxes, and mortgage insurance.

The three-bedroom models sold for $45,900 and required monthly payments of $540.93.

Some units had double carports and sold for $1,500 more.

Appraised higher

Oddly, the FHA appraisals came in much higher than the sale prices: $54,000 for the twos and $76,500 for the threes.

The reason the condos flopped the first time, but not when Bonaventures offered them, was price. New condos are generally offered at prices that are less than detached homes, but a bit more than renting the same unit.

Everything sells at market value. Idlewood just had to go through 20 years of denial by three owners before somebody could buy it cheap enough to sell it profitably.

FHA financing

Bonaventures got approval from FHA to offer their buyers 8.5% FHA mortgages [203(b) program]. The down payment was $1,800 on the twos and $2,000 on the threes. As always with FHA, getting the commitment was a pain in the neck. But as is also usually true, it was worth it.

FHA inspects the building and insists it meet stringent construction requirements. They also insist that 70% of the condos are sold before they will fund **any** of the loans. In Idlewood, they had to sell 65 x 70% = 46 units before any of the FHA-mortgaged deals could close. The delay in getting that 70% sold caused some of the original buyers to get antsy about closing. But they managed to close all of them—through FHA or VA.

Incentives to tenants

If you'll recall the old days when apartments were converted into condos, you may remember that it was standard to offer existing tenants a special deal to get them to buy. Bonaventures offered existing tenants a sneak-preview chance to buy along with discounts on carpet and such. Twelve bought. When you consider that **lowered** their monthly cost, it's a wonder there weren't more. Tenants could upgrade floor/wall coverings, kitchen appliances if they paid more.

Drainage work

Almost all real estate deals encounter unforeseen problems. But Tucker said the only one in this deal was that drainage work they **thought** would cost $2,000 to $3,000, cost about $10,000 instead. My book *Residential Property Acquisition Handbook* urges you to interview tenants to find out about drainage and similar problems. Tucker said they **did** interview several tenants and First Chicago told them there was a drainage problem. Bonaventures simply underestimated its cost.

Investors

Bonaventures has a team of investors who either put up cash or guarantee loans. The deal is structured as a loan from the investors to Tucker. The investors get a 25% or more annualized return. In Idlewood, two investors put up nothing but their credit. That is, they just guaranteed loans and were paid $125,000 each for their trouble.

$622,999 profit

Here are the Idlewood numbers:

Income:

Sales of condos	$2,940,404
Rents	$119,370
Other	$29,185

Total income $3,088,959

Expenses:

Purchase price	$1,560,000

Commissions	$126,043
Closing costs	$143,332
Operating expenses	$126,785
Salary, payroll taxes, medical insurance	$97,989
Interest to bank	$51,041
Advertising	$35,810
Origination fee	$32,000
Property taxes	$28,833
Insurance	$7,747
Professional fees	$6,380
Fee to investors who co-signed	$250,000
Total expenses:	$2,465,960

Profit: **$622,999**

The deal took 15 months.

Chattahoochee Terrace

In another deal, Bonaventures bought 27 2-bedroom townhouses in Dunwoody, GA from the RTC. Dunwoody is another northern suburb of Atlanta. Chattahoochee Terrace had originally been offered to the public at prices in the mid $60s to upper $70s. Bonaventures sold them for $48,900 to $51,900. Carrying costs were less than rents on comparable units.

Only **one** of Bonaventure's investors was needed for **this** deal. He got 7% interest plus $63,000 upon sellout. Chattahoochee Terrace sold out within five months of Bonaventure's buying it. Here are the numbers:

Income:	
Sales	$1,318,800
Rentals	$22,014
Total income:	$1,340,814

Expenses:	
Purchase price	$757,000
Commissions	$52,752
Closing costs	$39,727
Repairs, renovations, operating expenses	$69,146
Salary, payroll taxes, medical insurance	$71,203
Interest	$17,219
Advertising	$17,140
Property taxes	$10,323
Insurance	$7,448
Professional fees	$1,218
Fee to investor	$63,000
Total expenses:	$1,106,176

Profit: **$234,638**

Litigation

Say the word condo to real estate people and the first word that comes to many of their minds would be 'litigation.' A very high percentage of condo associations sue the builder who sold them the property for construction defects. When **conversions** were popular, they sued for failure to **disclose** defects.

Bonaventure has **not** been sued by Idlewood home owners. But they did go back and make some repairs requested by some homeowners to maintain goodwill.

This technique is part OREO and part condo conversion. It just shows once again that there are so many ways to skin the real estate cat. Or, to quote Tucker's letter to me,

No matter what happens, there's always a way to make money in real estate.

Tax Ramifications

This is dealer activity all the way. No depreciation, installment sale treatment, long-term capital gains treatment, or exchanging.

Special expertise required

Condo conversion became popular with investors in the seventies. It also became unpopular with tenants, especially in rent-controlled cities. So a great many anti-condo-conversion laws were passed. You need to find out if the location where you plan a conversion has such laws and comply with them or back away from the deal if the law makes it inadequately profitable.

Full-time or part-time possible

In general, I would say this is a full-time development-type activity. One might be able to do a small-scale condo reconversion—especially if you were in a related field like construction. but it would be hard to engage in such an intensive activity while holding down a nine-to-five job.

Ethical considerations

The temptations in this technique are lying to a lender, lying to prospective condo buyers about their likely homeowners dues or the condition of the property, and trying to report the deal as non-dealer property for tax purposes.

Environmental liability considerations

You can never be sure, but property that's been through the OREO process is the least likely to have unresolved environmental problems. Nowadays, lenders often have an environmental audit performed before they accept deed-in-lieu of foreclosure. You still must do your due diligence. But you should ask what environmental audits the previous owners have had performed as a way of possibly saving some money by avoiding duplication.

Need for secrecy

You should avoid bragging about OREO deals before they are consummated. And if you hope to buy from that lender again, you might want to avoid bragging about what a good deal you got even **after** the deal is consummated.

26

Assembly

How it works

Property can often be made more valuable by **combining** it with adjacent property. That's called **assembly**. It's the **opposite** of subdivision.

The value-increasing effect of combining smaller lots into a larger property more valuable than the sum of its parts is called **plottage**. Plottage creates buyers who overpay and logically so.

Plottage

More famous examples of plottage occur in New York City. In his book, *Land Rush*, Mark Stevens, tells how New York developers acquire adjoining city parcels in great secrecy. For example, they have a **different** straw buyer for each parcel. Each straw buyer uses a different law firm. If the property is a restaurant, the developers hire a retired restaurateur so he can talk ovens with the seller and operate the restaurant after purchase until the needed parcels are all bought.

The assemblers are deathly afraid that the owners of the parcels they have not yet bought will **find out** that they are assembling them into a larger, much more valuable parcel. Then they will demand far higher prices.

DisneyWorld

The acquisition of the land for DisneyWorld was an example of a huge assembly conducted in utmost secrecy. Disney's disguised front men acquired 27,443 acres in the Orlando area for about $5,000,000 ($182.20 per acre) in the early sixties. On November 15, 1965, Walt Disney revealed the plans to build DisneyWorld to the public. The land acquisition cost was just 5% of the total Disney expected to spend building the park. Clearly, they would have paid more than $182.20 for parcels they could not do without.

In its December 25, 1965 issue, *BusinessWeek* said more than 50 parcels had changed hands "...some at prices twelve times greater than before the Disney move was revealed." One 1965 investor offered $300 each for Orlando area lots that had sold at tax auction for $11 to $25 in '64. A property that was on the market in '64 for $10,000 was marked up to $70,000. The price increases didn't stop in '65 either. After DisneyWorld opened on

October 1, 1971, a 2,500 acre tract that was worth $2,000 an acre in '67 went up to $130,000 an acre.

Mineral King

But even Disney is not a sure thing in the assembly business. The U.S. Forest Service awarded Disney the contract to build the Mineral King resort in Sequoia National Forest in '67. But the Sierra Club filed suit to stop it so neither Disney nor anyone else built Mineral King.

Big or little deals

The assembly principle applies not only to mega developments like DisneyWorld. It appears in every nook and cranny of the U.S. on all sizes of deals. The bank drive-through window acquisition I describe below was a small-scale assembly which I could have profited from had I been smart enough to recognize it.

If you can spot an assembler, you can beat him out for one or more of the needed parcels. Then bargain hard when he gets to you. This is a tricky game because developers can sometimes build **around** holdouts who overplay their hand.

Assemblers are found in big cities or on farm land destined to become a theme park or in regular residential neighborhoods where a guy is trying to combine two undersized lots into one buildable one.

Landlocked land

There is profit in buying landlocked land at a depressed price due to its lack of access. Then you cure the lack of access by obtaining an easement or combining the parcel with one that **does** have access.

Example

Bob owns landlocked land which is useless. If he had road access, it would be worth $70,000. Sam owns the land between Bob's land and the road. To everyone but Bob, Sam's land is worth $100,000. But Bob could afford to pay as much as $150,000 or so. Because having it increases the value of his **first** property by $70,000. And putting a road across Sam's old property would probably not diminish its value by more than $5,000 or $10,000.

You could systematically seek out land which is the best access to landlocked land and try to sell the land or part of it or an easement to the landlocked owner at a premium over its market value. In the alternative, you could option the access property then buy the landlocked owner out at the low landlocked price then resell the property with road access for the higher unlandlocked price.

Case history

George Coats (818-339-0270) pulled that off with a 29-acre parcel in Kern County, CA. He owned a parcel which was **not** landlocked. He noticed that there **was** a landlocked parcel adjacent to his. He approached the owner of the landlocked parcel to see if he would sell.

George was willing to offer $400 an acre and would have gone higher if necessary. But the elderly owner rejected the approach out of hand without even hearing how much George was willing to pay.

Intestate estate sale

Later, George was reading the legal notices when he discovered that the owner of the landlocked parcel had died. Furthermore, he died **intestate** (no will) in L.A. So his property was being auctioned off by the Los Angeles County Administrator.

As is often the case with probates, the law requires an appraisal to protect the interests of the estate. Because the property was landlocked, it was appraised by the Administrator's appraiser at just $250 per acre—at least $150 less than George was willing to pay for it.

George was the only bidder and got it for $250 per acre. Assuming a value of $500 per acre at that time, when combined with a parcel which had access, he made 29 acres x $250/acre = $7,250. George sold the parcel some years later for $2,000 per acre or a $1,750 per acre x 29 acres = $50,750 profit.

Sliver with water view

A triangular lot smaller than 1/4 acre had been created in Hesperia, CA by the construction of the California Aqueduct. That is, a normal size property had been condemned and taken by the government through eminent domain proceedings. Then, after carving out the part they needed, the government resold the remaining triangle. George saw it advertised in a government announcement of sale and bought it from the state Department of Water Resources for a mere $175.

A buyer later agreed to buy it for $600 even though George told them they could **not** build on it without a variance or other special government approval. But when they belatedly discovered he was right, they yelled fraud.

So George bought it back for $500 keeping $100 of their money for his trouble. However, in the course of dealing with their real estate agent, he learned that an adjacent lot, which was **also** substandard as far as zoning was concerned, was available. He arranged to buy it, through the agent, for $1,100.

More than the sum of its parts

When the two substandard lots were combined, the resulting property was big enough to build on with**out** a variance. Because it was buildable, the new property was worth **$6,000** (in 1977).

But George's total cost, net of the aborted sale of the triangle, was just $175 - $100 profit on temporary sale + $1,100 = $1,175. That's a $6,000 - $1,175 = $4,825 ÷ $6,000 = 80% discount! In **today's** dollars, George made more than an $8,000 profit.

Low per-square-foot cost

The discounts in these cases were **huge**. In both cases, the property was available at a price much lower than comparable, problem-free property on a per-square-foot basis.

Working backwards, one could set that as one investment criterion, e.g., I will only buy property when I can get it for 40% or less of market value per square foot.

The second criterion would be that the **reason** the property is selling that cheap must be **correctable**. In both of Coats' deals, it was. Lack of access and inadequate dimensions are eminently correctable in many situations.

Two categories

Two kinds of buyers are willing to pay more than normal market value for some properties:

- lazy and/or incompetent buyers
- buyers who have a unique relationship to the property in question

There is a great desire for secrecy with these buyers. The lazy, incompetent ones don't want anyone to know that for obvious reasons. And those who have a unique reason to want a particular property strive mightily to keep that unique reason quiet.

One buyer will be willing to pay more than any other—let's say $100,000. He is the **high bidder** and he gets the property. The price he pays is the fair market value.

Perhaps two other buyers will pass at $100,000 but would have been willing to pay $99,000. Maybe four other buyers would have been willing to pay $98,000. At $97,000 there might have been seven buyers and so forth.

But this chapter is about situations where the number of buyers at each price would be **different**. In addition to the folks willing to pay $100,000 or less, there'd be one guy who'd be willing to pay, say, $110,000.

The trick is to systematically buy at market value or less—then sell to one of those few who will pay **more** than market value.

Case history

Listen to this disguised deal (amounts changed somewhat) which really took place in 1989. Investor spots piece of land next to hospital he knows wants to expand. Seller is in a hurry to sell. He gets the seller to agree to sell it to him for $400,000 putting a mere $8,000 deposit up. Then he offers it to the hospital for $790,000. They know they could have had it for $400,000 if they had been ready to act quickly. But their board requires months to approve such things so they just accepted the higher price. Aaaagh!

To us results-oriented entrepreneurs, that's insane. But in the narrow timid world of the process-oriented bureaucrat, following the policy manual—no matter how far astray it leads—is the way to survive.

Systematically tying up property in the path of expansion-minded bureaucracies is easier said than done, but worth the detective work it requires because it can lead to spectacular profits.

Value in use

Sometimes, it's logical for a buyer to pay more than market value—although it's **never** logical for him to **let the seller know** that. For example, when I sold my first duplex, the buyer said he did not want to inspect the inside of the property. Today, if a buyer said such a thing, I'd turn into a private investigator and find out who he was and why he **really** wanted my property. Back then, I sold him the property for market value.

Turns out he was a front man for a savings and loan whose branch was adjacent to my property. They needed my property to build a drive-through window. It was sensible for them to overpay by real estate standards because they had **non-real estate reasons** for wanting the property. Their alternatives were to continue to lose business or to move the entire branch to another location. Paying an extra $10,000 or so would have been no problem. That's why they concealed the true identity of the buyer.

Moving is expensive

Moving is very expensive for most businesses. So they will often overpay by normal real estate standards to avoid it. You could specialize in scoping out which businesses in your area want to expand and tying up property in their way. Or you could find which businesses have leases that are going to expire, buy out the landlord, then bargain hard on the renewal. The owners of property in the way of expansion or about-to-expire leases might even sell you options rather than forcing you to take title.

Lease option

Many nonresidential rental property owners who would **not** normally agree to a straight option **will** agree to an option-to-purchase clause being inserted in a lease. I don't know why they reject the one and accept the other. Maybe the lease option sounds like an afterthought whereas the straight option sounds like you're playing some angle.

So you might lease a property in order to get an option to purchase clause in the lease (the clause must be very detailed to be enforceable). You could sublease the property to a regular tenant at break-even, a profit, or small loss while you waited for your sale.

Homeowners do it

The May 23, 1984 *Wall Street Journal* contained an unusual example of plottage. Homeowners in the Atlanta were adjacent to a large office complex. Prior to construction of the office complex, the highest and best use of their land was for single-family homes. The construction of the office complex changed that. The homes were now on land which had a highest and best use of office buildings.

But the homes were in the way. The land was so valuable, it even made sense to remove them so that the office buildings could be built. The homeowners banded together and approached office building developers. As a result, they were able to sell their roughly $90,000 homes for roughly $180,000!

Office land was selling for $500,000 to $1,300,000 per acre in the area according to the article. I surmise that there were two or three homes per acre.

The January 1985 issue of *Changing Times* had a blurb about this idea. In it, they quoted Cecil Sears of the Urban Land Institute as advising that you

• hire an appraiser to establish a price for the combined properties
• use a commercial real estate agent to sell
• seek appropriate zoning
• and sell the houses separately from the land (by lifting them off their foundations and moving them) rather than just tearing them down

I saw a commercial developer try to assemble a similar plot in southern New Jersey. A bunch of old single-family houses had ended up in a pocket just below a major highway intersection. Unfortunately for the homeowners, too many of them refused to sell for any price. And the developer's offers were contingent on agreement of a certain minimum number of homes in certain strategic locations.

Oklahoma City deal

In Oklahoma City, four home owners across the street from Heritage Park Mall sold their properties to Circuit City who wanted to build a store there. The houses were worth about $60,000 a piece according to real estate educator Ron Starr. Circuit City paid $1.17 million or an average of $292,500 each for the lots. As stated above, they should have retained the right to the structures, had them moved, and installed on new lots. Circuit City only wanted the land.

Zoning a factor

Note that zoning is likely to be a factor in most plottage attempts. For example, the Atlanta homeowners land was probably zoned single-family residential. The office building developers would make their offer to purchase the home owners' properties **contingent** upon the land being **re**zoned and otherwise approved for the proposed office or other building. That zoning change would almost certainly be opposed by the homeowners adjacent to the land in question.

So this is easiest to do with pockets where there are no homeowners whose residential neighborhood is changed to nonresidential in part. By pocket I mean a group of homes which are surrounded by nonresidential uses like freeways or nonresidential properties.

Offering bigger lease space

"Plottage" works in leasing at times, too. Sometimes, prospective tenants are looking for **small** spaces; other times the market is stronger for **large** spaces. If the situation of the building in question is such that you can offer either small or large spaces, you can increase the building value by offering the more appropriate size. By situation I mean the architectural configuration and lease structure.

Again, there may be clauses in some leases which enable you to improve on a situation which appears at first glance to be unfavorable. Many nonresidential leases contain clauses which give the owner the right to **buy out** the tenant's lease. Or to move him to other space.

For example, you may have a 12,000 square foot floor with only one 2,000 square foot tenant in it—and a prospect who wants the whole floor. There may be a clause which enables the owner to force the little tenant to get out of the way—either through a buy out or a forced move to another part of the building. Or even a forced move to other "comparable space" in another building.

Why it works

Assembly works because of original mistakes or changes in market conditions. In order to realize the maximum value of any real estate, it must be of the most appropriate size and shape for the current market. Sometimes, the people who originally subdivide it blow it. They create landlocked parcels or parcels that are incorrect for the market even at that time. More often, the market—including zoning laws—changes thereby changing the most appropriate size and shape. Any time you can move the property closer to the most appropriate size and shape, you make money.

How to find them

Tax assessor's maps show the size and shape of virtually every lot. You may need to also consult other kinds of maps to determine whether a parcel has access. And you may need to drive by to confirm details of the land uses in the vicinity. But that's about all there is to finding assembly situations.

Financing ramifications

In general, you can only finance land purchases through seller financing. But many of these situations are so inexpensive that you do not need financing.

Tax Ramifications

If you consummate your assembly deals fast enough, you may be required to pay income taxes as a dealer. The law is not clear on who is and who is not a dealer.

Special expertise required

As I said in the beginning of this book, secrecy is often part of bargain purchases. The need for secrecy is highest in assemblies. It's so high, it qualifies as a special expertise.

You may also need expertise in obtaining zoning changes in a particular case.

Full-time or part-time possible

Smaller assembly deals can be done part-time. But the larger ones are heavy duty projects requiring even more than full-time effort at times.

27

Out-of-county land owners

Back in the late seventies, I sent away for a book I had seen advertised: *The Stephenson System* by Jim Stephenson. (It's no longer available for purchase.) In the spring of 1990, I tracked Stephenson down and interviewed him by phone.

The Stephenson System

Stephenson's system involves writing letters to out-of-county owners of rural raw land. He offers to buy their property. Some write back. And a few agree to sell their property to Stephenson for about 50% to 60% of market value. He then quickly resells the property for maybe 75% of market value—often at the same escrow.

You may wonder why he doesn't sell for full market value. He's getting the fast buck not the last buck. Trying to squeeze the last dollar out of a property takes far more time, usually requires seller financing in land, and is not worth the effort

Why it works

Raw land is difficult to appraise and easy to neglect. Comparable sales are not common knowledge among absentee land owners the way they are among owner-occupant home owners. Often, the owners of raw land inherited it. So they are subject to the easy-come-easy-go syndrome. They also frequently only own a partial interest. That diminishes their motivation to investigate the market value of the property and to negotiate hard over the sale price.

Sequence

Stephenson says to **write**, not call, the owners. Calling makes you seem too anxious.

He says the first response from the land owner is usually a return letter saying, "Make me an offer."

"Don't do it," says Stephenson who operates on the principle that the first one to mention a price loses. After waiting two weeks to give the owner further evidence that he is not anxious to buy the property, Stephenson writes back and says, in effect, "No, **you** make **me** an offer."

If the owner then offers to sell the property at a price far enough below market value to satisfy Stephenson, he waits a few more days then sends a letter saying, "I accept your offer."

If the owner's asking price is too high but close to what Stephenson needs, he'll **phone** and ask them to knock a bit more off the price. He emphasized that he does **not** try to knock any off a price which is already adequately low.

Response

Stephenson says many sellers want to know **why** he wants the property and what's going on in the area. I'm not sure exactly how he responds but I am sure he does not tell them so he can flip it for a quick profit. Your answers to such questions must either be "no comment" or words to that effect—or a scrupulously honest but minimal statement.

Stephenson says he also gets calls (his phone number is printed on the stationery he uses to solicit the owners) in which the owners say they need **cash** in a hurry.

The owner's response is often, "Yes, I'm interested in selling, but not now." As with other real estate systems, Stephenson and his wife often contacted the same owner repeatedly and did deals months or years after the first contact.

Ultra-high leverage

In the typical deal, Stephenson ties up the property for a small earnest money deposit in the $500 to $1,000 range. Then he resells it for a substantial markup—often a hundred times his cash outlay!

How to find the owners

Stephenson's wife simply went to the county court house and got the names and addresses of the current owners of land from the **tax assessor's records**. He suggests that you specialize in one county for starters. That is, you would only write to owners of raw land in that county—and only if they did not live in that county. In some areas, there are publishing services which sell the names and addresses of property owners. Ask real estate people or people who work in the tax assessor or county clerk's office in your area if they know of any such services there.

Some tax assessors will sell you **computer tapes or disks** of their records. That lets you put the records in your computer which, in turn, enables you to generate merged computer letters efficiently. Some private companies that gather this information offer it on-line through a computer modem—another way to generate merged computer letters efficiently.

The tax assessor records indicate the size of the property. Stephenson says only go after parcels of **one acre or more**.

Sometimes, the owners who are contacted say they don't want to sell the property in question but have **another** they would like to sell. Stephenson bought at least one of those.

Kill ratio

According to Stephenson, about one in eight letters sent by him results in a letter back saying, "Make me an offer." He does not know how many resulted in deals.

Finders fees

He has also found deals by paying **finders fees** to people who knew of his interest in buying land. That is illegal in some states unless the finder is a licensed real estate broker.

Unbelievably, one of his deals came from an owner who had previously sold to him. After he sold Stephenson one property for a $50,000 discount, he called him when he had **other** land to sell.

The letter

Stephenson's letter is brief and straightforward. It identifies the land in question and tells how he found the owner's name and address. It expresses his interest in buying and assures the owner that Stephenson is not a real estate agent so **no commission** will be due. It offers **cash** if necessary.

The letter is typed on printed stationery with his name, address, and phone number. No company name.

Expertise required

As with all forms of real estate investment, you have to know **property values** in the area in question. Again, there are usually services which sell that information to appraisers and real estate agents in your area. And you can see what's currently for sale by visiting a real estate agent or responding to for-sale-by-owner ads in the paper.

The assessor's records will show the assessed value. But those can be wildly inaccurate.

You need to know the values in your farm area **before** you send out your letters. That's because you may get a call a few days later from an owner who is willing to sell **quickly** at a bargain price for cash.

Partial interests

In many cases, Stephenson found that the land in question was owned by a group of **tenants in common**—often a dozen or more. He would get an acceptable offer from **one** then contact the other tenants in common who owned that property and ask if they would accept the same offer.

As I told you in chapter on partial interests, you can often get an **even better** bargain by buying out just one tenant in common. Stephenson was interested in tenant-in-common situations only when he could get them **all** to agree to sell.

He has since figured out that buying out just **one** can be as good a deal, if not better. Indeed, I would be leery of organizing all the tenants in common until I had an enforceable agreement to buy out at least one. Otherwise, your effort of organizing the owners may result in their offering the property on the open market and leaving you out.

Secrecy

In the course of investigating the value and liens of a target piece of land, be careful to tell as little as possible to anyone else—including assessor employees. If other land buyers or adjacent property owners get wind that the land is available—let alone at a bargain price—they will track down the owner immediately and likely kill your deal or at least diminish your bargain.

You get bargains by buying property that **nobody wants** or **nobody knows is for sale**. Stephenson's bargains are of the nobody-knows-is-for-sale variety. Keep it that way.

Case histories

Here are some of the deals done by Stephenson and others using his system. The sales are either double escrows or were sold shortly after they purchased the property.

Paid	Market value	Sold for
$60,000	unknown	$120,000
$86,000	unknown	$127,500
$35,750	$82,500	$57,750

Renovation

Stephenson often mows overgrown weeds, whitewashes fences, cleans up litter and underbrush on his land. He claims he gets back $1,000 in increased value for every $100 the "renovation" costs.

Conclusion

This is virtually a **management-free** program (no employees or tenants).

Environmental liability considerations

If you assign the purchase agreement rather than take title and sell, your name never appears in the chain of title which is good for **toxic liability** avoidance.

Financing ramifications

Long-term **financing** is difficult because land is difficult to mortgage. Although Stephenson does not hold the property long-term as a rule so he only needs short-term bank financing like a line of credit. And he often gets seller financing. (Which is fine as long as **you** are not the seller.)

Tax Ramifications

Taxwise, Stephenson and anyone following his approach would be a **dealer**. Although if you held onto one or more of the acquired properties, you would not be a dealer as to those properties and therefore you could **exchange** tax-free into or out of them.

Ethical considerations

There is nothing ethically or legally wrong with the Stephenson approach as long as you do **not** make **false** representations to the seller. A practitioner of the Stephenson System might be tempted to lie about his reason for buying the property or the current market value, for example. As long as you resist those temptations, you have done nothing wrong.

You should also check with a real estate attorney in your state to make sure your activities do not require a **real estate license** and that you would not be construed to have a **fiduciary** agent/client relationship with the seller. In some states, doing a certain number of deals a year—even for your own account—requires a real estate license.

Full-time or part-time possible

This is clearly a technique you can employ part-time. You need to get the names and addresses of the absentee land owners from government offices that are generally only open during normal business hours. That could interefere with your job if you work those same hours. But you could pay someone to get the names and addresses or use a private firm already in that business.

28

Environmental problem property

The Comprehensive Environmental Response, Compensation and Liability Act of 1980 (CERCLA) says landlords are strictly liable, without limit, for abatement of toxic substance hazards unless you can prove that you did not know or have reason to know of the hazard when you bought the property even though you conducted an investigation which was consistent with good commercial or customary practices [42 USC §9601(35)(A)(B)].

A couple court decisions say you are liable **regardless of fault** [*US v Nepacco*, 579 F Supp 839; *US v Argent*, 21 ERC, 354 BNA, Dist. NM].

Landlord's duties

According to Gary Andrews of Maxim Engineers, Inc. of Dallas, (800-526-2946) lawyers agree you have a common law duty to:

- **inspect** for toxics,
- **monitor** them continuously,
- **warn** your tenants if indeed you have hazardous toxics,
- **train** your employees to safeguard both the public's and their own health regarding proximity to or contact with toxics and
- **remove** or encapsulate any substances which are in a hazardous condition to the public using **state of the art**, not just legal minimum, methods.

Andrews says 99 out of 100 buildings which have asbestos do **not** need any more action than awareness, warning (ask your attorney), and monitoring.

Toxics are forever

You **never** escape responsibility for the removed toxics. Wherever it's taken, it's still yours. If the dump itself is later determined to be a hazard, you will be required to pay for removing your toxics from there and taking them to yet another dump.

Feds can bill you

If you fail to discharge your hazardous substance duties, the government has the authority to do it for you—and bill you.

Furthermore, there is the **personal injury lawsuit** liability from future tenant or employee or visitor suits. Even if you or the government remove the toxic substance immediately and by state-of-the-art removal technology, you may **still** be held liable for someone's illness by a jury if, for example, they feel you should have acted sooner.

Common sense tells us that these substances are more likely to cause harm if they are disturbed than if they are simply left alone. But when trial lawyers are part of the equation, common sense is an uncommon commodity.

Insurance and trash

You're generally **not** covered by your insurance policies for toxics. In recent years, insurance companies have added endorsements which **exclude** toxic substance coverage.

Trash collection companies are now slipping sweeping toxic clauses into the faint gray print on the back of container service agreements. One clause—which I crossed out on the contract pertaining to one of my properties—says,

"Non-hazardous waste only. Customer shall use the container only for the disposal of its non-hazardous solid waste, and agrees that if it places waste which is liquid, radioactive, reactive, toxic, ignitable, corrosive, pathological, acidic, or waste which is otherwise listed as a hazardous or toxic substance (as defined by local, state, provincial or federal laws or regulations) in the Equipment: (a) it shall indemnify company for any and all damages, losses or claims which may be incurred by Company; and that title to any such waste shall not pass to Company but shall remain with Customer. Customer shall not place any waste which requires special handling in the equipment, including but not limited to items such as tires, brush, demolition or construction waste, white goods, and foam products."

That clause prohibits most of the stuff you put in the trash. Furthermore, it makes **you** the trash company's insurer. If the trash company was faced with a suit or regulatory action which threatened to bankrupt its owners, they would likely sue all their customers who had signed these indemnification agreements.

The cost of all this

Maryland Bank & Trust Co. foreclosed on a $335,000 mortgage a couple years ago. So far, they've had to spend $500,000 cleaning up toxic waste they found on the property.

Four banks decided not to foreclose on a $57,000,000 mortgage they had made to a Colorado refinery. They feared toxic cleanup costs. Note that amount again: $57,000,000! A California jury awarded one tenant $600,000 in a "sick building" case.

According to *Means Repair & Remodeling Cost Data 1988*, it costs $2.86 to $3.13 per square foot to remove **ceiling** asbestos, a common application. The *1988 National Construction Estimator* puts the cost of removing asbestos **pipe** insulation at $3.02 to $10.96 per linear foot. Investor Ernie Kaluzhny adds that asbestos-removal contractors generally have a $1,000 to $1,500 minimum.

An executive of Brand Companies, a Park Ridge, IL asbestos removal contractor, says it costs $10 to $30 per square foot to remove asbestos. The September '88 issue of *Sunset* magazine has a diagram showing the common locations of asbestos in a house. That article puts the cost of a home inspection at $150 to $500 and the cost of removal from a ceiling at $3 to $30 per square foot. Restoring the ceiling to normal appearance is extra.

Underground worse

As bad as asbestos is, it's a picnic compared to underground toxics. And they can occur not only in industrial property but also in other property types because of a previous use or someone who dumped stuff on the premises.

Underground **tanks** can cause a buried toxics problem, too. In the Northeast, many houses and other buildings have buried tanks to hold heating oil. The Environmental Protection Agency says as many as 35% of motor fuel tanks leak. The percentage for heating oil tanks is probably higher.

Steps to take

You must take several precautions as a result of the new risk to real estate investors which toxics represent:

- Have the property **inspected** for toxics before you buy
- Investigate the **history** of the property regarding toxic-substances as best you can
- Seek **indemnification** agreements from sellers and tenants
- Take common-sense **precautions** to prevent injury
- Make full **disclosure** when you lease or sell
- **Fight** unreasonable cleanup demands and litigation

Inspection requires experts. For example, ascertaining whether asbestos is present often requires that samples be examined under an electron microscope (The fee for such microscopy is $330 to $580 according to *Means*).

You investigate the history of a property by talking to neighbors, the local fire department (which pays particular attention to properties where flammables are used), checking with the reference librarian for local history books, title chain search, and checking with concerned government agencies like the Environmental Protection Agency, state equivalents, local board of health, etc.

Indemnification

Seek indemnification by putting a clause in your purchase agreement which says the seller agrees to cover the cost of any toxic substance which was put on the property during or prior to his ownership. Make sure the clause survives closing. I suspect sellers will **refuse** such clauses except where virtually all buyers are demanding them. The more professional the average buyer for the property in question, the more likely all buyers will be demanding such clauses. That is, sellers of institutional-size properties will probably find they have to agree to such clauses. But sellers of homes, duplexes, etc. will probably find that they do **not**.

Prohibit your tenants from polluting your property—and make them promise to pay for it if they do. As with any prohibition clauses, remember that an ounce of **prevention** is worth a ton of litigation. So inspect periodically. Remember also that an indemnification clause is no better than the credit of the indemnifier.

Use an attorney to draw up indemnification clauses. That helps in two ways: attorneys are more likely to draw an effective clause and they and thereby, their errors and omissions insurance carriers, can be sued if they don't. The July '88 issue of *Leasing Professional* (602-860-0659) contains suggested hazardous waste lease clauses.

Consult with estate planning and bankruptcy attorneys on ways to rearrange your affairs so as to limit the amount of your net worth which can be taken if you are held liable for a cleanup.

Politics not health

Toxics are a **political** risk. Obviously, tobacco and alcohol kill far more people than leaking heating oil tanks or asbestos-containing ceiling coatings. But tobacco and alcohol companies reap billions in profits—in spite of the injuries they cause—while landlords may be ordered to give up their life savings—to fund cleanup of the remotest hazards—by methods which arguably do more harm than good. Clearly, these cleanup laws are the result of a dash of genuine health concern combined with a ton of dislike of landlords and big business.

Since cleanup laws are leftist- rather than health-inspired, you can expect that the laws will appear in a pattern similar to that of **rent control**. That is, leftist states and communities will pass such laws. And politically powerful groups like homeowners will be allowed to ignore the "hazard."

The profit opportunity

So where's the profit in all this? Many are **overreacting**. Maxim's Gary Andrews cites one example where a major insurance company owned a vacant 240,000 square foot office building in Dallas. It had asbestos. Consultants hired by the insurance company said it would cost $22 per square foot to remove. The insurance company decided to let the **new** owner remove it and offered the building for sale for $22 per square foot **less** than the asbestos-free market value.

Andrews' clients bought it because Andrews' firm said the correct removal cost was **$7** per square foot, not $22. Subsequent estimates from certified removal contractors confirmed that. Furthermore, Andrews said the asbestos-containing material was in good condition so a mere "operations and maintenance program," not removal, would suffice.

Andrews' clients bought the building for $22 - $7 = $15 x 240,000 = $3,600,000 less than market value if the asbestos has to be removed. And if they just went the operations and maintenance route, their bargain purchase price was $22 x 240,000 = $5,280,000 below market value even with the asbestos. Some people work all year to make that kind of money.

Andrews has seen many other similar cases. And I read of a Los Angeles office building which sold for a $90,000,000 discount when the asbestos removal cost was only $50,000,000.

Who is most likely to panic? Litigation-phobics and people and entities who usually respond to pressure for other leftist causes: governments, non-profit institutions, mass-market companies, people who invest in "socially conscious" mutual funds.

Opportunity won't last

I suspect that the window of opportunity for profiting from asbestos panic will be brief. The profits are too spectacular to last. Also, remember that the leftist communities will probably mandate not just monitoring but **removal** by owners of four units or more or non-residential buildings. Finally, remember that there's a big difference between toxics like asbestos—which can be accurately surveyed—and **underground** toxics which have spread God only knows how wide and deep.

How it works

The presence of environmental hazards means two things:

• the government may force you to clean it up or pay the cost of doing so
• litigation or the market may force you to clean it up or pay the cost of doing so.

Since environmental hazards usually involve astronomical costs, the presence of environmental hazards usually means a dramatic drop in the value of the property. In many cases, the property has a huge negative value. That is, the value of the property after it is cleaned up will be less than the cost of cleaning it up. More often, the cost of cleaning it up exceeds the equity the owner will have after he cleans it up.

Why it works

If everybody accurately identified their environmental problem and its cost, there would be no bargain purchase opportunity. But they don't. They frequently overreact. If the seller and other buyers think the cost of clean-up is, say, $100,000, when in fact it is only $23,000, you can make $100,000 - $23,000 = $77,000.

Incidence of this opportunity

In 1989, the Environmental Protection Agency estimated the national asbestos clean-up bill to be $51 billion. Private sector estimates on asbestos range from $100 to $200 billion. The number of new asbestos cases filed in federal court exceeds the number of old cases disposed of by two to one. One of every eight federal civil court cases involves asbestos. One in every three tort cases is an asbestos case. The number of asbestos cases about equals the number of civil rights cases in federal civil courts.

A 1990 survey of the members of the Mortgage Bankers Association found that 20% of all real properties in the U.S. had environmental problems. Asbestos was the problem half the time. In 20% of the 20%, the problem was severe enough to kill the mortgage application.

A 1986 study funded by EPA says 52% or 42 million of the nation's residential units have lead-based paint—generally properties built before 1980. HUD says 19 million apartments built before 1978 have lead-based paint.

According to a *Chicago Tribune* story, 35% of all new and remodeled commercial buildings have "sick building syndrome." Sick building syndrome is polluted interior air that causes illness or the psychosomatic "illnesses" that result from the mistaken belief that the interior air is polluted.

A study of 3,000 environmental audits revealed that 41% missed environmental problems.

How to find them

Environmental problems are generally discovered by environmental auditors. The obvious way to learn about them would be to befriend those auditors.

However, they would normally have a fiduciary relationship to their clients and therefore would not be able to share that information with you unless the client agreed.

Real estate agents also learn of the problem when their deals fall through because of adverse audits. Again, they have a fiduciary relationship to their clients and may not reveal this kind of information to third parties.

So the proper approach is to persuade those auditors and agents to tell their clients about you. Contact auditors and agents systematically and periodically and tell them you buy environmental problem property. Ask them to pass your name and phone number on to their clients. Auditors may welcome this because they normally deliver only bad news. Your name and number would be a good, "Maybe there's a way to salvage something out of the situation" piece of information the auditor could deliver along with the bad news.

Agents, of course, want their commission. If they think you might save their deal or some part of it, they will pass your name along. Indeed, their fiduciary duty requires them to do so.

You could also contact owners of large numbers of properties—namely the government and lenders—and tell them you are willing to consider buying some of their environmental problem property.

Financing ramifications

Institutional lenders do not want to get involved with environmental problem property. Some have, as I related above, with horrific results. Lenders are members of trade associations and subscribe to lender magazines. They are well aware of the problems some of their fellow lenders have had with environmental problem property. As a result, virtually all institutional lenders now require environmental audits of commercial property and will probably soon require them of single-family residential as well.

Lenders who are selling you one of their OREOs will probably not be willing to take back a mortgage as they often do with clean OREOs. Indeed, they will probably insist not only that you pay all cash but that you sign the most thorough agreement protecting them from any claims. RTC requires you to clean up the environmental problem property before closing your purchase from them.

Institutional lenders will, however, finance the building as soon as you get a clean audit.

Tax Ramifications

Environmental problems are such a new issue that the IRS, Congress, and courts have not yet addressed them much. IRS has on a couple occasions said that the cost of fixing environmental problems must be **capitalized**. That is, you must deduct it over 27.5 or 31.5 years. Investors would prefer deducting the full amount in the year it was spent.

Letter Ruling 9240004 (June 29, 1992) said you have to capitalize costs of removing and replacing asbestos insulation. The IRS said they were relying on IRC §§ 263 and 263A and appeared to rely on the U.S. Supreme Court's decision in *Indopco, Inc.* (112 S. Ct. 1039).

An unreleased technical advice memorandum from IRS requires capitalization of costs to clean up contaminated soil according to the April 16, 1993 *Tax Update* from the National Multi Housing Council. (202-659-3381)

Special expertise required

You have to know how to estimate the cost of cleaning up property and how to get it done. You need to know environmental law, such as it is. You may want to learn how to limit your liability in case you bite off more than you can chew on one deal.

Full-time or part-time possible

Although these properties probably are not hot in the sense that a lot of buyers are competing with you to buy them, the environmental area is nevertheless so complex that I hesitate to recommend it to a part-timer. A full-time environmental professional could probably do this kind of real estate investing part-time.

Regional variations

There are some regional variations in the way buildings are constructed. That may cause regional variations in the availability of environmental opportunities. There are definitely regional variations in environmental laws. For example, Massachusetts is by far the strictest when it comes to lead-based paint. In the early stages, that probably meant Massachusetts had more opportunities. But after a point, that strictness probably created widespread expertise on the subject. Widespread expertise is bad for bargain-seekers because it reduces the possibility that the seller and other buyers will overreact to the situation.

Ethical considerations

There is a powerful temptation to cover up rather than clean up environmental problems. That means you must be extra diligent at looking for such cover ups in today's market. And you must firmly resist the temptation to cover up yourself because the penalties are severe.

Need for secrecy

Since environmental problem properties are generally shunned, the whole idea of buying one need not be kept secret. But you'd better keep secret your clean-up estimate.

29

Corporate property

We're not in the real estate business.

That's the "Mating Call" of the businessperson who owns real estate as part of a **non**-real estate business. And therein lies an opportunity.

Non-residential users

This chapter is about non-residential **users** of real estate. A user is an owner-occupant. For example, a printing company may own and occupy an office-warehouse building. A chain of clothing stores may own some or all of the buildings it occupies. Etc.

When it comes to real estate, most non-residential users are **dumb**. Not because of low IQs. Rather they aren't interested.

The printer's balance sheet may show that his office-warehouse is 25% of his assets—but he thinks he's a **printer**, not a real estate investor.

Disdain for real estate

Not only are users ignorant of real estate. They **disdain** it. The real estate department of many large corporations is where they send you when you fall off the fast track—the elephant's graveyard of corporate bureaucrats—career Siberia.

Executives who do not have substantial equity in the company may be relatively unmotivated to get the best deal because it's not their money.

Smaller company executives and entrepreneurs bristle if someone hears that they own a building and says, "So, you're in real estate?"

*"Oh, no. I just own the building as part of my **printing** (or whatever) business. I'm a **printer** (or whatever)."*

Only when they get to their "true" profession does their chest pops out again. Therein lies an opportunity.

The opportunity

People who "aren't in the real estate business"—but own mucho real estate—probably don't know what their real estate is worth. And if they don't know what it's worth, you may be able to buy it from them for **less** than it's worth.

Mind you, these guys are rarely **total** fools. If you make them an offer, they'll probably make some effort to find out if it's a fair offer. Especially entrepreneurs. Corporate bureaucrats may just get a CYA appraisal—or less.

Appraisal not enough

But asking an appraiser and a friend in the real estate business often is not enough to ascertain true value. Case in point: Steve Roulac (415-925-1895) is a consultant who, among other services, tries to help large corporations **avoid** selling their real estate for less than market value. One of his clients had a piece of "surplus" land. They had it appraised by an M.A.I. and were about to sell it for the appraised value of $4,000,000.

Roulac's firm looked into the deal and said the present value of the property was **$16** million if developed as Roulac recommended.

From $1 to $1,000,000

One of Roulac's competitors, Hoffman Associates, had a client in the Northwest in the '70s. They had a "surplus" warehouse with 100,000 square feet as I recall. The client tried to **sell** it. No offers. They tried to **lease** it. No tenants. Finally, they tried to **give** it to the city for one dollar. No dice.

Hoffman Associates talked to other industrial tenants in the vicinity of the building. Many of them wanted to expand. But none needed 100,000 square feet.

So the client followed Hoffman's recommendation to divide the space into bays of the size the nearby tenants needed. The property leased up so that it had a capitalized value of about $1,000,000.

School boards are users. One of my seminar attendees told me of a case where the board declared a school "surplus." Two appraisers said it was worth $220,000 and $280,000. Fortunately for the school board, state law required them to **auction** the property. It sold for $475,000. So the typical user behavior of hiring an appraiser does not preclude bargains.

Sale-leasebacks

If you make users an offer to **buy** their building, you inspire them to make sure the property's not worth more than the offer. I suspect you'll have more success offering **sale-leasebacks**.

Let's say a company owns a building worth $1,000,000. You offer them a sale-leaseback on terms which give you a 12% cash-on-cash yield. To the seller, the deal looks like **financing**. Only it's a **better** deal than their banker will give them.

The banker wants a floating rate, short-term note. You are willing to give them a **long-term, fixed**-payment lease subject only to cost-of-living, not interest rate, increases. And your "loan-to-value" ratio is higher than what the bank is willing to do. So the seller gets more cash to put into his non-real estate business.

He may not see himself as being in the real estate business. But he sure sees himself as being in the business of getting **financing**. And you've just offered him a better deal than the normal financiers are willing to offer. So he evaluates the deal as a financing opportunity—not as a sale.

Not even an appraiser

Do business people hire appraisers to make sure the value the **lender's** using in his loan-to-value ratio is correct? No. So a sale-leaseback may enable you to buy for 20% or more below market by increasing the chances that the seller will not get up to speed on real estate values.

I oppose the use of unusual finance techniques to fool widows, orphans, and other unsophisticated folks. But I have no such qualms about successful business people who disdain real estate. They are fair game.

Become bilingual

You speak real estate. But that's **not** the language of the user. They're not in the real estate business, remember? You'll need to learn to speak **their** language. Do that by getting belly-to-belly with user decision makers. Keep your eyes and ears open. After you've tried to buy real estate from a half dozen or so users, you'll start to speak their language and understand what makes them tick.

"Surplus" real estate

Big corporations, school boards, and others often have "surplus" real estate. I have never regarded any of **my** real estate as surplus. Nor have I ever known a real estate investor who did.

Calling valuable property "surplus" is a telling manifestation of the attitude of the institutional bureaucrat toward property under his control. And it is one of the words you need to learn in order to speak the user's language.

Help these folks who are "not in the real estate business" rid themselves of their annoying "surplus."

How to find them

Systematically contact user-owners listed in tax assessor records and ask if they have any surplus real estate they might be interested in selling. You may find it worthwhile to drive around business areas looking for underutilized real estate. Many, if not most, surplus properties are listed for rent. You may find it profitable to make purchase offers to owners who were looking for tenants. Absentee owners are always prime prospects. We saw some evidence that absentee corporate owners of real estate-related assets can make dumb decisions.

Financing ramifications

You can probably get decent seller financing in some of these cases. Although not where you are holding out cash as an inducement to do the deal. You can get institutional financing—albeit with relatively low loan-to-value ratios—on general purpose property. Special purpose property is harder to finance. And you will probably have to have signed leases from tenants with decent credit to obtain institutional financing. This is a technique where cash can really be used as an offensive weapon.

Tax Ramifications

This is **non**residential real estate. That means you must use the 31.5-year recovery period instead of the 27.5-year period residential investors are used to.

Sale leasebacks may be construed to be mortgages if they have more of the characteristics of a mortgage than of a purchase. For example, a lease of 30 years or longer is considered a sale for tax purposes [Regulation § 1.1031(a)-1(c)(2)]. That is, when you buy the property then leases it back to him, your leaseback will be considered a sale back if the lease is 30 or more years.

Special expertise required

You must know nonresidential property values. And you must know how to talk to and deal with business people and bureaucrats. You may find it worthwhile to specialize in a particular type of business.

Accounting rules are often a factor. Public corporations play games with their earnings. Sometimes they decide to move events into the current quarter or year. If one of the events they want to move is selling a property, your ability to close before their self-imposed accounting deadline may be decisive in your getting the property.

Full-time or part-time possible

This is probably a full-time only activity. Vacant buildings are a major drag. Leasing or selling them takes hustle and shoe leather.

Regional variations

Industries are represented disproportionately in different regions. So opportunities to buy "surplus" buildings will vary by region according to how well the industry in question is doing.

Nonresidential vacancy rates also vary by region according to how much overbuilding was done there recently.

Although vacant space is a prerequisite to being "surplus," it may well be that healthy companies who nevertheless have some "surplus" real estate are easier prey because they are distracted by their business success. They may be too busy to focus on the "surplus" real estate. But a failing business may be in a liquidation mode and have become somewhat skilled at selling assets for market value.

Ethical considerations

There are two major ethical considerations:

• fraud
• suitability.

Fraud is wrong no matter whom you're dealing with. Suitability depends on whom your dealing with. I discussed suitability at length in the ethics chapter.

Causes of 'surplus' real estate

Thinking about the causes of corporate real estate becoming "surplus" in the minds of the corporation's executives is useful for figuring out where to look for such property.

One cause is shifting demographics. Cities used to have upscale department stores. When their customers moved to the suburbs, those inner city stores became "surplus."

Another cause is technological advances. A factory is generally a single-purpose building. It was specifically designed to manufacture a certain product. Products, like slide rules, and manufacturing technologies, like the Bessemer process of steel making, eventually become obsolete. When it is the manufacturing **technology** that's obsolete, the old factory often cannot economically be modified to use the now process.

In retail, approaches become obsolete. Retail used to be entirely storefront. Then catalog sales became widespread. Then shopping centers and malls were invented. Now we have the big-box, discount warehouse stores which are often in industrial space and locations rather than traditional high-visibility glass front retail buildings.

Plain old mismanagement makes real estate "surplus" in the eyes of many corporate executives. It may be that their managers of a particular store are incompetent. But they misdiagnose the problem as the location—and declare the store "surplus."

Downsizing industries create "surplus" real estate. Examples include **military** bases, military contractors, and business that depend on military bases that are downsizing or closing. The **bank and savings and loan** industries are definitely consolidating thereby creating "surplus" branches and administrative buildings. **Airlines** are restructuring. The famous Manhattan Pan Am building built on air rights above Grand Central Station is still there but it's not the Pan Am building anymore.

Roulac says utilities, transportation companies, agricultural companies and natural resources companies all tend to have lots of land. And those who have lots of it tend to regard some of it as "surplus." You can learn about which businesses are shrinking daily in your newspaper, magazines, or TV news.

Accounting rules, securities analysts, and regulators, like corporate bureaucrats, rarely understand real estate. And they encourage corporations to get rid of real estate as a result. For example, an accountant may carry real estate on the corporation's books at original cost. If the real estate has appreciated, that accounting rule gives a misleading picture of corporate management—a **less favorable** picture than if the property were sold an the cash put in the corporate bank account. Securities analysts, also, may fail to give the company credit for the market value of its real estate thereby making tying cash up in equity unattractive to management. And regulators, like those in the banking and savings and loan industries, believe deposit institutions should own only a limited amount of real estate.

Environmental liability considerations

On the other hand, it may be that you are not taking advantage of a businessman who ought to know better. Maybe **he's** taking advantage of **you** by not disclosing environmental contamination on the property. When he was mad at U.S. Steel for raising its prices, President John Kennedy said, "My father told me all businessmen were sons of bitches." President Kennedy's father was wrong. It's not all. But it may be most. Selling a property at a seeming big bargain may be a good way to get a buyer to let his guard down on pre-purchase inspections. You can't let your guard down in today's environmental battleground—especially when buying business properties which are the type most likely to be contaminated.

Need for secrecy

Secrecy is required for these deals. If the seller hears from anybody who knows they are selling too cheap, you'll almost certainly lose your deal. Also, business executives do not like their incompetence to be exposed—even after the fact. If it is, they may attack you to save their own neck.

30

Property-wanted ads

You've seen "Property wanted" ads in the newspaper all your life. Did you ever wonder if they work?

They do. The fact that they **continue** to run in the paper is proof of that. Advertising is funny that way. When it comes to ad copy-writing, it's hard for your competitors to keep any secrets because, by definition, it's publicly displayed. You can even figure out which copy works best by watching which ads run longest.

Wording of the ad

There aren't many variations of a property wanted ad. Virtually all seem to offer the same things:

- quick action
- no commission
- all cash
- will buy any property
- no inspections.

Many ads specify interest in foreclosures (**pre**-foreclosures actually) or in a particular property type. One foreclosure-seeker ad in the *LA Times* began, "Save your credit."

The general idea of most of the ads is that the guy who's running it has **cash**, will close practically **overnight**, and is **not choosy**. A property-wanted ad which appeared in the August 26, 1988 *Wall Street Journal* seemed to claim the **ultimate** in lack of choosiness:

"Fed up with due diligence buyers? Call us."

Due diligence buyers are people who check out a property before they buy it. Another advertiser in the *San Francisco Chronicle* claimed to represent "foreign buyers." Most people think foreign buyers are stupid and will grossly overpay.

Quick sale value

The quick action property-wanted advertisers offer is worth something to a guy who's in a hurry. And that's one reason these ads work. The advertisers are looking to buy at a discount off fair market value. They want to buy at **quick sale value**—or less.

Fair market value is the highest price a property will bring when exposed to the market for a **reasonable** period of time—like three to six months. Quick sale value is the highest price a property will bring when exposed to the market for a **short** period of time—like a week. Some property-wanted ads in the *LA Times* offer to close in two or three days. An ad in the *San Francisco Chronicle* said the buyer was in a hurry because of "Several Starker accounts." [Starker is the name of a court case (602 F2d 1341) which approved delayed exchanges and is now often used as a generic term for such exchanges even though the Tax Reform Act of 1984 superseded the Starker case in large part.]

In addition to the quick-sale discount, property-wanted advertisers hope to share commission and other **transaction cost savings** with the sellers. Finally, property-wanted advertisers hope to find sellers who **underestimate** the value of their property before those sellers learn the actual market value from a real estate agent or other buyers.

Bob Allen

You'll rarely find me recommending Bob Allen's books. He wrote *Nothing Down* and *Creating Wealth*. But in reading *Creating Wealth*, I found one chapter which had the ring of competence to it: Chapter Seven describes Allen's property-wanted ad experience.

Allen wanted to buy nothing down, in which case he was not concerned about price, or for at least 20% below market. You should **not** follow his example regarding nothing down purchases. The fact that you can get a property for nothing down does not make it a good deal. Indeed, since you typically **overpay** for those properties, they are the **opposite** of good deals. And they generally run negative cash flow because of the enormous debt burden.

Allen's ad read,

"FULL PRICE. We will pay full price for your property if you are willing to sell on flexible terms (little or no money down). Call Spencer 555-1234"

He says that ad, which only ran once a week, generated four to ten calls per week. Only two or three calls per month had potential. And of those, there would only be one property every other month which was good enough to "get excited about." Allen did not specify, but I presume he got that response from the Provo, Utah *Daily Herald* which had a circulation of 27,869 in the late seventies. *Creating Wealth* came out in 1983.

Allen's advice was that you should buy just one no-money-down house per year—that's one of the six "excited about" houses. (His theory was that inflation would increase the property's value enough to compensate you for the negative cash flow or negative amortization—plus adequately reward your effort and risk. In fact, that would only work in times of extraordinary appreciation.)

I recommend that you **not** use the phrase "Full price." Use "Fast closing" or "All Cash" or some such. It's possible that full price may be 20% below market in some cases where the seller is out of touch with the market. But that would be rare.

How much?

A two-line classified ad in the *San Francisco Chronicle* or *Examiner* costs $8.48 per day if you run it for at least 12 days or 365 x $8.48 = $3,095.20 per year.

If you only ran it in the weekly real estate section, it'd cost $21.50 per week or 52 x $21.50 = $1,118 a year.

Is it worth it? If it enabled you to get one property a year for 10% less than market—and the property in question was worth $31,000 or more—you'd be ahead as a result of running the ad.

Sequence

Allen, like many bargain purchasers, tried to accomplish as much as possible on the initial phone call from the respondent to the ad. He asked for a description of the property and location, whether there was assumable financing, whether the seller was willing to take back financing.

Criteria

Allen has a scoring system. I think scoring systems are a good idea because they get you to take action. But I don't like his system. Set up your own. There's no mystery to it. What's important is that you take prompt, decisive action when you get a good prospect.

Does it pay?

I was unable to find anyone who kept detailed books on the results of their property-wanted ads. But I found several investors who believed their ads were cost effective even though they did not have **detailed** proof. The Starker advertiser above, who turned out to be one of my subscribers, told me they were well-pleased with it. *"Tremendous response. Three or four calls on Saturday morning, which is high for a classified ad."*

Jay Kaplan used to be the head buyer for Consolidated Capital, a major syndicator. He said they only got **one** of their 400 acquisitions as a **direct** result of their property wanted ad in the Friday *Wall Street Journal*. But that another 200 resulted from **relationships** begun by those property wanted ads. Most of Con Cap's callers were brokers—which was fine with Con Cap. They tried other newspapers and magazines but found that only the Friday *Wall Street Journal* worked.

Experiment

Whether a property-wanted ad will work for the kind of property you seek in the market you have chosen remains to be seen. You need to experiment with:

- different newspapers
- different wording
- different ways of screening and responding to callers

Also, ads get stale after a time. When that happens, experiment again.

Case history

Glen Whitfield (509-448-5678) is a real estate investor who runs property wanted ads to find bargain purchases. Here is Whitfield's ad (the bottom one) from the Spokane, Washington daily *Spokesman-Review*.

It costs $1.36 per line to run daily. Like most property-wanted ads, his offers **quick** action and **cash**. He states his price range as a **screening** device. And he warns callers that they will probably get his answering machine in the hope that they will leave a message rather than hang up.

He mentions the word "**agent**" because he feels Washington state law requires him to do so.

Speed required

Many bargain-purchase techniques require that the buyer move at warp speed. Property-wanted ads are one such technique.

Most recent deal

In one homes-wanted ad transaction, Whitfield agreed to buy a house worth $55,000 for $43,000. That's a 22% discount which slightly exceeds my minimum recommended discount of 20%.

The house in question has two-bedrooms, one bath, 800-square feet, a one-car garage, and a full basement. The other houses in the neighborhood are similar. Whitfield says it was in "beautiful condition."

Investor/seller

The seller was an investor who was in a **hurry** because he was doing a tax-free exchange and moving out of the area. Delayed exchanges often cause those who arrange one end of the deal to be in a hurry to close the other end.

Drive by first

Whitfield found the call that led to this purchase on his answering machine. He drove by it—a step which struck me as dangerously time-consuming when a bargain purchase is in the offing—then called to make an appointment. The seller was a retired man who decided to invest in rental houses then abruptly decided to leave the area.

Negotiated down

The seller asked for $44,500. Although that was a bargain, Whitfield initially offered $42,000. Readers should be careful about trying to make clear bargains even better. Whitfield says he **was** careful making sure most of the negotiation was conducted face-to-face so he could tell if he was pushing it too far.

Whitfield also notes that it's sometimes dangerous to accept the seller's asking price because it may leave the seller thinking he sold too cheap. There's some truth to that. My first duplex was for sale for $16,500 (in 1969). When my initial offer of $14,000 was immediately accepted, I felt I should have offered less. (The property had gross rents of $230 and the mortgage interest rate was 7.5% so it was a good deal even at $14,000.)

Militant for sale by owner

Whitfield's negotiation took a split-the-difference tack and he got the seller to agree to pay $450 in points. Whitfield felt the key factor in his getting a bargain was that the seller was more determined to succeed at **not** using a real estate agent than he was in maximizing his net sale price. That's a common behavior pattern among For Sale By Owners who are invariably besieged by real estate agents who say or imply that the seller is making a mistake. The seller had also recently tried to sell his residence through a Realtor® without success so he was a bit miffed at the real-estate-brokerage profession.

Financing

Whitfield had to put down 30%—high by historical standards—but not so high for investors who own many houses today. Because he already owns more than four other mortgaged houses, Whitfield had difficulty obtaining a **fixed-rate** mortgage. He got a 10.5% ARM instead. I do not recommend ARMs. Look harder for a fixed rate. Foreclosure buyer Paul Thompson says he has to use five different banks to find his financing. Each will take about five of his deals then they say, "No more." So he goes to the next one. And the next. After a couple years he finds he can go back to the first one and go through the sequence again.

One-bedroom house

In another deal , Whitfield bought a one-bedroom, one bath, no-garage house on a 60' x 140' lot for $24,000. I think one-bedroom houses are one of the best-kept secrets in real estate investing—although not for lack of publicizing them on my part. I've written several articles pushing them.

Whitfield put $5,000 down on the house. It rents for $350 and has a monthly mortgage payment of $181. He figured it was worth $30,000 to $35,000 when he bought it.

Easy-come-easy-go syndrome

The sellers were investors who had bought the property just a few months before for **no money down** (they paid closing costs only). They were making a profit of over $4,000 even though they were selling at a bargain price to Whitfield. That's a phenomenon I've observed and written about on many occasions—investors who made a big profit on a property reselling it so cheaply that the **second** investor is still able to get it for at least 20% below market value.

Kill ratio

Whitfield says he usually gets about three calls a week in response to his property-wanted ad. The Spokane Sunday paper had a circulation of 121,474 according to one old newspaper directory. But he only buys about one property every three months. That's about 1 deal per 39 calls.

The number of deals per 39 calls would be **higher** if he were **full time**. He misses some deals because he also owns a real-estate-brokerage firm which often prevents him from responding quickly enough to the property-wanted-ad calls he gets.

For sale by owners

Whitfield also calls For Sale By Owners (FSBOs). He calls them first thing in the morning every day when he is not preoccupied with other deals. He has found that the first one there gets the best deals. In the Spokane area, which has a population of 360,000, he says you see about one good deal a week in the FSBO ads.

In one deal in April, Whitfield pounced on a FSBO and bought a $70,000 house for $55,000 with less than 10% down. He kept it and it now produces positive cash flow.

Multiple-bargain deal

Whitfield also did a successful almost-Nickerson deal as a result of one of his property-wanted ads. William Nickerson wrote the book, *How I Turned $1,000 into $3,000,000 in Real Estate in My Spare Time.* That book advocates buying run-down apartment buildings. Then you renovate them for half of what the rehab adds in market value. Whitfield's Nickerson deal, done in Bellingham, Washington in 1989, had a couple additional twists.

He bought a duplex and a four-plex for $85,000 from an estate. He spent $30,000 on fix up in addition to a lot of labor by a partner who lived in each unit as it was rehabbed. He also got the lot line moved.

The property consisted of two lots. But each lot had always had the same owner. So when they built on the lots, they paid no attention to where the lot line was. As a result, the four-plex **straddled** the lot line while the duplex was entirely on one lot. (See diagram below.) Whitfield got the city to move the lot line so each property had its own lot and could be sold separately. The lot-line change required two variances and cost Whitfield almost a thousand dollars for a special survey.

He doubled the rents after the renovation and sold the properties for a combined $205,000 within one year. Whitfield accounts for his overall $80,000 profit as follows:

Bargain buy from estate	$7,000
Moving lot line	$10,000
Market appreciation	$18,000
Renovation	$45,000
Total	$80,000

This was an **almost**-Nickerson deal because the renovation did not produce $2 for each $1 spent.

Tax Ramifications

If you hold for long-term, you may technically be required to capitalize the cost of your property-wanted ad as an acquisition cost. Otherwise, the property-wanted ad approach has no tax ramifications.

Full-time or part-time possible

Speed is important in this technique so full-time works best. Whitfield is part-time. But it has cost him deals.

Regional variations

As far as I know, property-wanted ads work in all regions. State laws may vary as to whether they require you to disclose if you have a real estate license. Disclosing that you have a real estate license probably depresses response to the ad.

Ethical considerations

In his book, *Creating Wealth*, Allen says he offers to pay the seller "full price" as determined by an FHA/VA appraiser. Then he says he hires "conservative" appraisers. That's a bit unethical. For one thing, it is unethical for an appraiser to be conservative. They are supposed to be accurate. Consequently, there should be no way to know whether an appraiser is conservative or not. If Allen tells the appraiser he wants "conservatism," he's making an unethical request. Since Allen was presumably a volume consumer of appraisal services, there is a temptation for the appraiser to give Allen what he wants—namely a **low** appraisal. Such a team would constitute a conspiracy.

I think bringing in an appraiser is fraught with ethical difficulties. Better you should just make the seller the offer you want to make.

False statements like "foreign buyers" or "Starker accounts" when you don't have any are unethical and may violate laws. Statements that you don't care about the property are either false or stupid. If you really don't care, you need your head examined. If you care but say you don't, you're a liar. If you're going to get into that whole question, you'd better limit it to, "Will consider all properties."

A

Pertinent references

Books and reports

Aggressive Tax Avoidance for Real Estate Investors by John T. Reed. Annual.

All About Escrow by Sandy Gadow. Express. 1981.

Black's Law Dictionary. West Publishing Company.

Buying Real Estate Superbargains at California Tax Sales by Ronal Starr. Unlimited Golden Opportunities Press.

California Title Insurance Practice. by John L. Hosack. Continuing Education of the Bar. 1992.

Complete Asset Protection Guide by Arthur Goldstein. Enterprise Publishing, Inc. 1990.

Creating Wealth by Robert Allen. Simon & Schuster. 1983. I do **not** recommend this book although the chapter on property-wanted ads seems valid except when discussing nothing-down purchases.

The Current Law of California Real Estate by Miller and Starr. Bancroft-Whitney Publishers. 1990.

Diamond Farming Probate Real Estate by Gary DiGrazia. Family Tree Publications. 1991.

Distressed Real Estate Times—Offensive and Defensive Strategy and Tactics by John T. Reed. Special Report. 1991.

Federal Estate and Gift Taxes by Lowndes, Kramer, and McCord. West Publishing Company.

Finding and Buying Your Place in the Country by Les Scher. Collier Books. 1974.

Forced Sale Workbook by John Beck. 1983.

Foreclosure Superbargains in California by John Beck and Ronald Starr. 1985.

Future Interests and Estate Planning 2d by Schwartz. W.H. Anderson

How I Turned $1,000 into $5,000,000 in Real Estate in My Spare Time by

William Nickerson. Simon & Schuster. 1969.

How to Avoid Probate Updated by Norman Dacey. Crown Publishers, Inc. 1980.

How to File For Bankruptcy by Elias, Renauer, and Leonard. Nolo Press. 1990.

How to Increase the Value of Real Estate by John T. Reed. 1986.

How to Make a Fortune in Real Estate: the Land Game by Albert Winnikoff. Wilshire Book Company. 1980.

How to Manage Residential Property for Maximum Cash Flow and Resale Value by John T. Reed. 1991.

How to Use Leverage to Maximize Your Real Estate Investment Return by John T. Reed. 1986.

The Language of Real Estate by John Reilly. Real Estate Education Company. 1977.

The Law of Future Interests 2d by Simes and Smith. West Publishing Company.

Means Repair and Remodeling Cost Data. R.S. Means Company, Inc. Annual.

National Construction Estimator. Craftsman Book Company. Annual.

Nothing Down by Robert Allen. Simon & Schuster. 1978. I do **not** recommend this book.

Office Building Acquisition Handbook by John T. Reed. 1987.

Owner Unknown—Your Guide to Real Estate Treasure Hunting by Jay Segal. Genealogical Publishing Company. 1991.

Researching the Title to Real Estate by Barry Adams. Available from John Beck Publishing.

Residential Property Acquisition Handbook by John T. Reed. 1991.

Single-Family Lease Options by John T. Reed. 1991.

Smart Trust Deed Investing in California by George Coats. Barr-Randol Publishing Company. 1991.

The Stephenson System by Jim Stephenson. Out of print.1977.

Take This House, Please! The complete guide to buying real estate owned by lenders by John Beck and Ronald Starr. John Beck Publishing. 1986

Your Illustrated Guide to Foreclosure Gold Mining by Ted Thomas. New Growth Financial. 1992.

Periodicals

Appraisal Journal, Quaterly. The Appraisal Institute.

The Blue Sheet. Probate listings in San Francisco.

Daily Commerce.

first tuesday. Realty Publications, Inc. Monthly.

Goodkin Real Estate Report/Florida by Lewis Goodkin.

Leasing Professional by Michael Chemodurow. Monthly ten months a year.

Real Estate Educator's Journal. Real Estate Educators Association. Quarterly.

Real Estate Investor's Monthly by John T. Reed.

Real Estate Issues. American Society of Real Estate Counselors (subsidiary of National Association of Realtors®).

Realtor® News. National Association of Realtors®

Urban Land. Urban Land Institute. Monthly.

Publishers' addresses

W.H. Anderson Company
Cincinnati, OH

Appraisal Institute
875 N. Michigan Avenue, Suite 2400
Chicago, IL 60611
312-335-4100

Bancroft-Whitney Law Publishers
3250 Van Ness Avenue
San Francisco, CA 94120
800-848-4000

Barr-Randol Publishing Co.
Box 4486
Covina, CA 91723
818-339-0270

John Beck Publishing
1024 Regent Street
Alameda, CA 94501
510-523-6115

Blue Sheet
P.O. Box 22399
San Francisco, CA
415-731-7941

Michael P. Chemodurow
P.O. Box 5675
Scottsdale, AZ 85261

Collier Books
866 Third Avenue
New York, NY 10022

Continuing Education of the Bar of
    California
2300 Shattuck Avenue
Berkeley, CA 94704

Craftsman Book Company
6058 Corte del Cedro
Carlsbad, CA 92008

Daily Commerce
P.O. Box 3511
Long Beach, CA 90803
714-858-8150

Enterprise Publishing, Inc.
725 North Market Street
Wilmington, DE 19801
800-533-2665

Genealogical Publishing Company
1001 N. Calvert Street
Baltimore, MD 21202
800-727-6687

Goodkin Real Estate Report/Florida
275 Commercial Boulevard
Lauderdale-by-the-Sea, FL 33308
305-493-5011

R.S. Means Company, Inc.
100 Construction Plaza
Kingston, MA 02364
617-747-1270

National Association of Realtors®
430 North Michigan Avenue
Chicago, IL 60611
312-329-8200

Nolo Press
950 Parker Street
Berkeley, CA 94710
510-549-1976

Real Estate Education Company
520 North Dearborn Street
Chicago, IL 60610
800-428-3846

Real Estate Educators Association
230 N. Michigan Avenue, Suite 1200
Chicago, IL 60601
312-372-9800

Realty Publications, Inc.
P.O. Box 20068
Riverside, CA 92516
714-781-7300

John T. Reed
342 Bryan Drive
Danville, CA 94526
800-635-5425

Simon & Schuster
1230 Avenue of the Americas
New York, NY 10020
212-245-6400

Unlimited Golden Opportunities Press
P.O. Box 27218
Oakland, CA 94602
510-534-6472

Urban Land Institute
625 Indiana Avenue, NW, Suite 400
Washington, DC 20004
202-624-7000

West Publishing Company
50 West Kellogg Boulevard
St. Paul, MN 55164

250

B

Definitions

Absolute auction—An auction with no minimum bid amount, that is, the highest bidder gets the property no matter how low the bid.

Annuity—Agreement to pay a certain amount of money per month for the life of a specified person or persons.

Assembly—Increasing property value by combining small parcels into a large parcel.

Assigned risk—Private insurers refuse to insure some properties and situations like vacant houses. To make sure insurance is available, states pass laws requiring private insurers to accept those policies by forcing them to participate in a pool where insurers take turns writing those policies.

Assignment—Transfer of the rights and responsibilities arising from an agreement to another person.

Bargain purchase—Purchase for 80% of current market value or less.

Bid chilling—Agreement among prospective bidders at an auction to refrain from bidding. Non-bidders are paid a fee for not bidding or are given a share of the winning bidder's extra profit from the bid-chilling agreement. This is unethical and is illegal in some situations.

Default judgment—Judgment against someone because they failed to show up in court.

Deficiency judgment—Court decision requiring a mortgage borrower to pay the lender the difference between the mortgage balance and the amount realized at foreclosure sale.

Descent, laws of—State laws that say who inherits what when a person dies without a will.

Due diligence—Inspections and other investigations of a property made before purchase to be sure it's a wise investment.

Due-on-sale clause—Clause in mortgage which says the lender has the option to make you pay off the mortgage if you sell, lease option, or lease for more than three years.

Equitable mortgage—A mortgage which is construed by law when the situation warrants even though no formal mortgage document exists. A possible recharacterization of the typical single-family lease option.

Escaped land—Land which is not listed in tax assessor's records.

Excess proceeds—Proceeds of a forced-sale auction which exceed the liens on the property. Excess proceeds generally belong to the person who owned the property at the time of the forced sale.

Execution sale—Forced sale by the sheriff of property owned by a judgment debtor who has not paid off the judgment as required.

Fee simple—Complete legal ownership of a property.

Finder's fee—Fee paid to a person who finds a real estate deal for you. In some states, it is illegal to pay such a fee to a person who is not a licensed real estate broker.

Foreclosure—Forced sale of property ordered by lender because of delinquency in mortgage payments.

Greenmail—Legalized extortion in which corporate executives pay hostile takeover raiders, with shareholders money, to refrain from taking over their company. Politicians who derive their power from the popularity of rent control appear to do a similar thing with landlords who sue seeking to overturn the rent control law on constitutional grounds.

Hedging—Avoiding or lessening the risk of a loss by making a counterbalancing bet.

Holding over—Occupant of a property remaining in it after their legal right to do so has ended.

Homestead exemption—Statutory bankruptcy exemption in some states for all or part of one's home equity. The amount in question is given to the bankrupt person and creditors can only get paid from what's left after the bankrupt person has received their homestead exemption amount.

Injunction—Court order requiring a person to do something or refrain from doing something that would hurt the person seeking the injunction. Preliminary injunctions are issued on an emergency basis before the full trial in the case.

Intestate—No will.

Involuntary lien—Lien against property stemming from a judgment. Less favored by the law than voluntary liens like mortgages.

Judgment—Court decision.

Judicial foreclosure—Foreclosure initiated by lawsuit against the defaulted borrower. In trust deed states, judicial foreclosure is more cumbersome and time-consuming than a trustee sale but may give the lender additional rights like the right to a deficiency judgment.

Kill ratio—Ratio of properties considered to properties purchased.

Land contract—Seller financing instrument which withholds the deed until a specified portion, usually 100%, of the loan is paid off.

Lease option—Combination of a lease with an option to purchase. A lease option structured in the most common fashion is an instrument of questionable legal standing. It could be construed as a sale at the outset of the lease option.

Leper properties—Properties that are generally shunned by the marketplace.

Lien release—Written agreement by lien holder to release a property from a lien. Lien release does not release the debtor from the obligation to pay the debt.

Life estate—The right to use a property during the lifetime of a specified person.

Lis pendens—Lawsuit pending.

Loan-to-value ratio—Mortgage balance divided by fair market value of property.

MLS—Multiple listing service run by local Realtor® associations.

Name lien—Lien recorded against a person but not mentioning specific property.

Nonconforming use—Property type or size which does not conform to current zoning law but did conform at the time it was built.

Nonrecourse mortgage—Mortgage in which no deficiency judgment is permitted either by agreement with the lender or by statute.

Option—The right to buy or lease something for a specified price during a specified time period.

OREO—Other Real Estate Owned by banks and savings and loans as a result of foreclosures where no other bidders appeared.

Paper—A note secured by a mortgage or trust deed.

Partition—Legal action to force a property that is owned by tenants in common to be divided up with each tenant in common receiving his share or sold with each tenant in common receiving his share of the proceeds.

Partition in kind—Dividing up a parcel into smaller parcels representing each co-tenant's share of ownership.

Personal liability—Opposite of nonrecourse. Borrower must pay debt even if the proceeds of foreclosure sale of the property pledged as security for the loan are not enough.

Plottage—The value-raising effect of combining small parcels into larger ones in a market where larger parcels are more valuable per square foot.

Pre-foreclosure—Period between when a mortgage borrower becomes delinquent and when their property is foreclosed upon.

Probate—Court supervised administration of an estate.

Quick-sale value—Ten to 15% below market value.

Quiet title—Lawsuit to eliminate title problems.

Quitclaim—The weakest form of deed. It means the grantor (person who signs the deed) is giving the grantee (buyer) whatever rights the grantor has in the property but makes no warranties about the rights others may have.

Remainder estate—The right to fee simple ownership of a property upon the death of a specified life tenant.

Reversion—Remainder estate owned by the creator of the life estate and remainder estate.

Right of redemption—Right to buy a property back for a limited period of time after it has been sold at a forced sale auction like a foreclosure, trustee sale, delinquent tax auction or sheriff's sale.

Specific performance—Lawsuit to force a party to a real estate agreement to comply with it.

Subordination agreement—Agreement by senior lien holder to make his lien junior to a subsequent lien.

Suitability—Whether an investment is appropriate for a given person based on that person's resources, education, training, and experience.

Superbargain purchase—Purchase for 67% of current market value or less.

Surplus real estate—Real estate owned by a non-real estate business which is no longer necessary for the conduct of that business.

Transfer tax—Tax on purchase of real estate.

Waste—Actions or neglect by a tenant which cause or permit deterioration of the property in question.

Zero-sum game—Negotiation in which neither party can improve their position except at the expense of the other. **All** negotiations are zero-sum games in part.

Index

Your Opinion of this Book is Important to Me

Please send me your comments on this book. I'm interested in both compliments and constructive ciriticism. Your compliments provide guidance on what you want. And, with your permission, I'd like to use your favorable comments to sell future editions of the book. Constructive criticism also helps make the book's next edition better.

Evaluation of *How to Buy Real Estate for at Least 20% Below Market*

Circle one: Excellent   Good   Satisfactory   Unsatisfactory

Circle one: Too Advanced   About Right   Too Basic

What part did you like best? _____

_____

What part did you like least? _____

_____

How can I improve the book? _____

_____

My promotional material includes brief comments by people who have read the book and their name, (company name in some cases), city, state, and occupation. I would appreciate any remarks you could give me for that purpose:

_____

_____

_____

Name _____ Occupation _____

Address _____

City _____ State _____ Zip _____

Feel free to leave blanks if you prefer not to answer all of these questions. I would appreciate receiving your evaluation even if you only fill out one line.

How long have you been a real estate investor? _____

What is the total value of your investment real estate? _____

What types of property do you own? _____

If your comments will not fit on this sheet, feel free to write them on the back of additional sheets. Please send your evaluation to:

**John T. Reed
342 Bryan Drive
Danville, CA 94526**

John T. Reed's Order Form

Newsletter

		Unit Price	Total
_____ one-year subscriptions to John T. Reed's Real Estate Investor's Monthly (12 monthly issues)		$121.00	$_____
_____ back issues (Please see catalog for list. <u>Minimum order is 3.</u>)	1 to 11 back issues	$ 8.50 ea.	$_____
	12 or more back issues	$ 8.00 ea.	$_____
	All back issues starting Feb. '86	$ 4.00ea.	$_____

Special reports (40 pages, or more)

	Unit Price	Total
_____ #1 Single-Family Lease Options	$ 29.95	$_____
_____ #2 Distressed Real Estate Times: Offensive and Defensive Strategy and Tactics	$ 29.95	$_____
_____ #3 How to Do a Delayed Exchange	$ 29.95	$_____

Books

	Unit Price	Total
_____ Aggressive Tax Avoidance for Real Estate Investors	$ 23.95	$_____
_____ Coaching Youth Football Defense	$ 19.95	$_____
_____ How to Buy Real Estate for At Least 20% Below Market Value	$ 19.95	$_____
_____ How to Increase the Value of Real Estate	$ 39.95	$_____
_____ How to Manage Residential Property for Maximum Cash Flow and Resale Value	$ 21.95	$_____
_____ How to Use Leverage to Maximize Your Real Estate Investment Return	$ 19.95	$_____
_____ Office Building Acquisition Handbook (loose leaf)	$ 39.95	$_____
_____ Real Estate Investor's Monthly on Real Estate Investment Strategy	$ 39.95	$_____
_____ Residential Property Acquisition Handbook	$ 39.95	$_____

Cassettes (Two 60-minute cassettes in a binder)

	Unit Price	Total
_____ High Leverage Real Estate Financing	$ 29.95	$_____
_____ How to Buy Real Estate for at Least 20% Below Market Value, Vol. I	$ 29.95	$_____
_____ How to Buy Real Estate for at Least 20% Below Market Value, Vol. II	$ 29.95	$_____
_____ How to Buy Residential Property	$ 29.95	$_____
_____ How to Find Deals That Make Sense in Today's Market	$ 29.95	$_____
_____ How to Manage Residential Property for Maximum Cash Flow and Resale Value	$ 29.95	$_____
_____ How to Do a Delayed Exchange	$ 29.95	$_____
_____ Offensive and Defensive Strategy for Distressed Real Estate Times	$ 29.95	$_____
_____ Single-Family Lease Options	$ 29.95	$_____

Software

	Unit Price	Total
_____ Landlording™ On Disk software by Leigh Robinson **IMPORTANT—CHECK ONE**: ☐ Macintosh ☐ IBM 5 1/4 ☐ IBM 3 1/2"	$ 39.95	$_____

	Subtotal	$_____
Discount 5% for two or more items totaling over $100	$_____	
California residents: add your area's **sales tax** (except newsletter subscriptions)	$_____	
Shipping: $4.00 for first item	$_____	
$2.00 for **EACH** additional item	$ 4.00	
For a **Rush Order,** add $5 more to the shipping costs.	$_____	
(There is **one** shipping charge for any number of newsletter back issues.)		
	Total	$_____

Satisfaction guaranteed or your money back

Method of Payment: _____ Check enclosed payable to John T. Reed   _____ Visa   _____ MasterCard   _____ Discover

Credit card # _____ Exp. Date _____ Signature _____

Ship to: Name _____

Street Address*_____

City _____ State _____ Zip _____ Telephone _____

UPS cannot deliver to P.O. boxes. Please allow 2-3 weeks for processing and delivery.
Please mail your order to: John T. Reed, P.O. Box 27311, Concord, CA 94527
These prices are effective June 1, 1993 and are subject to change. Source Code: 03

For faster service, phone toll-free: ☎
800-635-5425